A VOLUME IN THE SERIES

Culture and Society after Socialism

edited by Bruce Grant and Nancy Ries

For a full list of titles in the series, see www.cornellpress.cornell.edu

NEEDED BY NOBODY

HOMELESSNESS AND HUMANNESS IN POST-SOCIALIST RUSSIA

Tova Höjdestrand

CORNELL UNIVERSITY PRESS
Ithaca and London

First published 2009 by Cornell University Press
First printing, Cornell Paperbacks, 2009

Printed in the United States of America

Library of Congress Cataloging-in-publication Data

Höjdestrand, Tova, 1964–
  Needed by nobody : homelessness and humanness in
post-socialist Russia / Tova Höjdestrand.
      p. cm. — (Culture and society after socialism)
  Includes bibliographical references and index.
  ISBN 978-0-8014-4701-3 (cloth : alk. paper)
  ISBN 978-0-8014-7593-1 (pbk : alk. paper)
  1. Homelessness—Russia (Federation) 2. Russia
(Federation)—Social conditions—1991- I. Title.
II. Series: Culture and society after socialism.

  HV4577.2.A4H64   2009
  305.5'6920947—dc22
2009010906

Cornell University Press strives to use environmentally
responsible suppliers and materials to the fullest extent
possible in the publishing of its books. Such materials
include vegetable-based, low-VOC inks and acid-free
papers that are recycled, totally chlorine-free, or partly
composed of nonwood fibers. For further information,
visit our website at www.cornellpress.cornell.edu.

Cloth printing   10 9 8 7 6 5 4 3 2 1
Paperback printing   10 9 8 7 6 5 4 3 2 1

Contents

ACKNOWLEDGMENTS

This study owes a great deal to the encouragement and engagement of a large number of people. At the Department of Social Anthropology, Stockholm University, I thank all my colleagues for the ideas and encouragement I have received during the years. I am particularly grateful to Karin Norman, whose inspiring curiosity, careful attention, and critical eye have been indispensable in transforming my unbridled knack for telling stories into the serious ethnographic work I hope this book to be. I am also deeply indebted to Galina Lindquist, who initially was my partner in the "Coping with Misery in Post-Communist Russia" project, the original framework of this study, and whose close attention and insightful advice have been invaluable throughout. Her tragic death only months before the completion of this manuscript casts a shadow of grief over the relief and happiness that otherwise follow a finished publication, for she was, in the idiom of this book, indeed a "true human."

For extensive and valuable comments on this manuscript, I am especially grateful to Mark Graham, Åse Ottosson, Lissa Nordin, Johan Lindquist, Mattias Viktorin, Thomas Borén, Gudrun Dahl, Åsa Bartholdsson, and Åsa Aretun. I would like to thank the Institute of Anthropology in Copenhagen for a hospitable period of guest research in 2003 and its doctoral students for the inspiring seminars and conversations. In Copenhagen, my manuscript benefited greatly from the generous and constructive attention of Finn Sivert Nielsen, and I also thank Professor Michael Jackson for taking a keen interest in my work. In addition, I am grateful to the Department of Social Anthropology at Lund University, where I have enjoyed a number of greatly inspiring guest seminars throughout the years, and to the Centre for Independent Sociological Research in St. Petersburg, where I spent a rewarding period as a guest researcher in the spring of 2006.

The Bank of Sweden Tercentenary Foundation and the Swedish Institute provided the funding that made this project possible in the first place. I am deeply grateful for their invaluable support, and I also wish to thank the Nordic

Research Board and the Helge Ax:son Johnson Foundation for additional financial assistance.

As a reader for Cornell University Press, Dale Pesmen gave me a wonderful response with thoughtful and inspiring comments, and the careful attention, sound judgment, and indefatigable support of editors Nancy Ries and Bruce Grant have simply been priceless for the completion of this work. I also owe great thanks to Emily Zoss for patiently helping me out with a number of other issues.

Primarily, however, a large number of people in St. Petersburg deserve particular mention. My homeless informants generously spent their time on me instead of something more profitable. A number of others were nearly as invaluable. The help I have received from Igor Karlinsky with regard to legal matters was of great value, and I would never have completed—or even initiated—this project without help from the organization Nochlezhka and *Na Dne* and their staff, in particular Maksim Egorov. Professor Yakov Gilinsky, Institute of Sociology, Russian Academy of Sciences, has supported me with many practical issues and rewarding conversations. All my friends in the city have contributed to this study in some way or another, but I am especially grateful to Vladik Nakhimov, Maya Rusakova, Olga Ivanovna Rusakova, Larisa Petrova, and, in particular, Marina Dmitrieva, without whose patience with my endless questions and perpetual misunderstandings, this book would never have been written.

A Note on Transliteration and Translation

I have used the Library of Congress system for transliteration except when there is another commonly accepted English spelling, for instance in the case of names such as Fyodor or Berdyaev. Translations are my own.

NEEDED BY NOBODY

Introduction

One cold winter's evening in 1996, a friend and I went for a long walk through the center of St. Petersburg. We crossed the Field of Mars and approached the Eternal Flame, the memorial to the Unknown Soldier where newlyweds usually go to be photographed. An old man was stooping over the engraving on one of the marble blocks surrounding the memorial. It was a dedication to the victims of the German blockade during the Great Patriotic War (as the Russians call World War II), and he was apparently making a copy of the text by fervently rubbing a crayon over a large piece of paper placed over it. He looked like Lev Tolstoy, although his carefully composed folklore-style outfit was far more chic than anything ever worn by the great author. We went up to him and asked him what he was doing. He got up, stared hard at us, and said that he was going to send these copies to the International Court of Justice in The Hague, together with an application for a summons against the Russian state. Increasingly agitated, he continued to talk, but too fast for me to grasp everything he was saying. It was something about evil relatives and corrupt bureaucrats, and probably the latter were more important since he wanted to sue the state.

"You see," he ended up furiously, "they made me a *bomzh!*" He pulled out his domestic passport, the ID document, and showed it to my friend, who scrutinized it politely and nodded in sympathetic agreement. I asked them what a bomzh was. "A dirty drunkard, with *lice!*" the man bellowed.

"Sort of a beggar, like the ones we've seen everywhere during this walk," my friend explained, "poor, no place to live." I took bomzh to mean "homeless" and asked the old man where he was sleeping now. "So far where I've always lived," he said impatiently, "until they throw me out, that is. But that's not the point—I say *they made me a bomzh!* As if I haven't worked all my life, as if I'm a criminal or something, as if I'm not needed by anybody—as if I'm not *human!*" After this last outburst, he suddenly lost interest in us and went back to his rubbing, stubbornly ignoring further questions. My friend shrugged, and we went for some more vodka in one of the cheap bars that still existed in this district at the time.

More than a year before I even thought of a project about homelessness in Russia, this old man provided me with the basic concepts for such a study. Once I began my fieldwork in St. Petersburg in 1999, I heard the phrase "needed by nobody," *nikomu ne nuzhen,* and the words human (*chelovek*), people (*liudi*), and bomzh more or less every day. "Needed by nobody" is a set expression that conveys the worthlessness or rejection of something or someone. It can be used disparagingly to belittle others or, as the old man did, to convey subjective feelings of loneliness and vulnerability. As the logic goes, those who are not needed are, in Douglas's terms, matter out of place, dirt embodied, for real human beings are by definition immersed in social webs of mutual responsibility and protection (Douglas 1966, 34). Bomzhi (as the plural goes, emphasis on the last syllable) are, as the old man made clear, not needed; as if to emphasize this fact further, they are often talked about as *ostatki* (leftovers), *griaz'* (dirt), *der'mo* (dung), *drian'* (rubbish), *govno* (shit), *gadost'* (filth), or just *broshennye* (thrown away). Dirt appeared as a parable when they talked about themselves too. "If you are *treated* like shit," said one man, "you start to *feel* like it too, and then you'll *become* a piece of shit in no time at all." Therefore, he and others emphasized, it is crucial not to give in, to persist that in spite of everything, one *is* still human, and to do one's best to act accordingly. Not that the *real* thing was possible to achieve in this life, but at least it was something for the time being, to get through another day with at least a minimum measure of human dignity.

Regardless of how thrown away they may seem or feel, human beings are always able to manipulate, negotiate, and improvise their position in relation to others, and my main concern in this study is the resulting makeshift humanness; the bricolage of "as if" and "instead of" that is patched together by those who are deprived of the basic preconditions for a sense of human worth. Related issues are in which way and by whom one should be regarded as qualifying as a human; how one is displaced from these presumably humanizing social contexts; what means of survival are available outside of them;

and how reinterpretations and alternative meanings of humanness are utilized to negotiate the status as bomzh. The story is structured in accordance with the social contexts in which "not neededness" was experienced most tangibly by the homeless people I knew—different but intertwined clusters of social relationships that, from the viewpoint of the homeless, have their own regimes of exclusion and inclusion. It concerns the state and the formal social structure; the social aspects of the world of labor; the urban landscape in which physical bodies are situated; informal social networks from the time before homelessness; and the social relationships between the homeless. Throughout there run notion of "leftovers" and "dirt," which I finally bring up in a literal sense by focusing on cleanliness and physical appearance; not in itself a sphere in which social interaction takes place but a fundamental threshold to those that are mentioned.

The term "makeshift" applies not only to human existence, but also to the social orders that purportedly produce persons. Social waste is, as Bauman argues (2004), a result of modern social design as such. Any state-like formation always produces human "leftovers," for its resources—including housing—are always distributed according to some particular model of society and its members. These constructs are always makeshift since they can never encompass social reality in its entire complexity; as a result, someone is always lost in the process. Different designs result in different processes of expulsion; in most Western countries, for instance, homelessness has since the so-called neoliberal turn in the late 1900s proliferated due to increased housing costs and cuts in public expenditure (cf. Snow and Anderson 1993, 237–53; Wright 1997, 81–85; Kennet 1999). In Russia, by contrast, the production of this particular form of waste is less related to household economies than to administrative disjunctions and the inherent fallacies of Soviet social engineering. The state has always been equipped with plenty of mechanisms that efficiently and systematically deprive people of their homes, but until 1991 it also had a number of laws that equally effectively dispatched the victims behind bars if they dared to remind the public of their existence.

Razval, the "downfall" of the Soviet system, initiated a decade that was makeshift in every sense of the word. The period has gone down in history as "transition" or "transformation," terms that themselves indicate temporariness, while those who had to endure it referred to it as *bardak* (chaos, literally brothel) or *bezpredel* (boundlessness).[1] As "wild capitalism" confronted the Soviet bureaucracy, new discrepancies were added to the old ones, and novel routes to homelessness appeared. Recently displaced people joined an existing—but before then, concealed—displaced population, and in a few years homelessness was a conspicuous facet of metropolitan cityscapes. In the general tide of social calamities, this particular problem did not receive much attention or sympathy, for only a selected few had the privilege of escaping unscathed from hyperinflation, eroding structures of public support, proliferating criminality, and escalating corruption. In effect, everybody used whatever was at hand to make ends meet—or, in certain cases, to become very rich—and although the so-called bomzhi occupied the most marginal spaces in the general turmoil of "makeshifting," their strategies were in essence not different from those of others.

In large Russian cities, the turbulence calmed down in the second half of the 1990s, but the financial crisis of August 1998 put a temporary stop to the nascent stabilization. In 1999, people were once again cursing the neverending bardak and grieving their lost savings, with the exception of the homeless, who did not have anything to lose in the first place. Since the turn of the millennium, however, "transition" has moved into the past tense. A relative economic stability has incited private persons as well as the authorities to revamp the former decay and invest in the future; a process that, among other things, has fundamentally affected the mode of homelessness that I studied. The period of relative prosperity was interrupted by the economic crisis in late 2008, a worldwide recession that continues into 2009. Nonetheless, it will inscribe itself into history with a different name, be it "post-transition," "the Putin period," or something else. As the Soviet past becomes increasingly distant, the relevance of terms such as post-Soviet and post-Socialist diminish too. As Humphrey (2002a) argues, these concepts make sense only as long as the people we write about still identify with or relate to the Soviet past and as long as social scientists need them for historically informed studies. For these reasons, I keep the concepts. The administrative and legal framework that deprived the people I knew of their homes was and largely remains Soviet, and as persons, most of them were quite Soviet too. They grew up and lived their domestic lives in the Soviet era, and most of them became homeless in this period, even if some had the chance to experience a few transition years before it turned them into bomzhi. Their conceptualizations and values with regard to social existence and humanness were inculcated during this period of stagnation, and the imaginary home with which they juxtaposed homelessness was distinctly Soviet. This is indeed a story about the Soviet legacy, or about Soviet leftovers.

Dimensions of "Not Neededness"

"Homelessness" is not an emic concept. In the Soviet period, there was no need for such a word, since most social problems were officially nonexistent, and in the 1990s the term gained ground in the mass media and within academe mainly thanks to the conscious and tireless efforts of activist NGOs. To this day, few Russians refer to people who suffer from an apparent lack of housing as "homeless"—not even the homeless themselves, as a matter of fact. I use it for simplicity's sake and because of the strongly derogatory character of the term bomzh, which is the most common designation in popular parlance. During the last thirty years, it has gradually replaced older designations such vagrant (*brodiaga*) or *bich*, a joking acronym for *byvshii intelligentnyi chelovek*, "formerly intellectual person." Originally the term bich referred to intellectuals imprisoned by Stalin who had no place to live once Khrushchev released them (see Likhodei 2003). Homeless*ness* as a social condition is an equally novel term, but reads *bezdomnost'* when anyone cares to use it. The homeless usually used the expression "this life," however, which refers to a tough, dreary existence in general and is used by anyone who finds life unbearable or stifling.

Bomzh was originally an acronym too, one that comes from the state administrative apparatus. *Bez Opredelennogo Mesta Zhitel'stva* literally means "without a specific place of residence" and refers to a person without a so-called *propiska*, a compulsory registration at a permanent address, on which most civil rights and social benefits are based. It is displayed as a stamp in one's ID papers, which is why the old man at the Eternal Flame showed us his passport. As a bomzh in the administrative sense of the word, he no longer had the formal right to his municipal apartment (although he still occupied it), nor to pensions, medical care, even a work permit. Nor did he, as officially nonexistent, have access to any state structures of social support, and regardless of his respect for law and order, he was a lawbreaker as well, since it violates the passport laws to lack a propiska. Furthermore, the registration applies only locally. A person registered in Murmansk has no more rights in St. Petersburg than the old man had, and unless he or she registers temporarily after some time he or she is guilty of the same misdemeanor. Nowadays the offense incurs only fines, however, not imprisonment as in the Soviet period.

As Tikhonova argues, the absence of a propiska is basically the only indisputable criterion for social exclusion in Russia (2004, 109–15). Aside from that, the ubiquity of social hardship and deprivation since the downfall makes it difficult to pinpoint how certain categories have become more estranged than others from resources and social services (see Redmond and Hutton 2000, 8; De Soto and Dudwick 2002, 1–5). Still, it is not particularly unusual not to be registered: in 1999, an estimated three million Russian citizens (about 2 percent of the population) lacked a propiska, of whom between fifty and two hundred thousand lived in St. Petersburg (thus constituting some-where between 1 and 4 percent of the population).[2] To these an unknown (but probably even larger) number of subjects should be added: those who are registered, but in the wrong place. The vast majority of these "territorial misfits" have makeshift housing and jobs, albeit outside of official payrolls and registers, and frequently at the price of manifest discrimination and exploita-tion (Caldwell 2004, 137–39). My primary concern in this study is people who lack conventional housing rather than bomzhi in the administrative sense of the word, but there are no clear-cut boundaries separating the cat-egories. Certain roofless people have a propiska in places where they cannot live, and sometimes unregistered people with access to more or less makeshift housing have to resort to empty attics. It is merely a matter of different poles of a continuum along which individuals move, sometimes shuttling between "sleeping rough" and hospitable acquaintances, but often only in one direc-tion, further and further away from phenomena such as beds, privacy, or friends.

"Human" and "needed" are Russian articulations of what anthropologists usually call social personhood, which implies being a recognized co-actor, or agent-in-society, in a social whole of some sort. Like personhood, needed-ness is contextual, that is, construed in different but partially interconnected social settings, and may be bestowed upon someone in one context but not in another (cf. Harris 1989, 602–4). A bomzh in the administrative sense of the word is, as an example, rejected by the state but not necessarily by friends and family. A "bomzh-bum," however, is barred from a number of crucial spaces where social persons are conventionally created and maintained—a multi-leveled social exclusion that the Western concept of homelessness con-ventionally indicates, unless the term is used in a figurative sense (Wardhaugh 2000, 76ff.). Contemporary ethnographies on this topic try to give a first-hand account of everyday homeless life while at the same time showing how large-scale structures and processes emerge and are reflected at the individual level. The predicament itself, homelessness, is thereby seen as involving an ab-sence of conventional housing although it cannot be reduced to it. Roughly, it tends to be analyzed in relation to a macro-scale society in which housing, jobs, and social benefits are distributed; an intimate social level related to fam-ily and friends; and a moral dimension tied to social stigmatization (Snow and Anderson 1993; Wagner 1993; Passaro 1996; Wright 1997).[3]

The order of the chapters follows these levels of exclusion rather than the homeless hierarchy of importance and acquaints the reader with the home-less world and its people by drilling down from the macro perspective to an interpersonal level. Chapter 1 explains the state apparatus of administrative exclusion, the propiska, and its interconnection with allocated housing, access to work, legal sanctions on movement, and the construction of the stereotype bomzh as an outlaw and an Other. As complex as its historical development, my own account of this system is merely a brief overview that primarily highlights aspects that were relevant in my own field. (For a far more extensive and detailed account of the history of Russian homelessness, I wholeheartedly recommend Stephenson 2006.) My main focus is how the propiska, the cornerstone of Soviet and post-Soviet state surveillance and population management, permeates the most mundane aspects of the everyday lives of the citizens, locating them, keeping them in place, and regulating their moves. I pay particular attention to what Ledeneva has called the self-subversive nature of the system, or "the 'reverse side' of an over-controlling centre" (1998, 3). The gaze of power may aim at discipline and control (Foucault 1977), but the Soviet-Russian state is, and was always, quite shortsighted, for neither its main lens, the propiska, nor other strategies of vision are particularly efficient. The system itself excludes large categories from the administratively regulated structures of society, and it is also perpetually circumvented. The Socialist welfare state was not as caring and providing as the propaganda would have it, and in the Soviet era as well as later, subjects have always compensated for its wants by "seizing the moment" to pursue their own interests—manipulations that may result in homelessness, for those who cheat or for others (De Certeau 1984, 34–39).

The linking of civil rights to a place of permanent abode makes Russian homelessness more similar to the situation of undocumented international migrants than the one of homeless Western Europeans or North Americans. People who dare to enter desirable places without also being desired or desirable persons, are, as Bauman (2004, 32–33) argues, present-day versions of *Homo sacer*, Agamben's (1998) model of an excluded being: exempt from positive law through a deprivation of rights, but negatively included since the law prescribes that he may be killed (or, in this case, incarcerated or deported). However, nowhere is power exclusively located to the law and its representatives; in particular not in weak states such as the Socialist ones and their successors. As a substantial number of important studies of such societies has shown, the law amounts to little in comparison to informal sources of influence, regardless of whether the action takes place within the higher echelons of power or at considerably humbler levels (Wedel 1986; Handelman 1995; Ledeneva 1998; Humphrey 2002b; Nazpary 2002). While purported "political lives" rarely feel recognized as such by the state, the ubiquity of unofficial economic practices among grassroots in general opens up the scope for action also for seemingly "bare lives," whose essential dilemma is not legal exclusion (however cumbersome this may be) but a lack of reasonably reliable and supportive contacts. Such social capital, in Bourdieu's sense, differentiates a bomzh from someone who merely lacks registration or, more broadly, economic success in the common struggle for survival (1990, 35).[4]

Chapter 2 elucidates how homeless incomes are intertwined with the sustenance strategies of others while at the same time paying particular attention to the ways in which a strong work ethic is used to negotiate human dignity. Chapter 3 focuses on the utilization of urban space and highlights the importance of the organization of the cityscape for the survival of marginalized people. It also discusses violence and danger, for the relative absence of state control does not imply only freedom from effective surveillance but a withdrawal of protection as well. In both chapters I use waste as an organizing concept, because the Russian labor market is too permeated by so-called informal (and tax-evading) practices at all levels for the concept of a second, or shadow, economy to make much sense. Economic as well as spatial niches occupied by the homeless are accessible not because the state cannot see them but because nobody else wants them, which is why I prefer to think in terms of refuse space or refuse economics.

Chapters 4 and 5 take a close look at intimate social contexts, the second level of exclusion that qualitative researchers on homelessness tend to measure by. Homeless people are rarely if ever supported by the kind of networks that are counted by mainstream society—most notably, conventional family relations—and this aspect is even more crucial in societies where family and friends compensate for the deficiencies of feeble systems of state social support, as is the case in Russia and other post-Socialist countries (Shlapentokh 1984; Wedel 1986, 95–103; Pine 1996; Caldwell 2004). *Blizkie,* "close ones" as they are called in Russia, are, furthermore, also a moral and emotional nexus; the soil in which "real" human beings are primarily cultivated. The common factor among the homeless is nonexistent or fractured family ties. While chapter 4 addresses family and other social ties from the time before homelessness, chapter 5 deals with the social world of the homeless themselves, an ambiguous togetherness of sorts that for a number of reasons never becomes a satisfactory replacement for lost near and dear ones but remains a conflict-ridden mix of life-sustaining mutual support and ruthless self-interest. These two chapters largely address how neededness is embedded in notions of reciprocity and forms of exchange, and how understandings of human worth are affected by an inability to contribute and by the chronic contradiction between self-preservation and sociability.

Finally, homelessness implies exclusion from what might be called the moral community. Be it on the official level of society or more informally, homeless people are always stigmatized as purportedly unreliable nonpersons, and this fact certainly affects their options in finding a place to stay. The shift in meaning from "administrative absence of abode" into "dirty drunkard with lice" says enough about Russian popular prejudice (more about this in chapter 1), but a lack of territorial attachment seems to have an unnerving effect on settled people everywhere and at all times. Historically, vagrancy has been outlawed all over the modern world (Foucault 1977; Humphreys 1999; Torpey 2000); as noted by numerous researchers on contemporary unsettled or uprooted social categories such as the homeless, refugees, or traveling ethnic groups, their spatial indeterminacy is inexorably associated with moral elusiveness and symbolic pollution in Douglas's sense (see Malkki 1992; Sibley 1995; Stephenson 2006). The negative characteristics ascribed to bomzhi and the ways in which the homeless deal with those character-istics is a theme running through all of the chapters, one that becomes more central as the book proceeds. It is particularly highlighted in chapter 6, which discusses self-perception in the context of physical appearance and dirt in a literal sense, together with an elaboration on the complex relation-ship between alcohol and humanness, of the ways in which gender relates to homelessness, as well as how the homeless feel about trajectories, or, in their words, "getting used to it all."

Human Playgrounds: Society and Eternity

The homeless people I knew sometimes used the word bomzh as a neutral designation, to indicate whether or not someone was homeless or to specify homeless people as a group. If sharing and generosity was the subject, it could even be associated with positive qualities ("only bomzhi share everything they have"). As a rule, however, alternative meanings were not invested in the term, and nobody was fond of having it attributed to his or her own person. I discovered this during the very first days of my fieldwork, when I made the mistake of including "bomzh" in questions about whether or not people had a propiska. I reformulated my inquiry very quickly after irritated answers such as: "Bomzh? Well, in the *documents* perhaps, but not at *heart!*" "You shouldn't put impertinent questions to elderly people, young lady!" or "So what? Am I not a human being then?" The word became less charged as I became more acquainted with my interlocutors, but they were nonetheless conscientious in pointing out that "perhaps I'm a bomzh, but at least I'm not *typical.*"

Every move in these negotiations can be designated with the appropriate label from the symbolic interactionist supply of terms for stigma management, but I refrain from this kind of analysis. My concern is not the actual techniques used to improve spoiled identities or stigmatized selves (Goffman 1963) but rather the cultural understandings that imbue these actions and give them meaning, the "stuff" that is communicated. In particular, this concerns the word human, which in contrast to the relatively stable term bomzh could acquire meanings with quite disparate capacities to challenge or negotiate "not neededness." This is largely a story about the frequently awkward coexistence of two interdependent, but in my opinion quite distinct, articulations. The first and most common use of the word human was, as I have outlined above, basically synonymous to the quality of being needed, the state of being a mutually intelligible actor in the practical everyday world of routine responsibilities, the social universe conventionally referred to as society. As formulated by the homeless—and probably anyone whose referential framework was forged in the Soviet period—the emphasis on interdependence, cooperation, and inclusion may be stronger than in constructions of social personhood encompassed by Westerners or by younger or more successful Russians today, but as I shall show, not even among the homeless was collectivism as ubiquitous and unequivocal as frequent stereotypes about Russianness would often have it.

If social agents interact in the concrete society where everyday survival takes place, the other predominant articulation of humanness relates exclusively to what Turner (1974) called anti-structure: a different social modality or mode of experiencing and relating to social existence in which everybody is human in the mere capacity of being born, as a unique and undifferentiated part of a universal whole. When people talked about feeling human in this way, social distinctions such as bomzh simply lost all meaning. These were moments of spontaneity, philosophical reflection, or sincere introspection, quite unlike emotional outbursts of optimism or hope or grief or aggression. More often than not, alcohol was involved.

This mode of humanness is hardly specific to the homeless. Referred to as *dusha* (soul), it has for a couple of centuries been celebrated as the very essence of Russian culture and identity, by Russians and foreigners alike. In the neverending intellectual debate about Russia's position in relation to the West, intellectual giants such as Dostoevsky and Berdyaev have elaborated on the subject (Boym 1995), which is incidentally also Russia's most prominent foreign ambassador, promoted by numerous travel accounts and in many popular representations; Winston Churchill perhaps put dusha in its most memorable form when he called Russia "a riddle wrapped in a mystery inside an enigma." The qualities of soul are often likened to the vast, impenetrable Russian land with its obscure borders (Medvedev 1999), and they also appear to be anti-structural in a literal sense, since they are articulated as the very antithesis of all forms of predictable rationality and organization or the routine responsibilities of everyday life, what the Russians call *byt*, a belittling term denoting petty concerns of the material kind or the mundane, soul-killing necessities of the grey-hued "this life," cf. Pesmen 2000, 46–51). Elevated as truly human properties are instead irrationality, paradox, intuition, unpredictability, or even reckless anarchy; like dusha's propensity of embracing contradiction, it also turns suffering and weakness into virtues.

Although basically an intellectual construct, originally modeled on an idealized Orthodox peasantry prone to patience, suffering, and spirituality, dusha is fully sociologically observable as an "aesthetics, a way of feeling about and being in the world, a shifting focus and repertoire of discourses, rituals, beliefs, and practices" (Pesmen 2000, 9). Whether or not this "way of feeling" was always "there," it gives sociability, *obshchenie*, a very distinct spontaneity and intimacy (cf. Yurchak 2006, 148–51). The connotations of openness, deep feeling, and a communion of sorts are even more emphasized in the context of drinking, which, since it represents the epitome of togetherness and sharing, is simultaneously an expression and a vehicle of soulfulness or "a master trope for aspects of dusha" (Pesmen 2000, 187). A disregard of formal rules and social distinctions in favor of frank approaches "from a human to another human" also underpin reciprocal patterns that frequently are studied by social science, be it economies of favors (Ledeneva 1998) or the personification of trust (Humphrey 2000a, 83). Nonetheless, references to soulful social modalities are scarce within social science, perhaps as a conscious attempt to avoid romanticism and cliché (Pesmen 2000, 6). Pesmen's monograph on discourses and practices related to soul in the early 1990s is a noteworthy exception on which I rely extensively, as well as Ries's (1997) work on negotiations of cultural identity and notions of collective suffering during perestroika.

To people who by other definitions are not human at all, such a social modality comes in handy. The mundane expressions in my field were mostly related to openheartedness, sincerity, oneness (implying equality), conscience, and, not least, drinking, but the main thing, as emphasized by Pesmen as well as Ries, was an ability to feel deeply, and it was precisely through the given context and the emotions displayed in the word human that I knew what my informants were talking about. They rarely used the word dusha (see Wierzbicka 1992 for its semiotic aspects), and since the most important facet to them was an ability to experience and express togetherness with other people, I shall refer to the anti-structural mode of being human as fellow humanness, unless I make direct allusions to soul.

About the Field

Other anthropologists tend to be curious about my fieldwork, assuming that it was extremely tough, depressing, or even dangerous. That depends on how "tough" is defined. The most unnerving field stories I hear from colleagues describe suspicious, silent, and scornful informants-to-be, a problem that I never had to face. Studying "down," as it were, has certain advantages in this respect, at least if the people one studies feel lonely, despised, and rejected. Virtually everyone I met appreciated the fact that somebody was taking a serious interest in their lives and bothering to listen to them, even though they quite often did not want to talk about the subjects in which I was interested. They never made me feel like an intruder, but there was a range of other dilemmas that could easily fill a volume or two on methodology. Here I restrict myself to a summary of how the fieldwork was conducted, with a brief introduction to my main field sites.

I was already familiar with Russia when I planned this project. I traveled in the USSR a handful of times in the late perestroika period, and these trips resulted in a number of personal relationships with Russians and, gradually, some language skills. I lived in St. Petersburg for four months in 1996 (when I met the old man by the Eternal Flame) and spent a couple of months there as preparation for this project. I communicated somewhat fluently with middle-aged and elderly people (most of my informants were thirty or older), because youth slang is harder to understand because it changes all the time. *Mat,* the strongly sexualized curses that permeate colloquial Russian language everywhere, and criminal slang were not a problem since those who used it foresaw my ignorance and adjusted for it.

Initially I used organizations that help the homeless to find informants. A year and a half before my main fieldwork, I contacted an NGO called Nochlezhka and volunteered for a few weeks in a soup kitchen they were running. Among other things, they register people who lack a propiska in order to secure various civil rights for them by lobbying the city authorities.[5] They also distributed *Na Dne,* a street paper similar to *The Big Issue* or *Street News* to its homeless vendors. In 1999, *Na Dne* organized a writing contest for people who had experienced homelessness, and the contributions were later published in an anthology, *Tell Us Your Life,* which I have used as a complement to my own material (*Na Dne* 1999).

Their office was a sympathetically chaotic place where visitors were allowed to loiter even if they had no particular reason to be there. Most clients came to register or to receive advice on legal matters or to pick up clothes donated by private persons. I asked some about their particular problems (which they usually appreciated), while others spoke with me because I appeared to be idle. I also visited Nochlezhka's shelter or the halfway house, the best term for this building where the seventy or so inhabitants live more or less permanently. At the time, this was the only place of its kind in the entire city, but to my disappointment it closed unexpectedly for renovation in the summer. At the same address, Médecins Sans Frontières ran a clinic for homeless people in early 1999, but later they moved to one of the city's hospitals, and I never conducted fieldwork in their overcrowded waiting room.

Previously, I had also been in touch with two other organizations; the Caritas soup kitchen for homeless people and a corps of the Salvation Army that served the homeless. At Caritas I hung out some three or four times a week, joining the shifting crowds of visitors who stayed for a chat after finishing their meals. Many of them were also regular clients at the outdoor soup kitchen of the Salvation Army, a better place for mingling than the Salvation Army headquarters where I joined the other activities—Bible classes, discussion groups, hobbies—mostly out of politeness, spending as much time as possible with the visitors in the yard beforehand and afterwards. The most important field site was not a charity, however, but the largest and most central railway station in the city, the Moscow Station, where a long outdoor yard was the regular locus of some 100 to 150 more or less homeless people. I worked there some four times a week, usually in the company of the homeless man who initially took me there (to whom I shall return shortly).

Nochlezhka was the only place where one could spend an entire day. Any activity at the Salvation Army takes a few hours; Caritas is open only three hours a day; the residents of the shelter were usually "at home" only in the evenings; and after five hours at the station I was always exhausted because the place was so intense. In addition to my one day a week at Nochlezhka, I therefore went to two or more of these sites each day. Station regulars (as I call those who regularly hung out at the Moscow Station) were, with some exceptions, less prone to excursions, while the crowds at the NGOs overlapped each other, with the result that I often bumped into the same people more than once a day in different locations.

Regardless of site, my main approach was simply to hang around until somebody initiated a conversation with me or until I found a polite and natural reason to start talking to someone. "Someone" was as a rule more than one person, and most conversations were in reality unstructured group interviews of a sort in which the interviews lacked structure as much as the groups. Interlocutors and topics of conversation replaced each other continuously as people came, interrupted, changed the subject, and left as suddenly as they had appeared. The station was far more intense than the other places in this sense. Charity workers exercised no discipline—a genuinely unsympathetic police force tried to, with uneven results—and there were income opportunities as well as generous quantities of alcohol. With a seldom fulfilled promise to return later, interlocutors left promptly if they spotted deposit bottles and other opportunities for profit; moreover, most people—not only the homeless—drank habitually and hard. Because of all this, the general incoherence of all the field sites was even higher at the station, which made four or five hours there enough to shatter my brains completely.

There is no privacy in this neverending flow of people and events, no option to distance oneself from the here and now, be it physically, socially, or mentally. I received a hint of its destructive capacity when I tried to conduct private conversations. Participant observation grasps present events, but I also wanted in-depth interviews to get some notion of individual pasts and reflections. These crowded sites provided few if any places for confidential chats, however, and when I tried to invite my interviewees to cafes they would generally fall into an embarrassed silence because they felt that other people were staring at them—unless they promptly ordered vodka. The drink was meant to be humanizing, but in reality it just made the interviews more incoherent; since it would have been offensive to refuse my guests what they wanted, I gave up cafes entirely. Even when I managed to identify some secluded spot, I would have to make excuses to anyone who might feel excluded, after which I would be accused of playing favorites. Nor was there time for private conversations; my planned interlocutors always claimed to be too busy or in the wrong mood for a long talk, always suggesting that we meet later and elsewhere. All such appointments were a failure—not, I think, because they resented an interview as such but because in the homeless reality most preconceived plans tend to be thwarted by contingent and unforeseeable events. In addition, they wanted a long, private chat to be "from human to human," which presupposes a spontaneous desire to open up and reveal oneself. But this mood never appeared when it should, because homelessness does not provide options even to *think* beyond the here and now. If I brought up issues not directly relevant to the immediate context, they were infallibly misunderstood or met with silence, whether I did it in large groups or in some moment of unexpected privacy.

Finally, I gave up all aspirations to intimacy and surrendered to the continuous current of people, events, and talk that I had at hand. Each time I met a person, I received contingent and often contradictory fragments of his or her present and past life, and I was left with a huge and incomplete jigsaw puzzle to put together after the fact. There are aspects of homeless life that

I know nothing about because nobody ever mentioned them spontaneously, and vast chunks of individual life histories remain obscure because they were always overshadowed by present matters. What I did get, on the other hand, I got straight from the lived experience of the people concerned, not from moments of distanced reflection conditioned by myself as an interrogator.[6]

Judging from my field notes, I know *something* valuable about some two hundred persons. About 40 percent were women, which is more than the average 20 to 25 percent among the homeless registered at Nochlezhka in 1999. To a certain extent I paid particular attention to the women, for instance by hanging out more in the women's section of the shelter than in the men's section, but it is probably more significant that my most populated field site, the Moscow Station, featured a comparatively high proportion of females. Women as well as men were heterogeneous in terms of social background. As chapter 1 will show, almost half of them were former convicts, but many others had lived established lives until only a few years previously. Some had university degrees, although this was relatively unusual. In general, they were Russian or russified. The existing ethnic Others were mainly from the Caucasus, Moldavia, or Uzbekistan. Some were temporarily stuck in Russia while traveling, but most of them were living there when they became homeless and considered Russia to be their home. Groups of refugees from other former Soviet republics were frequent in St. Petersburg at the time, but they never mixed with the homeless population. Nor did the street children. My youngest informants were in their early twenties, and the oldest was eighty-two, although the majority were aged between thirty and sixty. Street children have their own hangouts, and they are reportedly not fond of any adult supervision (Fujimura 2002), let alone from bomzhi, seen by all as pathetic losers (Stephenson 2006, 47). Nor were drugs common. I knew four active users, youngsters who mainly kept to "drug-specific" hangouts where, as I understood it, few of their acquaintances were homeless. Some other young people had experience of heroin or home-made opiates but claimed that they were too expensive in their present situation. As for mental illness, I met three persons who suffered either from recurring psychoses or from perceptions of reality were distinctly different from those of others, and two of them were regularly admitted to mental hospitals. In 2002, however, I was told that the asylums were increasingly reluctant to admit patients without a local propiska, and the staff at Nochlezhka claimed that an increasing number of clients used narcotics or sold them in order to survive.

I met about a hundred people on such a regular basis that I felt obliged to remember their names. This was difficult; a third of my female informants at the station were in reality called Lena, and a third of the men whom I saw most often were called Sergei. To prevent the reader from getting lost, I have given each person an internally unique name of his or her own, or I omit names when they are unnecessary. Nonetheless, the number of characters rivals that of a great nineteenth-century Russian novel, and if they bewilder the reader, I can only offer the consolation that the homeless are no less confused. Their way of coping is to pay less attention to *who* and *when* and more to *what* and *why*. So did I, and it worked.

It goes without saying that I became closer with certain people than with others, even if I generally tried to avoid anything that could be interpreted as favoritism. "Becoming close with" does not imply "knowing everything about," and those whom I liked the most do not necessarily appear more frequently in the text than others. One main character was, however, also my closest buddy. His name was Vova, and he appointed himself my guide to the Moscow Station already on the first day of my fieldwork. I met him at Nochlezhka's office, the first place I went. Homeless or imprisoned for twenty of his forty-seven years and a permanent regular at the largest bomzh hangout in the city, he was an expert on "this life," he claimed, and educated enough to communicate with a *sotsiolog*.[7] I agreed, and he indeed proved to be of great value. His persistent explanations of everything that others said were not all that necessary, but I would not have been able to penetrate the station as quickly and conveniently without him. I had his acquaintances straight to hand, while he rescued me from exceptionally drunk and disturbing people by telling them off for me.

He made no secret of wanting to be paid for these services, so we struck a deal. For three or four days a week he would accompany me at the station, introduce me to others, and leave me alone with them if I wanted, and I would give him a good meal and fifty rubles a day, plus support in the event of certain unexpected needs.* I saw—and still see—the payment merely as a compensation for valuable time that he would otherwise have spent making ends meet, and initially I thought that I would have to pay others as well. However, most people regarded money as antithetical to a sincere relationship, and only very rarely did I have to compensate anyone for time

---

*In 1999, one U.S. dollar equaled about 27 rubles, but I find it more sensible to refer monetary sums to commodities that are relevant to the homeless. 50 rubles was then worth: 20 packs of cheap cigarettes *or* 6 bottles of beer *or* 7 loaves of good rye bread *or* 5 bottles of the most popular solvent. A chronically underpaid doctor made about 800 rubles per month, plus another 50 "on the side" for each consultation. The minimum pension was 225 rubles a month, about 9 US$, while pensions of 1,000 to 1,500 rubles were considered to be extremely good. Nonetheless, I estimate that it was difficult to survive on this sum of money. An income of 3,000 rubles per month was, according to my friends, not good, but enough for a relatively comfortable life.

or information. More often I was asked for support for the sake of friendship or *ot dushi,* "from the soul," and this is also how I spontaneously offered support. A traditional gift from the soul is a bottle or its contents, but I made it clear very early on that I would not give away cash or alcohol. My purpose was to get rid of some particularly thirsty and unabashed youngsters at the station who interrupted every conversation I had with requests for "something to drink," and to prevent similar nuisances in other places. Instead, I handed out cigarettes without restriction, a friendly gesture between fellow smokers that could serve as an equivalent to an offer of drink. My alcohol policy worked relatively well, although it was interpreted as a sign of moral fortitude and virtuous temperance, not as the merely pragmatic way of remaining sane it was. But I was respected for it, so I left people in this belief. I also helped out with medicines or food, passport photos (their ID documents disappear all the time), train tickets, handy objects such as immersion heaters, and, in some cases, cash. A less utilitarian but astoundingly popular request was that I act as a photographer and provide people with portraits of themselves, "as a memory." There are endless ways of interpreting this desire, but I take it as a wish to prove a continuously denied existence and a small compensation for all of the other material tokens of memory that these people had lost. At the Moscow Station, however, an annoyed FSB (formerly KGB) officer threatened to arrest me if I continued to photograph "strategic military objects"; since by that time, after a couple of months of fieldwork, I was tired of taking photos instead of talking to people, I obeyed him. The unfortunate effect is that I have few photos of the station as it looked at the time, and in the existing ones, my smiling informants are blocking the view.[8]

Vova made it clear from the start that he was a chronic alcoholic, which initially made me hesitant to undertake a monetary deal with him. Even if payment seemed OK with him, the ethical aspects of providing an alcoholic with the means to drink were dubious, and so was the practical side of it. I changed my mind after that first day at the station, after I realized that first of all, I would never find a guide to that place who was *not* a heavy drinker; second, that getting drunk at the station did not require much money, so he would drink without me as well; and third, if I wanted him to appear on time and in a relatively sober state, I had to give him what he required for the effort. To this day I have no idea what would have been ethically appropriate in this case. Anything I gave to anybody, medicine as well as bread, was potential currency in the general "booze exchange," so the only morally pure option would have been not to give away anything (which is itself immoral) or to avoid studying alcoholics in the first place.

I decided to deal with Vova's drinking habits pragmatically, which meant restricting the clause "unexpected expenses." He lost everything he owned each night in the obligatory drinking spree at the station, and after replacing three pairs of spectacles in one week, I refused him another. Thenceforth he lost them more rarely and found new ones on his own. We soon worked out some sort of implicit equilibrium with regard to gifts and support, mediated through a subtly shared sense of humor. He manipulated me excessively, either interpreting our "balanced" deal in his favor or appealing to me as a traditional Russian *khoziaika* (matron), who was to take care of all his needs as they appeared, in a loving, motherly, and nurturing way—until, that is, he once again profited from defining our relationship as strictly business. I insisted on the latter interpretation, but to my own benefit.

At the same time, we related to this game with some sort of ironic distance that made it possible to laugh together at our mutual attempts to exploit each other. It was, paradoxically, a very warm and straightforward relationship, albeit tarnished by the original unevenness in the distribution of power. Regardless of how many times he triumphantly left the battlefield with a substantial trophy straight from my wallet, I would win the game in total, for I was to go home and benefit from a book about him while he was to stay behind and remain as broke as ever, after drinking the last of my cash. We pretended that this difference did not exist, and sometimes our relationship felt almost like a friendship. Nonetheless, I refuse to call any of my homeless informants "friends." It would only be hypocritical; I was neither able nor prepared to do for them what both of us would expect from the kind of bond that we refer to as friendship. "Friends" in this book are non-homeless Russians whom I know through this project as well as independent of it.

Vova's drinking got out of hand in the summer. Since he missed our appointments, it was not my money he was using to destroy himself, but I felt guilty nonetheless, wanting to help him but realizing that there was nothing I could do. We could never talk about it. Vova was as distanced from himself as he was from his economic endeavors with me, and he related to his own "degradation" (as the other station regulars called it) with a mixture of denial and irony. In fact, this was his attitude to life as a whole, apart from a couple of rare occasions when he was so drunk that he just fell into my arms and wept. Usually, he seemed to get through by playacting. Depending on the situation, he was a naughty schoolboy, an experienced criminal, or a skilled veteran bomzh. (Vova was one of very few who did not mind this epithet, but obviously my research gave it some dignity—and provided him with a job.) The only role he played without even a touch of irony was that of doctor, his profession in a lost life that, I assume, was the only one he considered to be real enough to take seriously.

He was far from alone in cracking jokes about his miserable reality or in drinking to be able to bemoan it aloud. This emotional distance from oneself and one's fate is, according to Vova as well as others, one of the most important prerequisites for survival. Only recently dislocated people without a stigmatized past were willing to share their desperation and anguish as they actually experienced them. There were those—some of whom I knew very well—who simply refused to comment on their past, but most people with a long history of homelessness or imprisonment tended to approach past grievances as well as the humiliation and hopelessness of the present with a distinct dose of terse self-irony or even sarcasm. It may seem cynical, but the truth is that this fieldwork was as amusing and fun as it was deeply tragic—in spite of occasional lapses into wordless sobs.

It is difficult, not to say impossible, to write about these people in a key different from the one they offered me. My prose often resembles their idiom—distanced, curt, ironic. More than once I have tried to write about the processes that lie behind self-expressions of this kind; about the subjective experiences encompassed by these metonymic icebergs, these brisk punchlines; and about the feelings concealed behind each mountain of silence towering up before me. Every attempt has left me with a queasy feeling of infringing on somebody's integrity. I have tried to elaborate more on my own feelings too, but always with the uneasy sensation of stealing space from the people I set out to write about. When I told them that I was going to write about their lives, I meant, and they understood, that we were talking about the external world in which they live, not their insides. Finally I decided to convey their experiences in the same manner as they told them to me, without further comment. I believe that this is enough for the essence of this story to be conveyed—what it is to be needed by nobody, and what it takes to be human.

Chapter 1

"Excrement of the State"

The Soviet-Russian Production of Homelessness

The sociostructural mechanisms that expel "human refuse" from the Russian social organism are largely shaped by the legacy of Soviet social engineering and the attempts of early Socialist planners to position each subject precisely in the gigantic machine of state design. Hence an etiology of Soviet as well as of post-Soviet homelessness presupposes an elucidation of the main instrument to keep people in their proper places, in the most literal sense: the propiska, the obligatory registration at a permanent address. This system is best-known for its explicit restrictions on movement within the country, an aspect that in the Soviet time turned homelessness into a criminal offense. Without understating the coercion of the Soviet state, it is nonetheless important to underline that as the administrative cornerstone for a just distribution of social welfare, the propiska also achieved compliance through a more "fatherly" form of surveillance (Foucault 1991, 92) and that this governmental aspect was equally crucial for the production of "social waste."

The way in which political (or other) systems control their subjects is often framed in terms of seeing or legibility (Scott 1998), frequently with reference to Foucault's (1977) nightmare vision of panoptical surveillance—a classical model that seems difficult to avoid, in spite of recurring criticisms and calls for modification (Torpey 2000; Lyon 2006). One frequently invoked argument is that more attention must be paid to the responses of the purportedly controlled subjects, which I do by elucidating not only what De Certeau (1984) called strategy, the will of power to see and control, but also tactics, the manipulations of less compliant subjects to circumvent it. This implies an additional focus on systemic flaws. As Torpey argues, that modern states have monopolized the authority to control the movements of their subjects does not mean that they do it effectively (Torpey 2000, 5), and the Soviet system is notorious to this day for its inherent contradictions and chronic inefficiency. The characteristic mismatch between theory and actuality implied systemic contradictions that by themselves deprived people of their homes, but displacement and social exclusion were also the result of unsuccessful attempts of grassroots to compensate for the practical failure of the state to provide resources that it guaranteed in theory. Even though the state implicitly gave leeway for such improvisations as a provisional solution to its own disjunctions (Ledeneva 1998), these manipulations were always undertaken at the subjects' own risk.

The downfall obliterated certain overtly repressive mechanisms of displacement, and the introduction of the market economy created new shortcuts to housing, as money could now buy what formerly had been allocated by the state. Money also created novel routes to homelessness, although the legacy of the principle of just allocation in fact prevented the inability to pay rent from becoming one of them. Rather, the intersection of capitalism with the remaining administrative structure increased the scope for, and for many a citizen the necessity of, independent manipulations, which created novel routes to homelessness.

Keeping Matter out of Place out of Places that Matter

The restrictions on internal movement set by the propiska tend to be the main target of social researchers on the subject, Western as well as Russian, probably because this aspect is the most exotic to the former and the most infuriating to the latter. Historically, however, in Western Europe too, the movement of persons has always been circumscribed by various authorities. It is true that the Russian state exhibited the zealous ambition to control the physical movements of the population. Humphrey explains this with reference to a chronic anxiety about disunity and disintegration caused by the vastness of the land and its obscure borders, an anxiety that has always been managed by the exiling and containment of ideological dissent (2001, 339). The same logic may be expanded to differences in a broader sense, since the presumably incompatible urban and rural populations were separated from each other by serfdom and a passport system introduced by Peter the Great that prohibited residents from traveling without official permission.

However, Tsarist Russia was not unique in its attempts to make people stay put. Throughout Europe, population registers and restrictions on geographical movement date back to (at least) medieval times, but the modern nation-state has usurped the right to control this facet of social life (as well as others) from entities such as feudal lords, city authorities, the church, trade guilds, and so forth. The industrialization from the eighteenth century onward increasingly required a flexible workforce, while at the same time the extensive administrative infrastructures were developed that an effective monopoly on movement requires (Torpey 2000; see also Humphreys 1999). In Western Europe, internal restrictions of movement thus disappeared as the idea of the nation-state was institutionalized, and national borders rather than regional ones became the natural demarcations for the physical movement of citizens.

In Russia, too, the state administration gradually replaced lower-level authorities such as the landed gentry, but the empire remained a vast multiethnic, or multinational, state formation that never dissolved into nation-states (Steinwedel 2001). The abolishment of serfdom in 1861 facilitated a nascent industrialization, but the economic changes resulted in few other major alterations with regard to restrictions on movement. Only after the Revolution was the much-hated tsarist passport system abolished, although the new regime soon realized that some form of population register was necessary to administer the massive social transformations. Registers for the purpose of mobilizing labor thus appeared already in 1918 (Garcelon 2001; Stephenson 2006, 77), and in the 1920s attempts were made to solve a disastrous shortage of housing by confiscating and resettling large upper-class apartments, in which each registered tenant received a stipulated amount of *zhilploshchad'*, "living space" (I will return to these communal apartments, *kommunalki*, further on). Generally, the attempts of the state to control its subjects were relaxed during the New Economic Policy in the 1920s, gaining momentum only as Stalin initiated the extensive campaigns for industrialization and collectivization of agriculture in the early 1930s.

The present propiska system was created in 1932, when a new passport system was introduced that brought together obligatory work, access to housing, and restrictions on movement. Rural mass famine (caused by collectivization) and urban industrialization resulted in mass immigration to the large cities that had to be regulated (Matthews 1993, 27; Buckley 1995). The rapid and centrally planned Soviet industrialization differed from its

Western counterpart in that restrictions on movement were not obstructive but instrumental in the eyes of Socialist planners. Labor turnover was a serious problem, and some device was needed to direct cadres and keep them where they would be of most use (Kotkin 1995, 95–99).

The new passport system also served to enhance the revolutionary quality of urban populations. To live and work in the metropolitan centers, citizens had to obtain a new ID document, the domestic passport, a precondition of which was registration at a permanent address, the propiska (from the verb *propisat'*, "to register"). Recent peasant immigrants were denied propiski (and thereby passports) and had to leave these cities; somewhat later, former criminals, the unemployed, and political opponents were declared to be undesirable elements as well (for a record of such categories, see Popov 1995a, 1995b; Humphrey 2001, 337). As the system was gradually introduced throughout the country, the "misfits" were successively pushed further away (Popov 1995b). Collective farmers were not entitled to passports at all, which in practice made the system a socialistic variant of serfdom that disappeared only in the 1970s (Fitzpatrick 1994).

Throughout the Soviet period, the state was particularly attentive to the strategic cities and regions where the propiska system was first introduced.[1] They were to be protected against taking in too many people and, perhaps more important, the wrong *kind* of people. The huge differences in the standards of living between center and periphery in Russia were never erased by Communism, which resulted in a society characterized by territorial stratification rather than by class divisions based on capital, profession, or background (Zaslavsky 1982, 139–41). As social mobility was often simultaneously geographical, there was a constant flow of migrants to large cities in general and to Moscow, the hub of the centralized Soviet universe, in particular (Shlapentokh 1989, 86–88). The pressure was meant to be held at bay by the notorious Catch-22 situation that in Russian goes: *propiski net, raboty net—raboty net, propiski net* (no propiska, no job—no job, no propiska), meaning that, in accordance with the passport system, the one was always the prerequisite for the other.

Deportations, physical violence, and containment complemented the maintenance of the "sociopolitical hygiene" of these protected cities. However, these practices were in fact initially extra-legal (Stephenson 2006, 80–89). Arbitrary, secret deportations continue to this day, but for almost thirty years there was no codified legislation regulating physical movement. Only in 1960 a law (Paragraph 198 of the Criminal Code) was passed that prohibited "trespassing of the passport rules," that is, leaving one's region or city of registration for more than three days without reporting the journey to the authorities. The offense could, if repeated, result in a couple of years of incarceration, which was the case also with violations of Paragraph 209 of the Criminal Code, which prohibited vagrancy, begging, and *tuneiadstvo,* "parasitism" (in effect, long-term unemployment), which was passed at about the same time. In effect, Stephenson argues, the real object of criminalization was a social condition: displacement. Territorial transgressions were thus seen less as politically treacherous ill will or a mere breach of law, and more in terms of deviancy from a social normality that was based on attachment to a workplace and a permanent place of living.

In Agamben's (2005) terms, this legislation made permanent a state of exception. It codified a suspension of citizenship that initially was seen as an emergency measure, an extraordinary expulsion of allegedly hostile elements that was assumed to become redundant once the new and purified society was truly established. In a Foucauldian sense, these laws were also part and parcel of a general shift in emphasis between modes of domination. A Stalinist "sovereign despotism" obsessed with national security and political enemies gave way to a more governmental order characteristic of other modern welfare states, which also entailed an increased engagement in biopolitical concerns about the average "health and wealth" of the population (Foucault 1991, 1997). Between 1958 and 1961, a number of other laws appeared that aimed to improve the system of social welfare, and major reforms were launched with regard to education, pensions, orphanages, housing, and production of consumption goods (Madison 1968; Osborn 1970; George 1980). As the nurturing functions of the modern state have increased, so has its commitment to and reliance on strict demarcations of eligibility (Torpey 2000, 12). In the USSR, the difference between "the deserving" and "the undeserving" apparently became more crucial the more the propiska entitled its bearers to, and the improvement of civil rights presupposed a legal codification of the civic duty to be registered and stay in one place.

As the welfare society evolved, the propiska became the precondition for all benefits and civil rights: jobs, housing, medical insurance, public assistance, ration cards, education, the right to vote, even access to public libraries. Employment was the most crucial asset. Humphrey describes large Soviet workplaces as the primary units of society, collective "domains" that entirely encompassed the everyday lives of their workers by providing services such as garden plots, child care, holiday resorts, cultural resources, sporting facilities, and housing and, by extension, registrations (2002b, 21–28). Once transferred into the hands of local power-holders in the 1990s, these enterprises took on the character of quasi-feudal suzerainties that, particularly in peripheral areas, kept the workforce in place through nonmonetary benefits and cancelled payments of wages (Humphrey 2002b, 5–20; see also Verdery 1991, 204–28).

The propiska is only valid within an *oblast'*—a unit perhaps comparable to a very large county—or a region with a similar administrative status, which takes care of its own residents but has few duties with regard to others. Moscow and St. Petersburg are, in addition, administratively separate from their own oblasti for a radius of one hundred kilometers from the city center, the same boundary across which the first "metropolitan misfits" were deported in the early 1930s. A system of temporary registrations ensured services such as medical care outside of one's own area, but red-tape business, grudging bureaucrats, or just unexpected circumstances made this a less feasible option to many (somewhat cumbersomely, one was required to register at the new destination within three days if one was to stay there for more than ten days).

Spatial regulation also extended itself into the most intimate spheres of the lives of the subjects: their homes and their households. Since the introduction of communal apartments, *kommunalki,* in the 1920s, the propiska has regulated access to *zhilploshchad'* (living space) according to the so-called sanitary norm, a scientifically calculated standard for the amount of space needed by an adult person (during most of the Soviet era the norm was nine square meters, with additions for certain privileged categories). Large housing programs from Khrushchev onward finally outnumbered the kommunalki in the 1950s (Gerasimova 1999, 129), but the norm remained as a standard by which living space was distributed (see Kotkin 1995, 157–70). It imposed tight restrictions on the options of households to register anyone except for spouses, children, or elderly parents, since there had to be sufficient spare square meters available for the new household member. This was rarely the case because of the chronic housing shortages: in spite of gigantic construction campaigns in the Brezhnev years, many Soviet citizens never received even their stipulated living space. The risk of stray citizens registering permanently with friends or acquaintances was thereby eliminated by sheer equity, combined with crammed living.

A further incitement to make residents cherish their square meters was to give them a very strong entitlement to them. Once people were registered permanently, neither household members nor the state could easily get rid of them. Under certain circumstances, the law made it possible to evict residents on grounds of disturbing behavior (Matthews 1989, 142n10), but households failing to pay rent could only be evicted if the municipality provided a cheaper place to live (Matthews 1993, 47–48). I lack sufficient information on whether this happened in the Soviet era (even though rents were modest to say the least), but the housing administration in later years rarely had alternative housing solutions at its disposal to execute the law in practice, and to this day rent-evaders are not evicted.[2] The most common reason for eviction was instead absence: according to Article 60 of the Housing Code, municipal tenants who are proven not to have resided at their place of residence for more than six months may by a court decision be evicted and deprived of the propiska, and their flats or rooms are then given to people who presumably are in more need of them.

Ex-Convicts

Until 1995, Article 60 made no exceptions for involuntary absences caused by hospitalization (mental patients were especially affected) or, significantly, criminal conviction. People sentenced to more than six months incarceration were automatically deprived of the propiska, and if they had a place of their own before the conviction, they were deprived of it. They were supposed to be supported in finding jobs and housing by the local administration (Bodungen 1994; Zykov 1999), but the system was inefficient, and potential employers were usually unwilling to take on ex-convicts (Matthews 1993, 48). As an example, the homeless ex-cons I knew (almost half of my informants) claimed to know nothing about the existence of state support for former prisoners, even though most of them had served more than one sentence already in the Soviet period.[3] Since few prison sentences (or even pre-trial detentions) were shorter than six months, most released prisoners lacked a propiska and were thus vulnerable to charges for violation of the passport laws, vagrancy, and so forth.

The main sanctuary for most released prisoners was instead close family members, although the authorities could refuse a registration even with close relatives on the grounds that the household had no spare living space, as already stated. In addition, the family had to give its formal consent. I knew no former convict who made it even that far, however; as chapter 4 will show, some of them had no family in the first place, while others found out that their relatives had died or rejected them during their stay in the labor camp. A few of them had, moreover, been prohibited to come closer than one hundred kilometers to their hometown Leningrad (and, in effect, to their kin) after serving their sentences. Such forced exile, akin to the deportations of social and political "misfits" of the 1930s, usually befell political dissidents and perpetrators of serious crimes of violence, but I know people who were subjected to the sentence merely for parasitism. The practice, now abandoned, has even left orthographical marks in the popular representations of small towns and villages surrounding St. Petersburg; the phrase "101 kilometers" even today denotes the border between civilization and wilderness.

Vova's sixteen years behind bars fall into the middle range among adults of his age. As a twenty-five-year-old pediatrician, he was imprisoned for the first time in 1977 for having sold a bogus health certificate. His mother's suicide a year earlier triggered what he considers to be a latent alcoholism, and as a result his wife left him, taking their young child with her. In addition, he was arrested a few times for minor drinking offenses, infractions that undid his suspended sentence for the forgery and resulted in two years in the Zone, as the labor camps are called in everyday speech. Without a family, friends, a job, a propiska, or a place to live, he never returned to his hometown. He came to Leningrad by chance and drifted around between different "pads" populated by social outcasts of his own sort: ex-convicts, prostitutes, petty criminals. In 1980 he was detained for violating the passport regulations, and at the police department he was confronted with evidence proving that he had been involved in an armed robbery. According to Vova, he was just in the wrong place at the wrong time, and he was sentenced to eight years. Upon his release, he resumed his former life for a couple of years, until he was once again imprisoned. The offense was quite banal—I think it was shoplifting—but it resulted in six years of imprisonment since he was a recidivist (according to him, the long sentence reflected the court's prejudice against bomzhi). He finally left the Zone in 1997, roughly twenty years after he entered it for the first time.

Vova's career is fairly typical, except that his education sets him apart from other homeless ex-convicts. Few progressed past secondary school, and many started off in *maloletka,* youth prison. Vova's first imprisonment was an indirect effect of drinking, which in one way or another was related to most first offenses that I heard about. A number of ex-cons were initially imprisoned for hooliganism, a flexible term applied to a number of breaches of law and order, while other first-timers received a ten-year sentence right away because of drunken fights or even manslaughter. Crimes of violence were more common among men and thefts more frequent among women, but I knew a number of women who had served time for manslaughter or assault, and petty thefts are common in the criminal records of both sexes. (In the Soviet period, shoplifting, defined as theft of state property, was a serious crime.) In addition, a large number of men and women later faced charges of homelessness as such, that is, vagrancy, violating the passport laws, or parasitism. Sixteen years, the amount of time Vova spent behind bars, is not very much for a repeat offender, however. Furthermore, Vova was free for as long as two years between sentences, while others never managed more than a month or two before being imprisoned again.

During the course of my fieldwork, most formal ordinances that reinforced this bleak "treadmill" were abolished. According to some old-timers among the homeless, the persecution of bomzhi slackened already in the late 1980s (see also Stephenson 2006, 84ff.; and Starikov 1989); in late 1991, the paragraphs about parasitism, vagrancy, and violation of the passport laws were removed from the Criminal Code, although the latter remained as an administrative offense penalized by a fine.[4] In 1995, finally, the Constitutional Court declared it illegal to apply Article 60 in cases of criminal conviction and ruled that those concerned by the clause should be compensated. According to Soviet legislation, a propiska could only be cancelled by a separate court decision, which, as it turned out, never occurred in such cases.[5] Hence the proportion of ex-cons among younger homeless people is much lower; the proportion of released prisoners sentenced before 1995, of course, is also declining. Since a life on the margins of the established society often entails survival activities in the margins of the law, homeless people are particularly vulnerable to prosecution. In Russia, this might well entail imprisonment even for petty infringements, since the courts tend to sentence to incarceration those who are detained in custody before trial. A lack of a permanent residence is in itself a justification for detention since these defendants are believed unlikely to turn up in court (Karlinsky 2004, 46ff.).

People on the Move: Migrants and Others

In spite of all of the efforts to keep undesired provincials out of the big cities, a steady stream of migrants nonetheless trickled in. "The self-subversive nature of the Soviet system" was as manifest in the case of migration as in any other social process, and plenty of subjects defied the passport laws as well as sanitary norms by relocating illegally, in the hopes of a solution to appear by the time (Ledeneva 1998, 3). The most common migratory tactics were bogus marriages, bribes, and use of contacts (Matthews 1993, 51ff.; Buckley 1995, 905ff.), but there were other ways to make one's way into paradise, made possible by the system itself. The inherent tendency of the planned economy to hoard material and workers resulted in a chronic shortage of industrial labor, in particular high-skilled cadres (Verdery 1996, 20–23). Managers often solved the problem by tacitly overlooking the details in the documents of attractive applicants, so professional qualifications were a significant advantage (Zaslvasky 1982, 143ff.). There was also an official solution, the so-called *limit* system that allowed a planned quota, limit, of guest workers, *limitchiki,* to work on time-limited contracts with temporary propiski when the industry needed an influx of unskilled labor to fulfill its plans. These workers were often housed in *obshchezhitie,* a low-cost dormitory provided by most large workplaces that also provided a last hope for urban residents disfavored by the perennially inadequate housing system. A skilled worker could hope that residence at the obshchezhitie would result in a permanent propiska and thus permanent rights of residence. Workplaces often had their own quota of municipal housing units—unless they constructed houses on their own—and places to live were distributed through internal waiting lists or as bonuses to meritorious workers. These apartments or rooms remained with the employee even in the event of a change in employment. Many workers were entirely dependent on their jobs to be able to remain and ended up as part of a semi-housed, low-skilled pool of reserve labor, to be exploited or dismissed on demand. They were also feared and despised as part of a growing "lumpenproletariat," together with all of the other unsettled, itinerant, and illegal elements that populated the social margins of the centers of wealth (Zaslavsky 1982, 144–46; Starikov 1989; Pilkington 1994, 254; and Stephenson 2006, 108ff.). Their numbers are difficult to estimate: Zaslavsky mentions a 1970 census in Moscow when several hundred thousand unofficial inhabitants were revealed; when I was there for the first time in 1989, the common estimate was two or three million more inhabitants than the official number of eight million (1982, 144).

In the same way, it is difficult to estimate how the end of the Soviet regime affected migration to the large cities. The industrial decline made the former reserve labor force redundant and, in effect, vulnerable to homelessness as well (Stephenson 2006, 115ff.). Although the fiscal crisis was considerably more disastrous in the peripheries of Russia, migration was largely inhibited by the dependency of people on the nonmonetary privileges of their workplaces and their lack of liquid assets (Humphrey 2002b, 10, 21–28; Collier 2001, 43ff.). Officially, the demographic changes within Russia were surprisingly modest (Heleniak 1997), but migration from the "near abroad" (as the newly independent former Soviet republics are called) increased drastically, as rising poverty combined with other incentives to leave: the new nationalisms, ethnic persecution, war, or the threat of it (Heleniak 1997; Pilkington 1998).

Nevertheless, the cities remained as enticing as always in the 1990s. About a quarter of the homeless people I met were not able to organize housing after they arrived from other parts of Russia or from the former Soviet republics, but the vast majority was from northwestern Russia or had some previous connection to the city. I shall group them into a single category, in

spite of a vast heterogeneity with regard to length of stay (most of them disappeared from the area quite quickly) and the intention to migrate for good.
Not everybody was homeless due to migration, though; some had lost home
and propiska elsewhere and came to St. Petersburg to find work or a place to
live or simply to avoid the comments of former neighbors. Others were hiding from debts and unscrupulous creditors or had embezzled money themselves, and a large number of people were simply stuck. Distances are vast
in Russia, fares are expensive, and one also needs a valid ID to buy a ticket.
It is not unusual to have one's pockets picked during a journey and thus be
forced to organize tickets, money, and documents all over again. In certain
cases, such involuntary stays were prolonged extensively for any number of
reasons—documents could not be issued, relatives at home had no money
to send, or transferred money was stolen. Ex-convicts were particularly vulnerable to such delays. Upon release they are supposed to receive fare back
home—often a considerable distance—but the money is not always enough,
and frequently they have to pay for a large part of the journey themselves.

A handful of people had the additional disadvantage of being stuck in
the wrong country. Seasonal migrant labor is a common feature of the
Soviet Union, and in spite of the new borders many citizens from other
states still work part of the year in Russia (Dudwick 2002a, 228; 2002b, 13ff.;
De Soto and Dudwick 2002, 333). That is what the Armenians Papik and
his son Synchik (Vova simply replaced their unpronounceable names with
the diminutives for "father" and "son") did, but in 1998 their passports were
stolen. Papik was convinced that the Armenian embassy in Moscow was the
place to go, but he considered this to be a practical impossibility. Judging
from numerous other accounts about Moscow, his expectations were quite
realistic: "So—I arrive in Moscow. The police will immediately ask for my
documents because I look Armenian. I say that they've been stolen and that
I must go to the embassy. They say that that's not a new story. They beat me
up, steal my money, and throw me out of Moscow. When I return they'll do
the same. So why should I go to Moscow? If I had money I'd rather pay bribes
to get us through the borders than have it stolen by a cop."

Besides Papik and Synchik, I knew only a handful of people, ethnic Russians as well as others, from the near abroad. The general flow of such migrants into Russia declined after 1994 (Heleniak 1997; Pilkington 1998, 5),
but immigrants from the near abroad also appear to be more attracted to
Moscow (Stephenson 2006, 120).[6] The ones I met had chosen St. Petersburg
for particular reasons, usually because they had lived there at some point or
had relatives there. Formally, they should receive a formal status as "forced
migrants" (the term for Russian citizens) or "refugees" (non-Russian citizens)

that entitles them to settle where they like, but inconsistent legislation and bureaucratic hurdles often interfere. For example, the cities of Moscow and St. Petersburg made a local propiska a prerequisite for receiving the status of a forced migrant or refugee in the 1990s; the Constitutional Court later obliged these cities to change the policy, at least officially (Pilkington 1998, 40–42; Zaionchkovskaia 1998).[7] Nobody I knew was registered, although few of them cared, since the status in practice supplied neither a job nor a place to stay. Only two of them had fled open war or direct persecution; the others left, as is the case for most forced migrants, because of poverty and general insecurity about the future (Pilkington 1998, 116–40). Ethnic discrimination and the risk of war added to the gloomy scenarios but were usually not the main incentives for leaving.

Most homeless migrants came from the Russian peripheries, but they were as convinced as those from the near abroad that they had left their origins once and for all. "You can't live there any more," one man brusquely dismissed his own godforsaken northern village. "There are no jobs, no wages if you happen to have a job, no food in the shops if you should have money, and if you have something to cook there is no electricity anyway." For him there was no choice but to leave, he said, and he assured me that he was more content collecting deposit bottles at the Moscow Station in St. Petersburg than vegetating without hope in the place he had left. He was unusually talkative; most people took it for granted that I was familiar with the miserable living conditions in the provinces and left it at "You can't live there" or "There is nothing left there." Less remote places in northwest Russia or even nearby Leningrad oblast' are referred to in the same way, as if the relative proximity to St. Petersburg does not change their peripheral status. Most of my nonlocal informants were from these regions, and many of them still had a propiska and a place to live somewhere, sometimes even relatives. Nevertheless, they referred to these towns or villages as places where it would be useless to return.

Migrants from distant places sometimes had "nothing left" in a literal sense. In order to be able to move, they often had to sell everything they own, including their homes, but apartments and houses yield very little in depopulated regions, sometimes not even enough to cover the travel expenses. "Most of our friends and relatives moved long ago, and then our dad sold our house and everything in it so that we could leave too," said a teenage boy from Sakhalin who collected deposit bottles at the Moscow Station together with his younger sister. "It was a good house and they really got it for a bargain. The money wasn't enough even to get us here—we got as far as western Siberia, the rest we had to borrow from relatives there." Like most such migrants, this little family was counting on support from relatives in St. Petersburg but discovered too late that the "gatekeepers" were unwilling or unable to help: "My father's sister lives here in St. Petersburg, so he thought we could join her. But now we can't find her. She's never home, doesn't answer calls, and the neighbors say they know nothing. We're sure that she's hiding from us, she isn't better than those other relatives [in western Siberia]. They helped us with the tickets only to get rid of us, so now there is no help to get from them either."

The Scramble for Square Meters: Municipal Dwellings and Privatization

Throughout the twentieth century, everyday life for most Soviet and Russian citizens was permeated by a neverending quest for better and larger housing. Repeated efforts on the part of the authorities to solve the housing question, *zhilishchnyi vopros,* have never come close to satisfying the demand. Kommunalki, barracks, and other emergency solutions in the post-Revolution years were, as time passed, complemented and partially replaced with single-family apartments: in the 1950s Khrustiev's ill-reputed five-story buildings (*khrushcheby*) proliferated, and during the following decades most cities were gradually surrounded by gigantic *mikroraiony* (micro-districts) of tall tenement buildings. Nonetheless, dense living remained the rule; to this day, despite the sanitary norm, even single-family apartments tend to imply collective living since two or more generations of one family (including different branches of lateral kin such as siblings with families of their own) are often crowded together in one apartment (Shlapentokh 1989, 68). In the former capital St. Petersburg, where the central parts were once populated by nobility with spacious apartments, kommunalki are more common than anywhere else in the country; when I use the word *room* here, it always refers to a room in a kommunalka.[8]

In principle, the municipality should offer larger apartments or rooms to households with less space per person than the sanitary norm, and if a household wants to split up, its members are entitled to their respective square meters in separate domiciles. In the Soviet period, the housing administration was the sole agency responsible for the arrangement of such transfers, but according to most people the waiting list for municipal housing came to a standstill in the 1980s. Well before this stage, private persons were already finding it more expedient to organize these frequently very complicated exchanges on their own, and turn to the authorities for a formal approval only after the transaction was a fait accompli (Smith 1976, 100–105). Another way to enlarge one's living space was to register tactically, for instance with old relatives in order to acquire their living space when they died. (A municipal flat cannot be inherited as property, but if the formal proprietor dies, it is passed on to the remaining people registered there.) Even though most people endured overcrowded dwellings surprisingly well, the lack of space sometimes resulted in domestic conflicts that resulted in one or more participants being dispatched to the streets. At least a quarter of my informants became homeless due to family disagreements of some kind, before as well as after the downfall, but I prefer to discuss them in chapter 4, since their narratives have more to do with relationships among relatives than with housing conditions.

After 1991, it became legal for municipal housing to be privatized. Cities implemented housing reform in different ways (Ruble 1995; Gdaniec 2001); in St. Petersburg the system roughly developed as follows: the basic idea was that the municipality would keep a limited number of so-called social flats for the less privileged, on the assumption that everybody would privatize since it was free and entitled the owners to sell their apartment on the open market. However, to the individual households, privatization also implies responsibility for a certain amount of maintenance of the apartments and gives no financial advantages with regard to overall housing expenses. Given the dilapidated state of most apartment houses, privatization was not attractive to many people, and the process had already slowed down significantly by 1994 (Ambrose, Danemark, and Grinchel 1998, 79). Only about half of the housing stock was privatized during the 1990s, both in St. Petersburg and in Russia as a whole.[9]

In effect, there are two parallel housing systems and two parallel rules for registration to go with them. In the diminishing municipal sector, the sanitary norm still determines whether or not someone may register in a household and how many square meters a person is entitled to receive.[10] Privatized housing is, in contrast, not regulated by the norm, and thereby the propiska has become a commodity. Owners may register any number of people; an indignant employee at the office responsible for address registrations told to me about one twelve-square-meter room in which forty-six persons were registered. Other methods involve bribing administrators and using forged documents or stamps. In late 1999, you could obtain a permanent registration for about US$150 by calling anonymous phone numbers, many of which were carelessly glued to lampposts and telephone booths all over St. Petersburg. To my own informants the cost would have been insurmountable, however, and the few people who mentioned this solution at all were afraid of being ripped off.[11]

Clearly, privatization has placed additional pressure on an already overburdened state housing system. The reduced housing stock has made permanent the standstill of the waiting list for municipal housing, which is very harmful to vulnerable groups entitled to precedence in the queue. One such category is former inmates of orphanages. I will discuss them in more detail in chapter 4; here it is sufficient to note that they should be provided with housing, usually in kommunalki, but the shrinking supply of municipal housing makes it difficult for the authorities to realize these dwellings in practice. A similar category of people trapped by the immobile waiting list is ex-prisoners granted compensation for living space lost due to Article 60.

In addition to the reduction of the municipal sector, other factors have contributed to a drastic decrease in other types of accessible and cheap housing. The privatization and general decline of the state enterprises have more or less eliminated obshchezhitie, and a large proportion of the kommunalki have now reverted to prestigious single-family apartments for people wealthy enough to resettle the old tenants. It is now also possible to have more than one apartment or room at one's disposal. Once an apartment is privatized, it is not necessary to be registered there. Proprietors may live somewhere else and leave the spare one empty while waiting for a suitable moment to sell or sublet it. In 1999 the cheapest kommunalka rooms cost about three hundred rubles (US$12) per month, the same as the official rent for a large two-room municipal flat (which, in turn, could be sublet for US$300). Registering is usually impossible in a rented flat or room, not only because of the entitlement to living space granted by the propiska but also because of the possibility that a registration will reveal to the authorities that the landlord is making money by subletting and is thus liable to taxation.

The Scramble for Square Meters: Manipulation and Fraud

The main difference between the privatization of industry and the privatization of the housing stock was that in the former case, the initial "stake" allocated to each citizen took the form of privatization vouchers that soon ended up in the hands of a few oligarchs. In the case of housing, each person disposed of living space counted in square meters as initial capital, and the market for housing stock remained available to the grass roots or, if you prefer, to gangsters at the grass root level. The possibility of selling and buying real estate (whether legally or on the black market) and, not least, the privatization of the brokerage function that accompanied the housing reform deprived new categories of residents of their homes.

It is common to hear people say that the homeless are alcoholics who sell their flats and consume the money on the spot. I only knew two people who claim to have "sold and drunk," however—most homeless people say that they started to drink only after they became homeless, and the "sell and consume" theory is rarely reflected in their stories. More frequently they claim to have sold with the intention of buying something else but then lost the money due to unforeseen circumstances. Money may disappear in personal disasters: a burglary can cause a great deal of harm when the mattress is acting as a safe deposit box. Money may also disappear in national disasters; the Russian banks of the 1990s were not much safer than mattresses. The NGO Nochlezhka received numerous new clients who were ruined in the financial crash of August 1998, but I met only one victim of hyperinflation, a desperate construction engineer. He had gotten a divorce, moved out, and deregistered and was about to spend his savings on a new apartment when the bank simply disappeared, along with his money. The company where he worked went bankrupt as well, and the engineer ended up in a waiting hall at the Moscow Station.

The privatization reform made way for a wave of notorious criminality related to the real estate market. A recurrent theme in the mass media and in popular discourse was lonely, ill, old, and poor people, often alcoholics, who were threatened by criminal gangs to make them give up their flats—or even murdered. The stories I was told were more complicated, however, and more often involved suspiciously generous moneylenders, who would dupe naive and defenseless creditors into granting their living space as collateral. This story is really about social poverty and loneliness, because serious financial problems should be solved within a reliable circle of "one's own" people. Bank loans were not a realistic option: even if a bank was not bankrupt and someone against all precautions dared to trust it, the terms set for loans were too harsh for most private persons. Instead, people turned to friends and relatives for large sums of money. With old and reliable networks, problems can be negotiated if they appear, but people who have little or no close social environment may have to turn to contacts who are less familiar or who are known to be unforgiving.

Vova is one example. He experienced a "second coming" as a homeless person after his last release from the Zone in 1997. A friend from the labor camp allowed him to register with him in a small oblast' town, and then the friend happened to die, so the apartment became Vova's. Vova then mustered up the courage to propose marriage to a woman with whom he had exchanged letters in the camp. She consented, and they decided to exchange her St. Petersburg apartment and his place for a bigger one in his provincial town. Vova had some contacts from the Zone who were able to help with the deal. Unfortunately his fiancée changed her mind after he had already deregistered from his own place and promised the "fixers" a desirable apartment in St. Petersburg, and their money was by then invested in the apartment where Vova intended to live with the woman. Vova realized that his place was only a small compensation for what he owed them, and since they would wring more money out of him one way or another, he preferred to escape the scene for the anonymity of St. Petersburg.

The majority of all criminal real estate operations were entirely bloodless fraud cases. The police has identified some twenty to thirty main methods involving, among other things, corrupt administrators who turn a blind eye to forged documents or signatures, refrain from taking up police investigations, influence the result of court decisions, and so forth.[12] The most common theme among the homeless fraud victims I knew may be called "duping the victim to sign an authorization" (see Höjdestrand 2004, 2005). The procedure is similar regardless of whether the transaction concerns legal sale of privatized property, illegal sale of municipal property, or exchange of municipal property. The perpetrator, be it a broker or a private person, pretends to help out the contracting parties and secures authorizations and ID documents in order to first deregister the clients from their old addresses and then re-register them at the new ones. If the affair is a legal sale of a privatized flat, authorizations are also needed to purchase or sell the property in the name of the client. The broker or helper goes through with only half of the deal (deregistering and sale) and then disappears before the victim has realized what has happened.

Professional brokers were notorious for this kind of "grab and go" criminality, but since 1997 a certain self-organization of the business and new licensing rules have improved their reputation (Ambrose, Danemark, and Grinchel 1998). Criminal gangs used the same methods, worming themselves into the favor and trust of selected victims as ostensible "friends," and so did private individuals—strangers as well as kommunalka neighbors or even family members who wanted to deprive each other of living space. Criminals often deliberately targeted victims who were recently divorced, bereaved, or in other ways lonely. Without anybody to defend them, their yearning for friendship and personal attention easily prompted them to invest all their trust in strangers.

Gleb was a former economist in his mid-fifties. After a distressing divorce, he let people in his neighborhood know that he wanted to sell his privatized flat. One day some men of Caucasian origin entered his home and forced him to sign a sales contract on the flat. They then disappeared, and he reported the incident to the police; neither the intruders nor the contract were seen again. Later he understood, he said, that they were only part of a strategy to make him defenseless, and the incident certainly brought him to the verge of a nervous breakdown. At this time he met a man who gradually became a close friend. He had the patience to listen to Gleb, who was ill and depressed and felt that his other friends had deserted him when he needed to confide in somebody. The friend offered to help Gleb exchange the apartment. Gleb agreed, against warnings from relatives and other friends. When the friend came to Gleb's place with a heap of documents and papers to be signed, Gleb hesitated and admitted feeling awkward about turning over such important things to someone else. His friend (Gleb imitated his tearful voice) protested: "But Gleb—do you not trust me after all this time?" and the guilt-ridden Gleb blushed and quickly signed the authorizations that permitted the friend to deregister him from the address and sell the flat. He never saw the friend again, and after a few weeks some people arrived who could prove that they had bought his flat legally. Gleb filed a lawsuit, but two years later nothing had happened.

Gleb's case is one of many in which professional criminals discard the disguise of commercial agents and move right to developing personal trust by pretending to be friends. Even victims of deceitful real estate agents tended to legitimate their sometimes quite careless signing of documents by the fact that they trusted the *person,* that "they really made a good impression" or "they seemed to be good people, we related to each other almost like friends." The dimension of intimacy and of fellow humanness seems to be of paramount importance to both parties. When the market is only a few years old and no firms are old enough to have established a reputation of solidity and trustworthiness for themselves, the individual broker has to attract this trust to his or her person by appearing as reliable, helpful, and kind-hearted in an informal manner. In the 1990s business deals between firms were based mainly on personal trust as well (Humphrey 2000a). However, in the case of fraud on the estate market (and, presumably, in other branches too), personal confidence also has a retrospective value for the victim: it smoothes over mistakes and exonerates them. The goodness and righteousness associated with weakness and gullibility lend a streak of martyrdom to many fraud stories, for from a moral and humanist perspective, victims like Gleb do the right thing when they exchange suspicion and hostility for trust and faith in another human being.

Fraud victims are frequently unwilling to file charges against the perpetrators. The main reason is that, as in many other business deals, contracts are designed for the eyes of the tax office only; apartments are sold at a market price while the contracting parties agree to write a smaller sum in the documents (Humphrey 2000a). A court case will, if it succeeds, retrieve only the official sum, which many fraud victims do not consider worth the effort. It has happened, however, that victims turn to organized criminals to retrieve money swindled by other organized criminals.[13] Moreover, the weak evidence in cases of this kind tends to clog the criminal courts with lengthy civil cases. A common strategy among defendants is to refrain from turning up in court, which they can do for a year or more before a verdict is declared in their absence. If the fraud victim eventually wins, the buyers of the apartment will likely to file a charge too, arguing that they acted in good faith, which then extends the process by a few years more.

Frauds are far less common today, not only through self-regulation on the part of the real estate business but also through legislation. Since the lag in time and space between the deregistration and the new registration is vital for many types of illegal operations, the authorities brought in a rule in 1999 stating that, when places of residence are exchanged, the deregistration and the subsequent registration must take place at the same time. In addition, as time passes, people become more accustomed to business deals, contracts, and so forth. Frauds still occur, but the target is more often the municipality than private individuals, such as when a person without relatives dies and somebody else appropriates the place of residence with the help of a bribed bureaucrat and a forged propiska.[14]

Federal and Popular Views on Bomzhi and Vagrants

Although some raised concerns about the proliferation of vagrants (*brodiagi*) and *bichi* (a now abandoned term meaning "tramp") in the big cities as early as the late 1980s (for example, Starikov 1989), the presence of people with an apparent lack of housing became conspicuous only in the early 1990s, when the onset of the disastrous economic crisis coincided with the abolishment of the laws that in practice prohibited homelessness. At the same time, the industrial decline eliminated the limit system, and various forms of seasonal work disappeared that once provided a sanctuary of sorts to the itinerant and undocumented. Some of my informants had spent the last twenty years of the Soviet period working unofficially with agriculture and forestry, or as helpers at geological expeditions, but they were forced to leave for the big cities when these industries could no longer provide work (see also Stephenson 2006, 113ff.).

In comparison with the many other proliferating social problems, homelessness received little attention in the mass media as well as within social science or from the state. To the extent that research on vagrancy existed in the Soviet period, it was confined to the walls of the Ministry of the Interior, that is, the police (Likhodei 2003). Since the 1990s, a few studies of homelessness in Russia have been published by Russian researchers, in Russia and elsewhere. With the notable exception of Svetlana Stephenson's impressive work (1996; 1997; 2000a) and Karlinsky's analysis of homelessness and human rights (2004), these are mainly brief and often statistically based outlines of numbers, illnesses, income strategies, and so forth.[15] The tone is usually emphatic, even though a few of them are framed in terms of vagrancy or bomzhi instead of homelessness. That is not the case with the first post-Socialist state investigation, published by the Ministry of Work and Socialist Development, in which "the problem of persons without a permanent place of residence, BOMZh," is discussed in a manner that reveals how firmly entrenched Soviet understandings and conceptual tools may be in the minds of administrators and researchers:

A person without a permanent place of residence or occupation is a person who currently is located on Russian territory, who as a rule lacks documents verifying identity and occupation, who does not have a permanent place of residence on the territory where he is located, who currently lacks permanent employment or occupation and, thereby, also means for his survival, who as a rule displays signs of physical illness (mental, alcoholism, tuberculosis, venereal diseases), lice infection etc., a physical appearance that does not correspond to the physical norm of the human being (dirty clothes, dirty body), signs of degradation of the human being as a personality (Yulikova et al. 1997, 12).

Here, bomzh is defined first in terms of administrative status ("without a permanent place of registration"), after which it is narrowed down to unemployment, bad health, dirtiness, and, finally, personality and its "degradation." It is bluntly stated that "the whole tribe" lost its places of residence after the dismantling of the Soviet system of coercive alcohol rehabilitation (Yulikova et al. 1); the main object of the survey-based study is to verify or dismiss the widespread notion that bomzhi reject work and housing voluntarily. That they are legally entitled to neither is not mentioned, any more than the propiska system as a whole is discussed, and respondents who do not claim to be actively looking for jobs and housing (about 50 percent) are simply dismissed as lazy. In the same way, two draft laws of 2000 and 2003 targeted at "persons engaged in vagrancy" (*brodiazhnichestvo*) ignore the issue of registration, in spite of the stated intention of distinguishing the "deserving poor" from the "non-deserving" by their attitude to work.[16] Here too, the only objective criterion of the target category is the absence of a propiska, which is followed by unemployment and vague specifications like "traveling all over the Russian Federation." Neither draft law was ever passed, perhaps because it was never made clear whether the suggested reforms should apply to everybody who lacks registration or to unemployed people who travel, regardless of whether the proposals concerned targeted social support (the comparatively benign draft law of 2000), fifteen days of incarceration for vagrancy (the more condemnatory one of 2003), or—in the case of the investigation of the Ministry of Work and Social Development—forced labor for those bomzhi who are judged to be unwilling to work (Yulikova et al. 1997, 33). Nor is the propiska mentioned in a third draft law of 2007, which on the other hand introduces the term "homelessness."[17] The unintentionally homeless are distinguished from voluntary vagrants by their willingness to accept the treatment program of a planned system of rehabilitation centers. Those who refuse registration, medical treatment, professional training, and so forth are, it is suggested, to be subjected to incarceration and compulsory "work adaptation." However, after a very negative response from NGOs and the influential Orthodox Church, this draft law was reformulated into a far more humanistic variant lacking any mention of force or incarceration (as I write this, in early 2009, the law is still being prepared).[18]

People in general have no alternative "grand narrative" about the origins of the contingent lodgers in their stairways; usually they assume that the unfortunates are responsible for their predicament. Homeless people themselves did not, as I will show in the chapters to come, differ much from other Russians of the same age in their focus on moral character and willingness to work, although they were more prone than others to differentiate the deserving from the undeserving. People on the grassroots level can allow themselves to be inconsistent, however, and in a survey conducted on popular attitudes toward the homeless in St. Petersburg, it is apparent how easily condemnation and disgust are intertwined with empathy and compassion (Gerasimova 1998). My own experience also was that the same people who argued most fiercely that "the bloody bomzhi" ought to be deported to Siberia unless they "changed their attitude," in the next moment might well ask what they ought to do to help the poor unfortunates.

The relative lack of social stratification in the Soviet period has resulted in a remaining public unwillingness to accept that some social categories are structurally disadvantaged (Manning and Tikhonova 2004, 17, 30). In the same vein, grassroots and bureaucrats alike seem to think that socioeconomic upheaval and bureaucratic hurdles are not satisfactory explanations for homelessness. Everybody is going through the changes, they seem to think, and the standard reply to the question "Why precisely this person and why precisely now" is free will, or if not that then what I call intentionality by proxy, as in, "Since he wants to drink and not to work, he also wants to be homeless."[19] There is an alternative local view, however, that instead focuses on the incapacity of people to "want the right thing" in the first place. By this theory, revolution, civil war, Stalin's purges, and a system that privileged the mediocre rather than the gifted resulted in a literal elimination of the country's good brains and in a chronic failure to develop what was left of them (Gilinsky and Sokolov 1993; see also Starikov 1989). A cruder summary of the same theory was in fact given to me by a well-educated homeless woman in her early sixties, whose vehement contempt of bomzhi provided me with the title to this chapter. "*Excrement* of the state," Irina said, "that's what they are. Why? Because the state brought up the entire population to become bomzhi, made everybody lazy, irresponsible, immoral, uncultured. These idiots were cared for as long as they didn't ask for too much, but now there's nothing that prevents them from reaching their natural predestination, namely the garbage dump over there."

I read and heard more about this "brain drain theory" in the early period of perestroika than in later years, but private persons sometimes articulated it when they exonerated bomzhi as "weak people." As hapless victims, devoid of the strength needed to struggle with the present *bardak* (chaos) or with life in general, they are rendered a touch of spiritual or moral goodness that proves them to possess a sensitive soul (Ries 1997; Pesmen 2000), and that Gleb's martyrdom, for example, alludes to as well. In the 1990s, moreover, this idiom of mercy may have gained momentum since the contrasting stereotypes were not exactly positive: New Russians (the nouveaux riches of the period), oligarchs, the Mafia, and the Kremlin.

In the contemporary Western world, by contrast, homelessness tends to be explained in terms of medical pathologies, which is a result of the active involvement of modern science in defining and curing social problems (Foucault 1977). Medicalization merely surpasses moralization by entirely removing the subject from the field of penal correction into the hands of medical science. A century ago, "vagrants" were criminalized as morally deviant in Western countries too, but the explanatory frameworks gradually transformed their plight into "social disaffiliation" (Humphreys 1999) and, finally, in the late twentieth century, to mental illness and substance abuse (Koegel 1992; Mathieu 1993; Wright 1997). In the process the terminology changed from vagrancy to the more merciful homelessness. Individualizing approaches have never dominated the scientific discussion entirely, however, although research branches focusing on economical and political factors such as social stratification, distribution of low-income housing, and so forth are said to be less privileged with regard to funding than medical or socio-psychological disciplines. In particular, it is argued, this has been the case since the so-called neoliberal turn in the late twentieth century, since a focus on individuals conveniently distracts attention from the increased housing costs and the general dismantling of social welfare that coincided with enlarged homeless populations (Mathieu 1993; Wright 1997).

In the Soviet-Russian context, vagrancy remained a moral issue, even though other allegedly deviant characters (for instance lesbian women) were thoroughly investigated and "treated" by Soviet medical science (Essig 1999). It is true that neither mental illness nor drug abuse are frequent features among the Russian homeless (at least, when I was there; I suspect that this will change in the near future), but to a certain extent the difference also has to do with the academic ability to discuss things in the first place. If discourse is made up by a myriad of disparate and frequently contradictory strands, this plurality presupposes discussions and negotiations in which actors enjoy at least a modicum of freedom to position themselves (Foucault 1990). As I see it, these threads amount to little if they remain isolated from each other and if they are unable to literally inscribe themselves in history through publications. Judging from the work of Attwood, for example, scientists in fields such as pedagogy and psychology were able to exchange ideas among themselves that diverged somewhat from Marxist doctrine, even if these findings were made public by mass media only when they suited the purposes of the party (Attwood 1990, 165ff.). The theme of homelessness, by contrast, remained locked within the walls of the Ministry of the Interior and could therefore never be transferred from the politically charged and theoretically circumscribed field of sociology to the somewhat more relaxed fields of medicine or psychology.[20]

Local Care for the Homeless

In spite of indifference and prejudice at the federal level, homelessness received more attention in many local administrations, and during the 1990s supportive programs were initiated by a number of cities, sometimes in cooperation with local NGOs. This collaboration may be one reason why the municipal sector largely seems to have abandoned the terms vagrants or bomzhi in the favor of *bezdomnyi* (homeless). In St. Petersburg, persistent lobbying on the part of the NGO Nochlezhka resulted in the establishment of the municipal City Center for Registration of the Homeless (*Gorodskoi Punkt Registratsii Bezdomnykh*) in 1998, where a registration entitles citizens who had their most recent propiska in the city to medical insurance, support in applying for passports, and pensions.[21] Such registers have appeared in other Russian cities as well, but the first of its kind was set up by Nochlezhka as early as 1990. The organization persuaded the city to entitle their enlisted clients to ration cards, since which time registration has entitled them to vote in local elections and receive medical care and other services depending on the fluctuating agreements with the city and with other NGOs.

Medical care has always been central to these deals. Patients who lack a propiska are not denied emergency treatment at ordinary hospitals, but without agreements of this kind in place, they tend to be released prematurely; furthermore, they are not entitled to preventive health care at clinics. In 1999, Nochlezhka's registration ensured that nonlocal patients would receive the treatment that they needed at city hospitals, while local homeless people were cared for by the aforementioned city center. As I was told by locals as well as nonlocals, however, the significance of both registrations decreased in the following years since clinics, in spite of the deals struck by the politicians, nevertheless were not paid for homeless patients and therefore to an increasing extent hesitated to accept them. An alternative was instead Médecins Sans Frontières, whose clinic for local as well as nonlocal homeless people was situated first in Nochlezhka's buildings and later (in cooperation with the municipality) at the Botkin Hospital near the Moscow Station.

Another important office was the Commission for the Prevention of Homelessness, which was set up in each city to compensate former prisoners whose residences had been confiscated due to the now illegal application of Article 60 of the Housing Code. Approved applicants are granted precedence in the queue for municipal housing, but the process tends to be lengthy because the commission needs full documentation of the applicants' whereabouts after the cancellation of the propiska in order to confirm that they are not homeless for other reasons. As mentioned above, the shortage of municipal housing complicates the task further, and applicants may have to spend a considerable time waiting for an apartment or a room. There are also other hurdles, for instance kommunalka neighbors filing charges because they consider themselves to be eligible to receive the vacant room given to the ex-convict, and only one of the five applicants I knew who were approved in 1999 had moved in somewhere when I last met them in 2003.

The needs of ex-convicts were also overseen by two municipal centers for the rehabilitation of male ex-prisoners, both functioning as halfway houses where clients received temporary propiski and were assisted in applications to the commission or in finding jobs or places in homes for the elderly or the disabled. Since 2000, similar centers for homeless people have been set up in most districts of St. Petersburg, but their impact has not been thoroughly investigated. According to local human rights activists, there is still not enough funding, and the new structures have unfortunately retained the administrative logic of the propiska system. The support of each center is restricted to "its own" people, that is, those whose last registration was in that particular district, but since the homeless population is considerably more itinerant and heterogeneous than the planners expected, the centers have difficulty finding the appropriate clients.[22]

A main concern of most of these offices is to make the clients *vosstanovit' dokumenty*, "prepare the documents." *Bez bumazhki ty bukashka, s bumazhkoi ty chelovek,* the proverb goes: "Without papers you are an insect, with papers you are a human being"; in this case that holds true in a twofold sense. The propiska is only one stamp in a sea of documents necessary in everyday life, and *khodit' po instantsiiam,* "walking around the offices [that produce the documents]," is part and parcel of the everyday life of any Russian. Any move in the universe of officialdom requires its share of documents, but in spite of the increased computerization of public administration, files are seldom coordinated. People must get themselves to the different office responsible for each document and personally deliver them to whichever administrative body requires them. The homeless lack most necessary papers, and my informants were primarily engaged in retrieving or otherwise obtaining certificates of birth; current and former places of registration; records of prior incarceration or hospitalization; contracts on places of residence; certificates of marriages, divorces, and births; and so on. These papers are needed to organize a number of compulsory documents such as the *trudovaia knizhka,* the employment record in which all one's jobs are listed, or the men's *voennyi bilet,* the "military ticket," which has information about military service, and, in particular, the internal passport, the most central document (see Humphrey 2002b, 26).

Street dwellers perpetually lose their ID documents due to theft or because they trade them—there is a black market for domestic passports even without the propiska stamp—unless they sell them on their own behalf, as some claim. Registered citizens restore stolen or lost passports at their local police station, and today the regular police force assists the unregistered too. Before 2002, however, the issuing of a new passport to an unregistered person entailed ten days of incarceration. This was a legacy from the Soviet time, when "violators of the passport laws" were first brought to a special police department to have their identities established before being dispatched further. After 1991, the sole function of the "passport detention center," as I call it, was to issue ID documents for unregistered citizens, but the applicants were nonetheless held for ten days while documents proving their identity were retrieved from other administrative levels.[23] Due to bureaucratic inertia and slow postal services, most applicants nonetheless left without a passport and received their documents afterward. Industrious applicants tried to organize as many documents as possible beforehand, which also was the case with many of the clients of the Commission for the Prevention of Homelessness, which had to gather a bulky file of papers before their cases could be handled.

I refrain from plunging deeper into the sea of documents, commissions, and courts that I was told about. Regrettably, I was not able to follow some portion of these cases as closely as I would have liked, but I had to accept very soon that I would need another year of fieldwork *and* informants with permanent whereabouts before I could grasp the full breadth of events, papers, paragraphs, offices, and powerful bureaucrats that I was told about. The persistence and endurance of these people were impressive, however, and I wish that more of them had managed to regain an official profile in the form of a propiska, and not only a makeshift "state personhood" bestowed by a register of homeless people—although for some, even this paltry status seemed to provide some semblance of humanness. Repeatedly I witnessed how distressed clients came to Nochlezhka's office and left somewhat calmer—still with a very vague idea about the organization, but apparently comforted by the mere fact being recorded *somewhere,* regardless of purpose.

To a certain extent, the efforts of the social workers to make people restore their documents was therapeutic. Regardless of the result, felt the staff at Nochlezhka, the mere process of acquiring papers kept people active, and then they would be industrious in other respects too. Passivity was dangerous, for if people "unlearned to work" (*otuchilis' rabotat'*), the likelihood that they could regain their social status would be virtually nil. Ironically, this opinion was shared by the very people who made the social workers sigh and question their mission; "philosophers" who had submitted to their fate and stated frankly that the mere thought of endless walks "along the offices" was a complete waste of time. No papers in the world would help them, they said with an indifferent shrug, not least since documents on the whole were of little support to *anyone* these days. There were rich men driving Mercedes who lacked a propiska, while others were homeless in spite of having that vital stamp in their passports. If one wanted to get by, they argued, to feel oneself like a human, one just had to be willing to work, and work did not depend on documents and official permissions but on one's ability to make the best out of what was at hand. I therefore proceed to a closer examination of the understandings of work and willingness, and how they played out in the transitional economic climate in which papers may not have mattered as they once did, but in which, in my opinion, the "just" preceding "willing to work" was far less trivial than the abovementioned philosophers would have had it.

CHAPTER 2

Refuse Economics

Getting By with the Help of Waste

"You're writing about bomzhi? But what's new about that? They just *don't want to work,* that's all there is to it! All they want is to drink!" Most non-homeless people I met had opinions on my "weird" job, and this was the most frequent response that I received, by far. In the same vein as the state investigation discussed in the previous chapter (Yulikova et al. 1997), people simply took it for granted that bomzhi reject work voluntarily and that this is the cause of their homelessness. If you work, you don't end up in an attic, it was as simple as that. Homeless people were basically of the same opinion, although with the crucial modification that *typical* bomzhi—a category that has the indisputable advantage of always being pinned on other people—just didn't want to work, while my interlocutors were "bomzh perhaps, but at least I'm *working.*"

Perhaps their income strategies would have passed as work in the eyes of some of their detractors, had these been aware of the wide variety of activities in which these inhabitants of attics and basements were engaged all day long. Others would dismiss it all as scavenging, admittedly a not entirely inapt label. With the exception of a limited supply of charities, the main livelihood of the homeless consists of dealing with objects and tasks that others do not want, the core of what I call the refuse economy. By definition, the refuse economy consists of informal practices, since nothing that homeless people do is recorded or seen by the state, but I find concepts such as "the second economy," "the informal sector," or "interstitial, liminal spaces" all but meaningless in this context. The Russian economy is much too infused by officially unsanctioned activities for such concepts to make sense, and such legal or academic divisions say little about the social environment in which transactions are embedded (Ledeneva 1998, 48ff.). Nor do they explain how work constitutes meaningful persons, which is a main discussion here.

The purported laziness of bomzhi is merely an marker for their antisocial behavior, for work is a contribution to an exchange of sorts in which the reward is a recognized position in a social whole. Nonetheless, the extreme focus on work in the condemnations of bomzhi may seem somewhat odd in a cultural context in which *byt,* material everyday concerns, are traditionally seen as soul-killing but necessary evils, and that only ten years earlier was characterized by an "oppositional cult of non-work" (Verdery 1996, 23), a sentiment aptly summarized in the Soviet saying "We pretend to work and they pretend to pay us." To perceive work as a plight does not imply that one thinks that nobody should do it, however; perhaps the most annoying aspect of the perceived laziness of others is that they try to escape a burden that everybody else has to share. Furthermore, although the inefficiency of Soviet workplaces is notorious, they were nonetheless crucial sites for social belonging. Frequently the workplace permeated the entire lives of the workers by providing social services and leisure facilities, and as such they were crucial for a sense of inclusion and a socially recognized identity. *Having* a job was thus more important that exactly whatever was achieved during work hours, and those who were not encompassed by these quasi-feudal corporations were indeed outcasts in a very real way (Humphrey 2002b, 21–39). Nonetheless, workplaces were sites of hard work, although not as a devout accomplishment of the plans of the employer. As reservoirs of resources— social networks, things, services, or just time—they were independently expropriated by employees at all levels for the benefit of themselves and their family and friends (Simis 1982; Ledeneva 1998, 125–38; Pesmen 2000, 135). The mutual obligations within these networks constituted, and continue to constitute, the work that matters most, and when bomzhi today are accused of being lazy, it is rather responsibilities of this kind that are implied than jobs in a proper sense.

Charity and Humanness

Much of the information I have about homeless work opportunities was gathered during long conversations at soup kitchens and other charities,

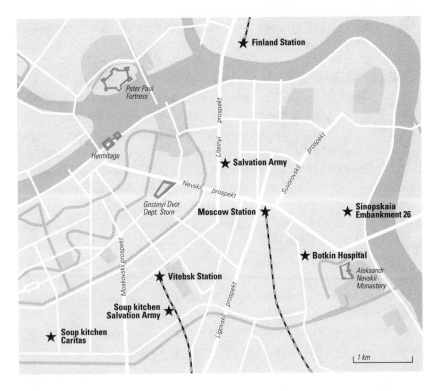

FIGURE 1. Central St. Petersburg. Map drawn by Oskar Karlin.

which is why they receive more attention here than they deserve from a purely nutritional perspective. There were, moreover, not many of them in the first place. In 1999, only a handful of organizations in St. Petersburg were dedicated to helping at the homeless: the municipal City Center for Registration of the Homeless and the charities Nochlezhka, Médecins Sans Frontières, the Salvation Army, and Caritas's soup kitchens. (In addition, there was Mother Teresa's home for elderly and handicapped homeless people, where, as noted previously, I never worked.) The first three of these had conveniently been assigned localities at the same address by the city council. Nochlezhka had already moved into a dilapidated *obshchezhitie* at Sinopskaia Embankment 26 by 1997, to be joined by the City Center a year later, at about the same time that MSF opened its clinic for the homeless in one of the apartments after a thorough renovation (this clinic was relocated to the Botkin Hospital by late 1999).

Nochlezhka and the City Center distributed clothes and sometimes food but primarily provided legal advice and support with various official documents and bureaucratic matters. Clients were often directed to other agencies, supported by written pleas for assistance directed to, for example, the passport detention center, the housing administration, the Commission for the Prevention of Homelessness, or other NGOs. As mentioned, it was their implicit mission to keep clients active, and the most important device in this struggle was Nochlezhka's street newspaper *Na Dne,* which all visitors to the office were encouraged to sell. (*Nochlezhka,* "Night Shelter," and *Na Dne,* "On the Bottom," are the two titles of Maxim Gorky's famous play *The Lower Depths.*) In 1999, there were some fifty people who bought the paper for eighty kopecks and sold it for two rubles. Cold weather, perpetual risk of police harassment, and apparently unstable and meager profits prevented many even from trying. Many cited a personal lack of competence in salesmanship, reflecting a lingering Soviet resentment against speculation in the early 1990s (Humphrey 2002b, 40–63; Pesmen 2001, 128–30) that was particularly salient in conceptualizations of masculinity (Kiblitskaya 2000, 101; Nazpary 2002, 52ff.). Such objections were infrequent, however, and I believe that any former disinclination to earn money was reconsidered quite quickly in the face of destitute want, be it due to homelessness or transitional poverty. The most common argument was that *Na Dne* was too serious. The vendors complained that the persistent focus on social journalism and avant-garde culture repelled tired would-be readers who only wanted a crossword puzzle on their way home from work. Others found this a good job, however, and the most active vendors could on rare occasions make as much as five hundred rubles a week—the cheapest possible *kommunalka* room cost about three hundred rubles a month in 1999 (Solovieva 2001).

Nochlezhka's very name suggests the existence of a night shelter, and the organization indeed ran one, although it was chronically overcrowded. The original intention was to give the inhabitants a propiska at the address, which would enable them to find work and other forms of housing. However, the health department and the local police blocked the plan on the grounds that the buildings were not fit for human habitation. The house was indeed run down and lice-infected, in spite of laborious efforts on the part of Nochlezhka to renovate it. In 1998, the organization decided that a dilapidated shelter was better than no shelter at all, and in spite of the disagreement with the health department the house was settled with seventy or so people who lived there more or less permanently. I usually visited the section for women and families, which was usually quite peaceful. In the other sections—one for men only and one for couples—the recurring incidents of drinking and violence were blamed on a minority of less than remorseful ex-cons. When two people were stabbed in the summer of 1999 (both victims were out of hospital within days), Nochlezhka closed the shelter and reorganized it thoroughly.

After its reopening in late 1999, it was exclusively aimed at women, old or disabled men, and the vendors of *Na Dne.*

From Sinopskaia, a small number of shelter residents regularly took a streetcar straight to Liteinyi Prospekt 44 and the main office of the Salvation Army. A doctor saw patients on a regular basis, and the facility also distributed clothes and useful things such as spectacles or crutches. Every day, there was some activity, *programma,* involving religious education or hobby activities such as films, book readings, handicrafts (for women), table tennis, and so on. For a while, there was also an AA group. Sundays were particularly busy with programs in the morning as well as the evening, in addition to a long service in the afternoon. In effect a handful of faithful regulars rarely left the Salvation Army at all, especially not in the winter, when the main hall was opened up at night so that people could sit and sleep there (it lacked economic resources for a proper night shelter). Probably only a minority of the visitors would name faith as an important factor in their lives, but many of them claimed that they appreciated the Bible classes as welcome intellectual stimulation in their otherwise dreary lives. Many visitors just dozed off, however, satisfied with a nap and something to eat, as every program ended with a standard meal of tea, bread, and broth.

Three times a week, a van drove from the main office to the Vitebsk Station with crates of bread and canteens of tomato soup and tea. This mobile soup kitchen was aimed at anyone in need, and many recipients were non-homeless impoverished pensioners, usually female. At first, the food was distributed right next to Vitebsk Station, but the station authorities did not appreciate the presence of two hundred purported bomzhi in the vicinity and forced the Salvation Army to move to a more secluded place a few hundred meters away. Later it was pushed further to an even more peripheral place. The appearance of a small garbage dump was blamed on the kitchen's clients, even though the amount of discarded car parts made the nearby petrol station nearby a more reasonable guess. The only leftovers from the kitchen used to be a disproportionate number of empty 1.5-liter plastic bottles cut in half, the swiftest solution of the problem with dishes, which were the recipients' responsibility.

Quite a few of the recipients arrived straight from Caritas's soup kitchen, which was situated a forty-minute walk away at Obvodnyi Kanal, near the Baltic Station. Together with another branch situated in the vicinity (they were merged in 2001), it took in some five hundred people in all per day. It was a good field site thanks to a small green yard outside and a couple of benches, where people would gather and chat after finishing their brief meals, usually broth, bread, tea, and a piece of sausage or cheese. Many had their first drink of the day there, beyond the sensitive noses of the staff; after this, some would seek out bottles of the all-purpose solvent Ldinka and end the day passing out in the bushes behind the kitchen.

The kitchen at Obvodnyi Kanal was originally aimed at the chronically ill, although the clientele was always mixed due to the proximity to the metro. Caritas provided general health controls and, more important, medical tests for tuberculosis, a common disease among ex-cons and thus also among the homeless at large.[1] It is latent until malnutrition and a hard life in general make it "open itself up," as the expression goes. Only then is the patient's health considered to be critical; at that point, he or she may be sent to the TB sanatorium in Pavlovsk, an idyllic suburb south of the city, for an extended stay, usually for at least six months. Unless they are without doubt contagious, patients move about relatively freely even outside the hospital grounds, and quite a few of them regularly complemented the poor food in Pavlovsk (so they told me) with a meal at Caritas.

That charities give away something for free, without demands for work in return, was slightly controversial, and officials and homeless people alike frequently expressed concerns about the moral implications of such philanthropy. For instance, the sociologists of the Ministry of Work and Social Development worried about the suspected unwillingness of bomzhi to work, speculating that charities are "enabling those bomzhi who so desire to go on with their lifestyle" (Yulikova et al. 1997, 18). It might console them that a diet consisting only of the food at Caritas and the Salvation Army would lead to imminent malnutrition, even more so that plenty of homeless people considered soup kitchens a waste of time: "After all, it takes some two-three hours in all," as one person said, "and in that time I can make more money on my own than the cost of that food ration." In addition, many of them agreed that charity merely permits the idle to eschew honest work, although they were more concerned about the moral implications of receiving aid than of providing it. The homeless people genuinely appreciated the support of Caritas, while there were plenty of irritated remarks about "lazy bomzhi who only want to live *na khaliavu*" (at the expense of others).

Frequently such complaints evolved into reflections about the Russian national character. Many discussions were punctuated with a comment to the effect that Russians cannot work or do not want to work, either because they are incapable as such or because of Communism or because of the dismantling of Communism (the difference deriving from the political slant of the speaker). Such reflections—admittedly encouraged by my presence and the Western funding of the food—often sparked a discussion among Russians in general that Russia belongs to an "uncivilized" East, characterized by irresponsibility, dishonesty, and drinking, in contrast to the civilizing virtues of a presumably "cultured" West (see Pesmen 2000, 282ff.).

When, at some point, forty-eight-year-old Ksenia accused the staff at Caritas of pilfering, she and everybody else thus reduced the problem to Russianness: "Our people are too corrupt. It has to be *your* people there, not *ours,*" they told me. I heard similar accusations against all charities, the rumors escalating in proportion to their dependence on foreign goods and money. Bruno interprets such suspicions against Russians working for Western NGOs as a proliferated belief that anyone in control of resources will use them for their personal benefit, just as the privileged and corrupt party people of the Soviet past did (1998, 179). In her case, which was not the only one I learned about, the rage is thus directed against a group of "them" that is distinguished from an "us" by their particular power and venality. Ksenia, in contrast, seemed to blame what she considered to be a weak spot common to all Russians, including herself, implying that now as well as before, everybody pilfers who is given the opportunity.

In my experience, the choice of scapegoat is situational. When people feel like decent, accountable humans-in-society, the blame is put on *them,* the more powerful "not us." The idea that all Russians are natural scoundrels, on the other hand, indicates a shift in the definition of "human" toward the soulfully erring variant, in the idiom of which human (or Russian) flaws and the regrettable state of the world (or Russia) are linked by a law of causality. External circumstances may exonerate individual weakness, as in the regretful assertion that in "this life"—be it Russia, the present *bardak,* or just the general cussedness of life—it is not possible to be honest in the first place. With an ironic twist, however, the causality is reversed, and the deplorable state of "this life" (however it is to be understood) becomes merely a result of a Russian "mentality" that is perceived to be "too vast to be virtuous, neat, rational, or stable" (Pesmen 2000, 282). "Homeless" due to the split between East and West, such a mentality can only aim at boundlessness, which surfaces as an incapacity to conform that inevitably erodes any attempt at social order—an order that, as the popular conclusion often goes, is not truly human anyway, as it is too boring.

In an instant, the reference for "being human" switches from the dutifulness and diligence of the West to the anarchy, unpredictability, and soulfulness of the Eastern "land of miracles" or "land of fools" (Ries 1997, 44–51; Pesmen 2000, 69ff.), and the lazy and undisciplined Russian becomes the hero instead. At the soup kitchen, laments about pilfering were thus frequently concluded with an ironic remark that pictured the charitable foreigners as being weak and a bit stupid, otherwise they would not be outwitted by such rascals. The theme connects to a seemingly inexhaustible repertoire of anecdotes on the theme of "a German, an Englishman, and a Russian...," in which the lazy, disloyal, and undisciplined Russian one-ups the rational and morally impeccable Westerners with his stupidity or under-handed tricks. They relate to that traditional genre of anecdote in which a mischievous folk hero gets even with the powerful; in the Soviet period similarly unmanageable personages defied the discipline of the system (Ries 1997, 65–80).

Down to the last detail, the tarnished characters of the stereotypes "typical bomzh" and "rascal Russian" (usually he is referred to as "Vania," diminutive for Ivan) are identical, and so are the negative impact of the homeless "this life" and the Russian "this life" on qualities such as diligence, sobriety, and orderliness. One might think that the similarities may cast a beam of mercy on the homeless by reminding others that they are not all that different. Alas, this is not the case; while many a Russian would admit, roaring with laughter, that all Russians are really bomzhi, it actually occurs to few of them that most bomzhi are in fact ordinary Russians.

Even fierce critics of a lifestyle na khaliavu might admit that a visit to a soup kitchen or to Nochlezhka sometimes was worthwhile, because it could lead to "honest work" of some sort. Besides issuing the street paper *Na Dne,* Nochlezhka for some time arranged odd jobs in the neighborhood for qualified shelter residents, although, as we shall see, the attempt was not very successful. At the Salvation Army and Caritas, homeless regulars frequently appeared as regular workers, so-called volunteers. Ksenia was one, until she accused the staff of stealing and left her position. As an assistant and cleaner at Obvodnyi Kanal, she did not receive money for her three hours of work every day, only food and priority for the clothes that were occasionally distributed. Still, the in-kind salary was not her main motivation: "Idleness gets on my nerves," she said, "and you lose the incitement to work if you're passive—just look at the bomzhi here, they've unlearned [*otuchilis'*] whatever capabilities they once had!" I heard similar arguments from a number of men who in the same way simultaneously survived and "felt needed" at monasteries, where visitors often receive food and lodging in return for work. Hare Krishna offered the same deal and had a particularly good reputation for rewarding construction work with delicious food and friendly treatment.

Some jobs of this kind involved monetary payment. At the Salvation Army, "volunteers" mended donated shoes and other items, performed housework, worked as janitors, or helped out at the mobile soup kitchen. The reward was three good meals a day, priority for clothes, and a small salary that clearly represented a compromise among the strained finances of the agency, the

Figure 2. Outside the Caritas soup kitchen. Photograph by the author.

personal situation of the worker, and the work hours expected. One man in his mid-thirties, Lyosha, received fifty rubles a week in cash, regardless of whether he was a doorman, cloakroom attendant, janitor, or a receptionist, whereas his predecessor as a janitor was finally paid 180 rubles, but then he had a wife and a baby to support. Lyosha did not mind that others were paid more. As a (mostly) sober alcoholic, he preferred in-kind rewards, he said, since more cash than an absolute minimum needed for cigarettes only tempted him to drink.

Once in a while, Lyosha disappeared for days or weeks, only to return as an emaciated wreck. Such binges were not unusual among the volunteers, and they were also caught stealing or exploiting their positions in other ways. A young man who used to keep the waiting line in order at Caritas told me that he and his mates demanded money from soup kitchen clients for not dismissing them on the grounds of purported drunkenness. The regular staff never found out, but later he and his friends were nonetheless let go for drinking on the job. At Caritas the dismissal was definite, while the Salvation Army was more patient because of its more explicit mission of spiritual reform. Prodigal sons and daughters were usually allowed back after a suitable period of penitence, at least if drinking was the only offense. They were offered more menial positions, perhaps, but as far as I know nobody really cast suspicion upon them later on. Rather, they were approached with an indulgent air of "we know that you cannot be trusted but we love you anyway" that accorded with a general atmosphere of intimacy and friendliness at the corps.

Visits to the soup kitchens were also legitimized with a need to update oneself, because like any place where homeless people gather, these hangouts served as exchange centers for goods as well as information. They swapped useful items like clothes or the highly valued pensioner's certificates that provided free public transport. Advice and tip-offs were shared about issues such as charity: whether the Salvation Army would open up its main hall for the night; if there were plenty of clothes there or vacant beds at Nochlezhka's shelter; or what one currently got for registering at any of the offices at Sinopskaia Embankment. Other free-of-charge opportunities were discussed, such as discount public baths, vocational colleges for hairdressers, or the much-talked-about *pel'meni* factory that fed bearers of a pensioner's certificate for free once a day.[2] Bureaucracy was an inexhaustible topic: where to get which certificate for what purpose; what papers one needed to apply to the Commission for Prevention of Homelessness; if the wait at the passport detention center was long and whether the temporary incarceration involved should be regarded as an infringement on one's rights or, on the contrary, as a holiday with full board.

Dreams, Deceit, and Distrust: "Real" Jobs

Work was continuously on the agenda at the soup kitchens. That homeless-ness in Russia is not necessarily the end of a long process of social exclusion makes the homeless population quite heterogeneous when it comes to work history, although the average educational level is below the national average (Stephenson 1997, 12). Caritas fed both people with professional qualifica-tions who were utterly frustrated at not being able to use them and old ex-convicts out of touch with official society for decades. Moreover, since the market conditions of today provide less seasonal work than the Soviet period did, people who lost their propiska decades earlier may nevertheless have been working most of the time.

Although most homeless incomes stem from gathering or various inde-pendent enterprises, the issue at stake at the soup kitchens was rather jobs in a more conventional sense: the kind of work that an employer asks for up front and that is performed on a regular basis or for an agreed-upon period of time, for a fixed monetary reward. Such jobs were risky and hard to find, which presumably was why people felt the need to discuss them all the time—deposit bottles were too self-evident to be interesting. As noted in the previous chapter, far from everybody considered their lack of a propiska to be a problem, but as I will show this depended largely on which kind of jobs they sought. The registration was required by most employers in 1999: ambiguous legislation made those overlooking it subject to fines, and in many cases an official address would represent their only available means of control over the employee.[3] A lack of documents could frequently be negotiated with personal contacts, however, and I knew plenty of people without a St. Petersburg propiska whose extensive social networks and special skills always kept them professionally engaged and well-paid. Since contacts were (and remain) crucial on the legal labor market too (Ledeneva 1998, 207ff.; Yakubovich and Kozina 2000), lack of social capital was far more inhibiting than an absence of documents.

The most discussed job among the homeless could even provide a prop-iska, or at least somewhere to sleep. A *dvornik* is a street cleaner and janitor who is responsible for a few apartment houses or a block. The job is hard, underpaid, and dirty, but in the Soviet period it was attractive since it in-cluded accommodation and thereby a propiska. Today the lodging is not understood to be automatic, but some sort of place for storing the cleaning equipment and tools is often available, and to a homeless person this is bet-ter than nothing. After Nochlezhkas shelter closed, a former resident named Galia found such a job through a woman she knew from the *bania* (public bath). She cleaned staircases and yards and was supposed to have a general overview of the houses eight hours a day, seven days a week. The wages were very low, but thanks to a kind-hearted boss she finally managed to secure a propiska through this job. As I understood her, she slept and was registered in what was basically the broom cupboard.

Far less popular, but always available, was the vegetable *baza,* which might be translated as a wholesale warehouse but in reality is a concept all of its own. In the Soviet era, only managers were employed at the baza, and the actual work of sorting out rotten fruit was done by students and the like, as compulsory social service on a one-day-a-month basis.[4] When this system was abolished, the baza became one of the few workplaces where nobody cared about the propiska because of the extreme turnover of labor. "I can't afford to work there," people often frowned, moaning that thirty rubles per day for eight or more backbreaking hours carrying heavy crates in a sea of rotten vegetables was not acceptable, particularly since there were no fringe benefits like the implicit permission to take fruit.

Women and men discussed, applied for, and acquired jobs as dvornik or at the baza to about the same extent. Otherwise women were at a clear disadvantage. The jobs that they conceptualized as "real"—often related to trade, care, or cleaning—frequently required a "proper" appearance that a homeless reality makes very difficult, and they tended to be confined to the sector of regular employment where managers cannot overlook the propiska as easily as an independent entrepreneur who strikes a deal about a temporary assignment. Male jobs were usually of this kind, in particular within the construction sector, which is (as everywhere) extreme in its reliance on informal practices and untaxed labor. There was a good deal of self-esteem invested in such assignments, and men liked to emphasize that this or that decent employer wanted them because of their special skills, often as the leader of a crew. Quite a few female job applicants would happily have accepted construction jobs too, as a second-best alternative to the scarce feminine jobs they would have preferred. Like generations of Russian women, moreover, many of them had always performed hard physical labor, regardless of cultural ideals and individual wishes. The construction sector suffered a serious downturn after the financial crash in August 1998, however, and during 1999 there were few such jobs available, even for able-bodied men.

Even toward the end of 1999, when building projects received a new impetus, the homeless job market was considerably more gender-equal than the legitimate one. The negative impact of market reforms on women's work opportunities all over the post-Socialist space is well known, but in the case of the homeless, most men are, sad to say, as disqualified as women from the rare "real" jobs, due to old age or bad health.[5] While non-homeless women often turned to trading, homeless women stood a better chance than homeless men in what I came to call "self-invented micro-entrepreneurship" (cf. Bridger, Kay, and Pinnick 1996, 147–64; Ivleva and Pachenkov 2003; Lindquist 2003). The shelter resident Marina did an interesting variant of this before a prison sentence rendered her homeless. Through contacts she had permission to hang out in a hospital ward, where she offered herself as an alternative to the overworked and sometimes careless employed staff. The patients or their kin hired Marina to change sheets, buy medicine, wash the patients, and so on, tasks that relatives are more or less expected to do. Quite a few female jobs are of that kind: taking over unwanted tasks from employees at workplaces or, in Marina's case, from private individuals with other burdens.

Marina wanted a *real* job, and she worked hard to find one, but her hopes merely fueled endless walks each day, all over the city. Before prison she worked in shops, and she was also a hairdresser. For a while she hoped to be accepted as a cleaner at a hospital; a homeless acquaintance of hers sometimes made a few rubles running errands there, and two of her roommates at the shelter cleaned at another hospital. But after some hesitation, the administrator said that she did not dare to take somebody on without proper documents. After that Marina mainly tried for cafes, but the only result of her job-seeking walks, she said ironically, was feet too swollen to fit into her fashionable boots that leaked water but looked good enough for a job interview. The only job she got was delivering advertisements to people's mailboxes, but after a brief hospitalization due to a heart attack she found herself replaced.

If female "real jobs" are unobtainable as such, the problem with their male counterparts is rather that the payment turns out to be out of reach. Employers do not always pay as agreed, and some systematically cheat homeless workers. One notorious case was that of the Armenian. His first victim, a man called Oleg, was talking a lot about an assignment to dig cables for the national telephone company, a two-week job that he thought would be safe since it was for a state enterprise. But it turned out that the Armenian who hired Oleg and his homeless co-workers was an entrepreneur. "He said he would pay once we were back in town," said Oleg afterwards, "and once there he told us that he would be back the next day with the money. But he didn't turn up, and when we went looking for him they told us that he had left for some other assignment and nobody would say where. And they didn't even feed us properly—twelve hours work a day for more than two weeks out in the forest, eating only porridge!" A few weeks later another man at the soup kitchen mentioned a job for the telephone company, and a short interrogation by Oleg confirmed that it was for the same Armenian.

This is a fairly common practice. The homeless are vulnerable, and certain employers go straight to the soup kitchen to pick up a hopeful workforce that they later refuse to pay. There are no written contracts, and the police would never give a bomzh the benefit of the doubt over a wealthy businessman. In addition, the Armenian probably profited from the assumption that the assignment was a state job. Banned from the shrinking supply of regular public employment, homeless people are totally in the hands of private entrepreneurs and fully aware that they depend on the goodwill of their patrons. The discussions about the Armenian disclosed that, even though the state is hardly conceptualized as a structure of trust in general, there is still a persistent hope that a state employer would at least pay as agreed.

The distrust is mutual. The employer has no reason to trust homeless workers either, another kitchen client explained. "They often drink," he said, "or sometimes they steal or just do a bad job. The employer can take the passport [the ID document is often held as a kind of collateral security] and pay only when the work is finished, and if the worker doesn't behave he naturally loses the money." As an outsider, he emphasized, I heard only one side of the truth, the stories of deceit told by the homeless. Employers would probably have *their* stories if they were asked. Judging from him, the job situation is governed by bad faith. The trust of an employer presupposes some form of continuity—personal knowledge or a place where the employee can reliably be found—but homeless workers are by definition contingent and impossible to control. Alternative precautions on the part of the employer are taken as a sign of distrust, which provokes disloyalty and what Scott (1985) has called hidden resistance on the part of the employees, whose suspicions that there will be no payment at all end up legitimizing an immediate acquisition in compensation for the anticipated loss. Hence the attempts by Nochlezhka to organize jobs for their clients ended after a few months since, in the words of the staff member responsible: "I just got sick of always being cheated; either the guy ordering the job wouldn't pay, or my own men would steal his tools or just screw up the job in general."

Bad faith was, moreover, no less common in transactions among the homeless than they were between workers and employers. Those who claimed to have been cheated were sometimes suspected of being cheaters themselves, deserving of their fate because of bad work or theft, or else they were assumed to be victims of their own gullibility. Potential workers were therefore not necessarily discouraged by the bad reputation of certain employers. The man who understood himself to be negotiating with Oleg's treacherous

Armenian finally accepted the job, although I know nothing about the result. On another occasion, I was told a story of a director of a pioneer camp[6] who was notorious for taking on seasonal labor and never paying. "Some guys are going there now to work for her," the teller emphasized, "even though they know everything about her." I asked him why, were they that desperate? "No," he said with a sardonic smile, "they do it because everybody believes himself to be the one smart dude (*tot krutoi*) whom she cannot fool!"

Criminality: A Problematic Masculinity

More than once, upset visitors to the soup kitchen told me about confrontations with arrogant bureaucrats or policemen, who scornfully encouraged them to start stealing straightaway since there was no other support for people of their kind. In particular, male ex-convicts seemed to carry on continuous negotiations with themselves about where they stood on the issue. As one man in his mid-forties concluded: "I don't have any place in this new society. I don't *want* to go on stealing, I wouldn't survive another sentence, but apparently I have no choice." Such discussions were usually quite matter-of-fact, sometimes heated because of the anger at having to choose at all, but always juxtaposing distinct moral standpoints of equal value. It is in principle wrong to steal, but after all, reality does not offer much of a choice. A frequent additional argument for "going stealing" derived from the general awareness about the moral and legal shadiness of the present power. Writing about pilfering at work, Birdsall calls it righteous indignation (1999, 158): if things had been the way they should be I wouldn't have to consider this, but now that those at the top—the Kremlin, the oligarchs, the New Russians—also steal, why shouldn't I?

Another factor relates particularly to men, namely the particular Russian articulation of criminality as an alternative masculinity in Connell's sense (1995). As Kukhterin notes, work as *the* expression of masculinity is a complication for men with inferior roles in the labor market. He suggests that the solution may be to express manliness in ways that are implicitly culturally endorsed but not, for that reason, being supported by explicit mainstream morals, such as drinking (Kukhterin 2000, 84; see also Zdravomyslova and Chikadze 2000). A great deal has been written about the Soviet-Russian criminal world, and it indeed offers a masculinity as good as any (Chalidze 1977; Abramkin and Chizhov 1992; Handelman 1997; Konstantinov and Dikselius 1997). The divorce from the state and established society prescribed by the traditional ethos of the thieves, *blatnye,* implies a rejection also of institutions such as the propiska, family life, regular employment (or, inside the Zone, forced labor), private property, and personal monetary gain. Instead, the supposedly wise and disinterested leaders, *vory v zakone* ("thieves in the law," the internal rules of the criminal underworld), should provide for the entire community, including brothers held up in the Zone.

Criminal subcultures are subject to the vicissitudes of the day too, however, and post-Soviet *avtoritety* (authorities) are less faithful to tradition and considerably more business-minded and individualistic than their predecessors (Ledeneva and Kurkchiyan 2000). The old ethos still permeates the Zone, however, which may be one reason why homeless men with a penchant for a criminal lifestyle still embrace it. An equally plausible explanation is that the traditional code ought to come in handy to a released and homeless man; after all, it rejects precisely the humanizing contexts of established society that he is persistently denied. In particular, it justifies one's lack of a job and makes a virtue out of the necessity to steal. "Money should be given by friends, won in gambling, or stolen, and nothing else," as I was told by a proud old ex-con who carefully concealed that once in a while, in a quite honest way, he unloaded trucks at the market where he later claimed to have stolen wallets (told to me in confidence by two accomplices).

The refusal to work should be interpreted as a redefinition of the work ethos rather than a denial of it, because these ex-cons were no less moralistic than others about the despicability of living na khaliavu (to which stealing apparently did not pertain). In a conversation with me about his activities at the time, a regular at the Moscow Station called "Andrei Half-Finger" once heatedly emphasized: "Tova—you know very well that I haven't worked one day in my entire life!" A little later he suddenly pointed at some ragged men who were collecting bottles nearby and said indignantly: "Do you know how many of these ragamuffins I've tried to fix jobs for? I know this executive at a *kolkhoz* and he would take them, but they just *don't want* to work!" I made an ironic remark about his lack of consistency, and he frowned and said in an almost pedagogical fashion: "*I* live a little on the side, you know that, but nobody can call me *lazy!*"

The ready-made image of "the criminal" thus provides a kit of ways in which to think, act, and, for that matter, look, talk, and gesture, and it is flexible enough to allow men to dispense with the codes that do not suit their practical life. It also brings men together, as they unite in lamentations about society being taken over by materialism and lack of respect and extol the Zone as the only place where morality, decency, and sound rules of behavior still hold sway. Nonetheless, comparatively few men unambiguously identified themselves with the "thieves' world," regardless of its potential to turn a bomzh into a man. One persuasive reason for this might be that real thieves do not end up homeless in the first place, which makes such allegiances less convincing. To what extent the men who talked about "going stealing" actually went through with it, I cannot say—according to Stephenson, the homeless representation in the criminal statistics is marginal—but the salience and persuasiveness of criminality make it an *issue,* something one explicitly has to define oneself in relation to, in particular if one is a sentenced male (2006, 28). This does not mean that women were any less affected by the apparent dead end in which stealing appears to be the only reasonable alternative, but they seemingly felt less pressure to make a conscious stand about how to relate to it.

Homeless Hangouts: Surviving (at) the Station

Instead of chasing risky jobs all over the city, it is possible to simply stick to a place where income opportunities are already all around, or even where they come straight to you. In St. Petersburg, there used to be plenty of such potentially profitable hangouts. At any site where petty, unpretentious commerce took place, a crew of homeless people somehow survived in the margins of other activities. The railway stations had the worst reputation among them, and most visitors to the soup kitchens would never set foot there since the sleaziness of these places, they said, led to nothing but destruction. It is true that the homeless regulars (as I call those who spent most of their time there) at the Moscow Station differed somewhat from most visitors to the charities: however different they were in other respects, they seemed to appreciate an intensive life in which interesting things happen all the time, and most of them were habitual and hard drinkers. Nonetheless, even if the tolerance level for crime, prostitution, and drinking was indeed higher at the station than in other places, it was also inhabited by homeless people who managed well enough to dismiss most forms of charity and who survived on what most people—even their critics at the soup kitchens—would call honest work.

The main hangout at the station was a long yard alongside the main building where two of the main sources of income were concentrated: travelers heading for long-distance trains, and people who were drinking. On both sides along the yard, an abundance of small kiosks and cafes provided alcohol for thirsty travelers, their companions seeing them off, and those who went to the station the way others set out for the pub. A number of fast-food stands offered *shaverma* (chicken kebab) and various greasy pastries, other kiosks sold groceries or pharmaceuticals, and the pirate cassette stands drowned the entire area in loud Russian pop music. I knew about fifty regulars at the time, not even half of those whom I understood to be homeless. The categories were blurred; not all regulars were homeless, and others periodically stayed with acquaintances or rented rooms. Poor pensioners collected bottles there too, most of the prostitutes were not homeless, and a significant number of people with more or less obvious drinking problems had a place to live but worked as the homeless did at the station or just went there to drink. Regulars related to each other in more or less the same way, and, as I explain in chapter 5, it was not unusual for homeless regulars to stay temporarily with *domashnie* (domestics).

Nor were all homeless people regulars. The station was a thoroughfare as much as it was a terminal, and many who dwelled there did not themselves know what designation applied to them. Vova used to call newcomers *zaletnye,* "in-flyers," his voice rich with disdain. They were nonlocal tramps, he said, who came to St. Petersburg expecting a better life. (He never seemed to consider it relevant that once upon a time he "flew in" too.) Pastures are indeed greener in St. Petersburg than in many other places, and I met people from small towns who regularly went to St. Petersburg for medical care at the MSF clinic or for similar errands. Others commuted between Moscow and St. Petersburg. The former city is said to offer more free-of-charge services such as soup kitchens and shelters, whereas the latter is a little easier when it comes to police violence and enforcement of the propiska laws. Those who had figured out where the respective local train systems of the two cities interconnect could in fact travel all the way for free.[7]

Gathering Glass and Garbage

The ubiquitous drinking made the station a goldmine for the main subsistence reserve of the most impoverished: deposit bottles, which constitute the core of the refuse economy. To some regulars, they were merely a complement to their tiny pensions or other forms of work, while others collected them full-time, optimizing their share with all means available. The Armenian Papik and his son Synchik always calculated time and space with almost scientific precision when working out in which order to attend the departures of the long-distance trains, knowing from experience which groups of people making their farewells would be most profitable. Plenty of competitors had the same bottles in mind, but Papik and Synchik were sober and they cooperated, and as such they were difficult to defeat.

Public consumption of alcohol was not limited to the station; in those years, drinking beer on public transport or in the streets was as commonplace as eating ice cream. Until the 2007 prohibition against drinking in public, the leftovers from the omnipresent intake of beer littered the entire city center. In 1999, a beer cost about nine rubles, whereas an empty bottle yielded one ruble, about the same as vodka bottles. Due to stagnant rewards for bottles and substantial inflation, bottle gathering has become increasingly less lucrative, and I assume that the value of other types of useful waste has declined as well. Quite a few people gathered aluminum cans, usually from long drinks such as Gin and Tonic or Vodka Cranberry, although this is less rewarding since they yield only their weight in metal. Most kiosks take beer bottles, whereas particular deposit stations all around the city accept other bottles, metal, or even rags or paper.

Nobody thought twice about taking bottles: they were the target of everybody who needed a little extra income, and clinking bags were the constant accompaniment of my friends and my homeless informants alike. Metal did not seem to be a sensitive matter either, but quite a few homeless people had an ambivalent attitude toward garbage. It is embarrassing to root around in dirt, I was told, but considerate people often place usable items neatly *beside* the bin, which somehow transforms the objects into humanitarian aid or gifts. There were differing viewpoints on this, however. Shelter resident Marina was always well-dressed in secondhand clothes, but she found them at the charities and would never touch the same garments if they were lying beside a dustbin. Yet others regarded scavenging as a fully fledged profession and displayed profound knowledge and skill about where to look for different things and what their value was likely to be.

Micro-Entrepreneurship and Good Relations

Vova often kept company with a couple called Olga and Kostia who worked for a kiosk attendant. The deal was simple: for taking a large parasol and some high tables from a storeroom and arranging them outside the kiosk in the morning, then keeping the tables clean from bottles and litter during the day and finally removing parasol, tables, and rubbish before closing up at night, they enjoyed a monopoly on the deposit bottles left at the tables. In principle, the bottle belongs to the buyer who has paid for it, but few customers bothered about this, and in any case Olga or Kostia made sure that it came off the table before anyone had any opportunity for second thoughts. During the hot summer of 1999, they sometimes made eighty rubles a day, and even if this sum is exceptional—only Papik and Synchik occasionally made more—they usually exceeded the salary of a doctor of eight hundred rubles a month, with the consideration that the doctor probably made more outside of the official payroll. Without any rent to pay, Olga and Kostia had quite low expenses. The money was enough for food; that summer Olga was pregnant and craved kefir and expensive tomatoes, and most days she could have this. She was also satisfied with the job because they could get boiled water in the kiosk and make noodle soup (eight rubles) or coffee (two rubles) from single-portion instant bags that they bought themselves.

All kiosks or cafes selling alcohol had a station regular performing this kind of "self-invented micro-entrepreneurship," as I call it, since it was the worker who took the initiative by finding a way to be useful. The employer was rarely dependent on the proposed favor even if it came in handy, and there were always equally capable competitors around. Therefore an element of goodwill was inescapable in most such deals, and workers accordingly explained them as the products of "good relations" (khoroshye otnosheniia). Basically, the deal implied that the worker dispose of the "refuse" from the employer's job by liberating him or her from tedious tasks. The reward was sometimes, as in the case of kiosks and cafes, only the permission to use a profitable space, but in other cases the compensation was monetary.

Train wagons were, for instance, rarely if ever cleaned by the staff that was ostensibly responsible for the job. On Russian trains, each wagon has its own provodnik, a caretaker who is responsible for everything from collecting tickets to distributing bed sheets and making tea. Part of the real income of the provodnik comes from what Birdsall (1999) has called covert earning schemes: selling alcoholic beverages on the side or taking bribes for giving away empty seats. A portion of the money gained outside the formal payroll can be spent on a micro-entrepreneur who takes care of the cleaning. At the station, most cleaners had a number of regular provodniki who expected them to be ready for work when the train arrived. In 1999, the standard fee was forty rubles per wagon, and those who were strong and industrious enough to complete a number of jobs each day even made enough money to rent rooms.

Outside of the station, a similar way to make money was to unload trucks or to hang out in parking lots and offer to wash cars. These incomes were insecure, and people usually looked for a more permanent income by establishing contacts with salespeople at markets or the clusters of kiosks that used to surround the entrances to the metro. The reward could be a monopoly on bottles, as was the case at the station, while the payment for putting up stalls and unloading goods at markets amounted to some thirty or forty rubles a day. The money was meager, but the laborer had plenty of time left over for soup kitchens and other ways of earning money. One method was to buy cheap goods in the suburbs and sell them at a profit in the center, a seemingly more independent enterprise that nonetheless benefited significantly from regular contacts. The retailer I knew best managed rather well, not least since his clients often paid him for other errands as well, like unloading goods or acting as a lookout for unexpected tax inspectors. Payment could also be in-kind: the most ingenious variant of vending I heard of was the woman who collected empty plastic bottles (worthless at the deposit stations), washed them, and took them to a market where one stall sold vegetable oil by the liter. The customers always needed empty bottles, so the salesman gave her a couple of full bottles in exchange, which she in turn exchanged for food at other stalls.

Micro-entrepreneurship was predominantly a female income strategy. It consisted of taking over the most simple and menial tasks from employees within conventionally female sectors such as trade and catering, and most homeless entrepreneurs were women too. Hence the proportion of women at the station (roughly half) was twice the average among the homeless in St. Petersburg (in 1999 about a fourth). Kiosk jobs and wagon cleaning were nonetheless not exclusively female domains, I should emphasize, nor were the homeless inclined to gender these activities by, for example, referring to them as female or unmanly. Still, women were generally assumed to have an advantageous position at the station since they, in the words of one man, "are more responsible and better at dealing with people."

"Good relations" were not necessarily durable. Olga and Kostia worked for half a year or more at their kiosk, but otherwise the labor turnover was rapid. Homelessness is associated with neither punctuality nor sobriety, and if a worker did not arrive as agreed or turned up drunk, the position was by definition vacant. On the other hand, the failing party always had a fair chance of working up good relations somewhere else. Thus a mate of Vova's, fifty-year-old Raia, had at some point or other worked in every cafe at the station. In spite of being a hard worker and a very kind and likable person, she was also, in her own words, an incurable alcoholic with a notoriously vile temper when drunk. A workday for Raia thus consisted of a number of moves according to a pattern determined by old conflicts and new agreements. When A was in charge of one of the cafes, Raia worked there, but not when A's shift was taken over by B, with whom Raia had had a fight. Then C worked in another cafe and Raia wiped tables there until D, with whom she also had argued, took over and Raia once again left for another patron, E, with whom she had not up to that point quarreled.

FIGURE 3. Raia at one of her jobs at Moscow Station. Photograph by the author.

Raia's drunken disagreements confused her nightly whereabouts as much as it complicated her working pattern. In the washrooms, one section was usually closed to visitors, and in these toilet stalls Raia and some other women used to sleep, either seated or curled up beside the odorous holes in the floor. Raia had argued with the washroom attendants too, and according to Nina, a longtime antagonist of the same age, she was now denied access by two shifts out of four. "People [travelers] pay three rubles to get in," Nina explained, "of course they don't want lots of drunken bomzhi roaming about." The problem with Raia was, according to Nina, that she could not handle alcohol, while Nina herself could be completely plastered but always knew how to behave herself. Usually, the attendants admitted regulars for free, but if their tolerance was misused, she argued, they might become more restrictive to everybody, not only to drunkards like Raia.

The washroom was indeed crucial, for hygienic purposes and as a sleeping place and a refuge from bad weather or ill-willed policemen, and the attendants were probably the most valuable "good relations" at the station. Nonetheless I never heard of return favors or small gifts as a token of appreciation, often considered appropriate for favors that are either too small or too significant to be repaid (Ledeneva 1998, 152–55). Nina for one regularly gave, as she put it, "cakes and other presents" to a doctor at Botkin Hospital who hospitalized her whenever she felt ill or tired, but in the washroom, everyone who did not abuse the tolerance of the attendants seemed to be able to count on their goodwill. I suppose that they found it easier to simply let the regulars in than to argue about money every time they appeared.

Prostitution

The washroom attendants were particularly important to the women who sold sex at the station. As twenty-five-year-old Zhanna described her working day, it usually started in the afternoon with a steady glass of vodka at one of the cafes, roughly followed by the pattern "vodka-client-washroom-vodka-client-washroom" until the cafes finally closed late at night. Throughout the evening, the attendants acted as safe deposit boxes. Clients always paid in advance, and since neither Zhanna nor her colleagues had pimps, the money was handed over to the washroom staff who took care of it until the service was conveyed. According to Zhanna, the women solicited customers on their own or with the help of other station regulars. "Unless," she added, "a girl has a boyfriend anyway. If so, he keeps the money while she takes care of the client."

Vokzalnye prostitutki, "railway prostitutes," are popularly said to occupy the lowest rung in the professional hierarchy, and the mass media outlets like to depict them as down-and-out bomzhi whose compulsive drinking compels them to trade sex for vodka. Since there are virtually no *other* representations of homeless women, one easily gets the impression that this is the main livelihood of all homeless females. Stephenson gives a more truthful account by depicting sex as an occasional item for trade, be it for money or just a shower and somewhere to sleep, with a clientele that is nearly as poor and marginalized as the women themselves (2006, 25ff.). Personally, however, I saw very little of women exchanging sex for money or favors outside the station (unless certain love affairs are to be interpreted as such, which I discuss in chapter 5), and even there, the distinctions were blurred by the fact that the more successfully one manages to sell *any* commodity, the less one has to worry about a roof over one's head.[8]

Zhanna and her closest colleagues had nothing whatsoever in common with the stereotypical railway prostitute. I identified her, her sister Katia (nicknamed "the Colonel" because of her fierceness), and a handful of other female sex-sellers as homeless only because they slept in a waiting hall where many others spent their nights as well. They could charge up to five hundred rubles for their services, and when the hall was closed for renovation in the summer, this clique could afford to rent rooms instead. Generally, these women seemed to relate to their trade as they would to any other job, even a qualified one. Thirty-three-year-old Katia (the Colonel), who had worked for several years at the station, claimed that her own success depended on her brains and four years at law school. "If they want some cute little girlie doll, they have plenty to choose from," she stated firmly, "but I can offer them some intellectual company too." On the same occasion she nevertheless admitted that she was fed up with the station and opted for a well-paid job in a grocery store instead, but "that bloody stamp," her propiska from a small town outside Murmansk, eliminated all such hopes. Regardless of her occasional doubts, the other station regulars uniformly respected her and the others as hard-working professionals who made their own money and kept themselves clean and tidy, an important issue at the station. Younger women looked up to them, and elderly women related to them as if they were the only representatives of the younger generation at the station who deserved approval.

This elite notwithstanding, there was a clique of younger girls at the station whose homelessness was less disputable and whose interaction with domestic men involved material benefits as well as sex. I heard a male regular refer to one of them as a "coincidental fifty-ruble girl," but in my opinion their liberal (indeed, suicidal) drinking habits made it difficult to define it as trade in the first place or, if so, what precisely was exchanged. They were usually too drunk or too dulled by hangovers to be interested in coherent conversation, but many disparate comments over a long period formed a picture, however opaque and sketchy. Usually they would start out with an ordinary drinking spree together with one or more domestics, with whom they might or might not have sex before passing out, which they might or might not remember afterwards. Sometimes they provided the drinks themselves, on the implicit understanding that the one who contributes the alcohol is allowed to stay the night, and, again, sex might occur or not. In these commonplace situations, sex did not seem to be the most relevant of issues, compared with alcohol, nor was it necessarily included in a deal just because it often appeared as a consequence.[9]

Means and Ends: Drinking

I found it somewhat ironic that the homeless, many of whom were hard drinkers, lived to a large extent off the drinking of others. Most station regulars did in some way or another profit from various side effects of alcohol consumption, be it emptied bottles, dirty beer tables, or illicit alcohol trade on the trains. Even the regular cleaners at the station hired a bomzh to do their job when they wanted to party. Drinking was also the precondition for a kind of contingent income that for instance Vova relied upon. He usually turned up at the station only when the yard started to become a bit busy in the early afternoon. Once there, he simply spent the day hanging out and waiting for opportunities to crop up by themselves, which they usually did. As the day turned into evening, the income potentials of those who hung out in this fashion tended to rise with the average level of drunkenness. Not only did the deposit bottles multiply, but tipsy travelers always show their gratitude to those who carry their bags more graciously than sober ones, and they are also more likely to lose their luggage, in which case it must be taken care of before someone else steals it. As the hours passed, drunken men wanting willing women paid more to those who found them, and the reward from the grateful girls increased as their stacks of cash grew in the washroom. Late in the evening, odd-job men like Vova were considerably less hungry and thirsty than a few hours earlier, not least because payments at the station often were in kind, in particular the liquid kind.

The money that was gained during the evening was generally pooled with the resources of others and spent on the purported facial lotion Bomi. Bomi

was said to cause itching and to be of lower quality than Ldinka, but it was
slightly cheaper and appreciated for the remarkable swiftness with which
it put a tired body to sleep. Both bottles contained some 250 grams of 160
proof alcohol (spirits in quantities of half a liter or less are always measured
in grams in Russia) and cost about ten rubles. Towards the end of 1999,
the kiosks were prohibited from selling these solvents (they used to be on
display alongside beer and sweet alcoholic drinks), and the station regulars
changed to a herbal mixture made from hawthorn, *Boiaryshnika,* on sale in
the frequent pharmacy kiosks. Pharmacies have always provided a number of
alternatives out of reach from the law, just as paint shops and hardware stores
do. The tradition of drinking substitutes is old in Russia, and elderly informants talked nostalgically about the standard drink of the old days, *Krasnaia
Shapochka* ("Little Red Riding Hood," literally "red cap"). Ries notes that
men in particular liked to boast and joke about drinking substitutes in the
early 1990s, but she expresses doubts about the extent to which these liquids
actually were consumed (1997, 68). A fine example of the genre are the
classical drinking recipes of eau de cologne, dandruff shampoo, shoe polish,
and so forth recommended by the equally classical bomzh immortalized by
Venedikt Erofeev (1990). According to White, however, the increase in consumption of such substitutes increased during these years to such an extent
that in certain parts of the country, the sale of perfumes and other alcohol-
based or intoxicating products (including glue and window-cleaning fluid)
was limited to particular hours of the day or a limited number of bottles per
person (1996, 126ff.).

Anybody who contributed to the bottle had a share, but a substantial part
of the collected money came from panhandling travelers and other visitors
to the station. This might seem contradictory to the general work ethic and
the dislike of living na khaliavu, and these drinkers did not differ from other
homeless people in finding it humiliating for an able-bodied adult to ask
strangers for food or money. This pride was, admittedly, to some extent a
virtue made out of a necessity, because everybody knew that only the old and
the handicapped could extract some pity from the public. The only full-time
beggars I knew were an acquaintance of Vova's who had no legs, a man at
the station who walked on crutches, and a *dedushka* (grandfather) who was
old enough to have been imprisoned for the first time in 1942. Others who
knew him laughingly said that they would not mind trying the same thing,
but with competition like that, they would hardly get anything.

As begging was conceptualized, however, it did not pertain to a plea for
a drink or even for money aimed at alcohol. Rather, it presupposed that
donor and receiver were strangers to each other, but strangeness was not only

determined *by whom* one asked but also by *how* one did it and *what* the plea concerned. I was, for example, not a stranger, and thus I was frequently approached with requests for food, medicine, and other favors. The intimacy that simultaneously presupposed and was confirmed by my support was underlined by expressions such as "for friendship's sake" or "from the soul," *ot dushi,* even if I did not know the person very well. (Thus I was ostensibly the best friend in the world of a gang of industrious youngsters who systematically exchanged the bread I bought for Bomi behind my back.) People who without doubt were strangers were instead familiarized by an informal and straightforward approach, in contrast to the submissive body posture of the ubiquitous (and frequently kneeling) beggars who worked all over the city center at the time.

The main factor was, however, the alcohol itself, which carries associations of brotherhood and intimacy in most places where it is drunk. In Russia, its symbolic allusions to communion and oneness are extremely salient, in the words of Pesmen: "Drinking, as the epitome of hospitality and communion, related to exchange of all sorts of substances, physical and spiritual. Drinking, like dusha [soul], united people and domains felt to be fractured by life." As such, alcohol has a unique capacity to integrate seemingly irreconcilable binaries such as sociability versus economic rationality, and a bottle of cognac as a gift thereby transforms an act of bribery into one of closeness and friendship (Pesmen 2000, 137, 181, 187). In the station yard, that a request concerned drinking and nothing else transformed condescending patronage into an unproblematic, friendly favor between comrades on an equal footing. This is not to say that the mere reference to drinking always turns all Russians into generous fellow humans, in particular not if they are asked for cash by a tipsy bomzh, but panhandlers could still rely enough on the generosity of drunken potential donors to state openly what the money was aimed at. In any case, this proved to be more effective than saying that one was hungry. "You can get drunk for free here as easy as anything," Vova sighed at some point, "but nobody gives you a kopeck if you say 'bread.'"

Since alcohol connotes spiritual communion, in certain extraordinary cases it was enough to appeal straight to fellow humanness. Thus an unknown man (who for some reason knew my name) once ran up to me in the station yard, put his hand on his heart, and appealed dramatically and passionately: "Tova—I ask you this only as one *human* to another *human*—you're my last hope, give me 150 rubles for a ticket back home!" My companions, Vova and some others, were so moved by his request that I had to give him the money. (When I bumped into him a couple of months later, he admitted that he had cheated me.)

The connection between drinking and incomes was underlined further by the widespread opinion that most ways of making money at the station in fact required a drink. For example, Nina never questioned Raia's alcoholism per se, only her drunken temper. As she and most other saw it, drinking was a necessary and indisputable defense against cold weather, boredom, and depressing thoughts. According to Nina, who made her money washing cars in a nearby parking lot, it was in any case self-perpetuating since the money she received for each car, ten rubles, was the exact price of a bottle of Bomi, which was precisely what she needed after washing a car. To Vova, who always emphasized that "here, you mustn't be afraid, and never embarrassed either," a certain degree of tipsiness was the perfect remedy against these impediments. It was not natural for a human being to compete with aggressive porters or to snatch bottles from others or to attempt at more or less obvious thefts. To be bold one has to drink, he said. This sentiment found a fine expression in a conversation I once overheard. A man was trying to persuade Vova to take part in a theft, but Vova declined on the grounds that the man was too drunk to go through with it. The man promptly replied: "But *of course* I'm drunk! I *have* to be drunk for this, otherwise I would be ashamed, what else do you think?"

This man was suggesting that alcohol exonerates immoral acts that for the moment may seem unavoidable. Vova's opinion that qualities like boldness and shamelessness presuppose drunkenness features the same dilemma, but in a more generalized sense: to be the kind of person who survives, one has to drink, because true humans do not possess the (implicitly) negative characteristics of survivors and winners. Nonetheless, even the virtuously weak have to make the perpetual choice between Scylla and Charybdis: to get by as an agent in society at the expense of others or to perish as a fellow human. To claim one's need for intoxication in order to be somebody whom one essentially despises is an emphatic way of objecting to the state of things while going through with the unavoidable.

Ambition and Disillusion

Stephenson (1997) argues that among her Moscow informants, progressive social exclusion leads to an increasing incapacity to make long-term plans, which affects means of survival as much as anything else. Snow and Anderson describe how homeless people in the United States gradually abandon all hope of wage labor in favor of scavenging, theft, and the like (1993, 133ff.). The tendency is not very surprising: by definition, those who succeed disappear from the field and cease being homeless, and it would be strange if the remaining ones do not change tactics after a prolonged period of perpetual failure. In my own case, this development pertained mainly to the job-hunting minority who pinned their faith on the relatively established work market of construction, dvornik jobs, cleaning hospitals, and so on. As time passed and professional failures mounted, their optimism tended to fade, and gradually they redirected their efforts from "jobs" to "anything that pays." I should underline, however, that the pattern was neither ubiquitous nor clear-cut. To begin with, the group of people I was observing had very low persistence, making longitudinal processes difficult to observe—even if *I* returned there regularly for four years, most of the people I knew would not. It is also true that some people are more stubborn than others in pursuing their ideas about the essence of work, life, and, in effect, themselves as human beings. In this case it does not really matter what they actually do; the point is rather the social worlds in which they situate themselves.

Thus Marina always talked about would-be jobs when we met, but she was less informative about the fact that most of her job-seeking days resulted in the same thing as the efforts of her less ambitious roommates: a bag or two filled with deposit bottles and aluminum. I do not know if she really believed that she ever would get a job, but her persistent search and her scorn for the refuse that sustained her were nonetheless fundamental to her sense of remaining human. To her and to people like her, work was more than survival: it constituted meaningful persons insofar that the more "real" your job is, with normal work hours and workmates to talk to, the more included you are in the world of equally real humans and the less you have in common with scavenging bomzhi.

Marina was unusually tenacious, but the determination of many others was steadily eroded by repeated dismissals and deceitful employers, and in the end they seemed to accept that in their own reality, conventional ways to make oneself human only lead to further dehumanization. In this perspective, scavenging is not all that demeaning, in particular since bottles are fair game to most poor people (and most people are poor). Furthermore, the value of work, or the meaning of work for one's sense of self, is possible to renegotiate in one's own favor by shifting emphasis from one aspect to another. Work is the epitome of a societal dimension of humanness that is indeed a matter of reciprocity and inclusion, but this mutuality presupposes that nobody is anybody else's burden. The only choice for those who find themselves unable to be decent humans by cooperation and togetherness is therefore at least to avoid being parasites. "Perhaps I'm a bomzh," as everybody said, "but I don't live na khaliavu."

Fortunately, the preconditions of independent income were optimal in St. Petersburg in those years. In addition to the omnipresent drinking and the generous ratio of filled bottles to emptied ones, this world of work was not, as too often is the case for Western homeless people, limited to the two extremes of conventional jobs and solitary scavenging. Some displaced people never tried for proper jobs in the first place but headed straight for the station and the range of sustenance strategies involved with self-invented micro-entrepreneurship. This type of income presupposes a certain degree of corruption, however, or at least a notable lack of regulation and surveillance. The jobs of the employers must by themselves generate some form of payment for the workers, such as money from covert earning schemes or leftovers that nobody else takes an interest in. Another requirement is that no superior officials or controlling authorities prevent their employees from putting out their own tasks to tender or from allowing station regulars to hang out at cafes or to enter the trains. Crucial for homeless work opportunities is thus a slack regulation, not only of economic and material resources but also of urban space, an aspect that the next chapter investigates.

CHAPTER 3

Perilous Places

The Use and Abuse of Space and Bodies

Homeless people always cause anxiety because they use space in ways that it was not intended. They challenge conventional notions about the boundary between private and public, and their obvious poverty also defies the meanings invested in space by city planners, commercial actors, and the general public (Wright 1997). Such violations are punished if they cannot be prevented in the first place, but the ways of effecting discipline depend on the political and economic system. In St. Petersburg, the 1990s constituted a liminal period between what I found to be different systems of spatial regulation. As in the case of refuse economics, a profound lack of state regulation and surveillance simultaneously gave the homeless access to resources—in this case urban space—*and* exposed them to various forms of abuse. Although my discussion of the homeless work market conveys an image of a fairly peaceful urban environment, the presence of bomzhi in the urban landscape was nonetheless heavily contested by a variety of actors. The prevalence of ruthless evictions, assaults, or even murders in the everyday lives of my informants was in fact so salient that the first spontaneous comment I received when talking about my project was frequently: "So you want to know what it's like to be bomzh? They chase us and they beat us, *that's* how we live!"

Space is not equal in the eyes of the "housed" society. Places that are considered to be valuable for some reason are meticulously safeguarded against trespassers, while others appear as forgotten spatial leftovers. In reality, the latter are not as unused as they appear to be, but they tend to be occupied by equally neglected nonpersons. I use Wright's (1997) term refuse space for these often unwittingly ignored sites of varying shapes and sizes: they can be peripheral areas on the margins of cities or vacant lots inside them or just a few square meters behind a corner. In St. Petersburg in 1999, refuse space usually consisted of abandoned building sites or unused spaces inside residential houses. For the opposite, space that in some way is significant for the housed society, I use Snow and Anderson's (1991) term prime space.[1] Since these categories are defined by human practice, they are relative and flexible. Refuse space is swiftly transformed into prime space when actors more powerful than the homeless suddenly decide to use it, and in addition there is a temporal coefficient involved since certain places are abandoned by nonhomeless people only at particular times, most notably at night (Lovell 1992, 100ff.). Homeless people split their time between the two types of space: to survive, they need to occupy themselves in prime space, while they use refuse space to sleep and rest.[2]

In contemporary metropolises all over the world, refuse space is retracting. To conclude the arguments of Lovell (1992), Wright (1997), Snow and Mulcahy (2001), and Amster (2003) about the development of the spatial situation for the homeless in U.S. cities, centrally located refuse spaces are increasingly being appropriated by commercial interests and public agencies. As city centers are transformed to suit the needs of business actors and wealthy consumers, city authorities consciously try to eradicate traces of poverty in general, and the presence of homeless people in particular, by making urban space generally inaccessible and difficult for them to use. This strategy also implies an increasing surveillance of prime space. Paradoxically, these measures compel the homeless to spend *more* time in prime space since they literally have nowhere else to go, and their presence therefore also brings a certain measure of legally sanctioned violence. Amster (2003) argues that the homeless are successively being criminalized as a category due to the arrival of (usually local) laws prohibiting behavior that a homeless person can hardly avoid—sitting on pavement, sleeping in parks, loitering, camping, panhandling, and so on. Laws of this kind are not as easy to implement in all countries, but the tendency to purge profitable and prestigious metropolitan spaces from undesired human bodies seems general also in an international perspective. Homeless people, street children, and beggars are rarely welcomed in areas where the wealthy live, work, consume, or relax.

The Soviet system dealt with homelessness exclusively by criminalization. The passport laws prohibited "behavior" such as vagrancy and unemployment, and when this legislation disappeared in 1991, there were no other mechanisms available to obscure the existence of homeless people. No new laws replaced the old ones, but more important is the way in which cities, not least their central parts, were constructed. During Socialism, urban space did not have more commercial value than anything else, and there was thus no economic incentive to appropriate every single spot and put it to effective use. A general lack of maintenance of buildings and outdoor space contributed to a city infused with refuse space everywhere—inside residential buildings as well as on vacant lots sprinkled all over the urban landscape. In consequence, there existed a social space (mainly constituted by residents and janitors) in which the homeless had certain options to negotiate and legitimize their own presence, albeit always at the risk of being rejected. Extensive renovation schemes were initiated in the late 1990s, but the August 1998 financial crash caused a temporary standstill that made the city seem relatively static during my main fieldwork. The redevelopment was soon in full swing again, and today refuse space is gradually meeting the same fate as in Western metropolises. An additional incentive for the authorities to eliminate it was already making itself felt in 1999, but it became of central importance only during the succeeding years: fear of terrorism.

If the Soviet mode of spatial exclusion forced the homeless underground by outlawing them, the "capitalist" mode instead exposes them by literally eliminating the underground. Amster's comment about the proliferation of laws targeted at the homeless in the United States shows the continuities between the two modes: the capitalist attempts to exclude misfits from prestigious city spaces cannot but fail, and the complement seems to be the very device that the Soviet mode relied upon—various expressions of anti-vagrancy legislation.

Permissive Poverty: The Homeless and the Outdoor Cityscape

In 1999, central St. Petersburg was a patchwork of grey Sovietness and the bright colors of capitalist ambition. Not even the facades along Nevsky Prospekt, the aorta of the city, were renovated in full, and the grandiose buildings, tip-top renovated Western-style restaurants, fast-food chains, and hotels uneasily straddled shops, administrative offices, and museums of a distinctly Soviet kind—tiny windows guarded by thick curtains; small doors situated where potential customers and clients were least likely to find them; and a slightly run-down, colorless, albeit clean interiority.[3] *Evroremont* was the word of the day, and this "renovation to European standards" attracted wealthy tenants to expensive apartments and prestigiously situated commercial localities. With evroremont the scarcity and poor quality of the Soviet era were literally discarded, as faded wallpapers and porcelain kitchen sinks were replaced with the purported Western quality that once had to be chased, traded, or purchased underground. The best jobs that my male informants could think of were such renovations: not only did they pay well, but the skill required to turn East into West was also a prestigious sign of good craftsmanship. Eurospace, as I call space subjected to evroremont, was arbitrarily studded into the old cityscape. Among dozens of old-style grocery stores and bookshops on any central street, the large, shining windows of a gussied-up fashion shop stuck out like a gold tooth in a Soviet mouth, and evroremont apartments were hidden behind layers of steel doors in decrepit apartment blocs full of overcrowded *kommunalki,* with dark, dilapidated, dirty stairways, where some of my informants might be found sleeping on the top landing.

The Western or capitalist mode of spatial regulation is part and parcel of a larger metropolitan strategy to conceal, expel, and contain poverty (Wright 1997). In St. Petersburg in the late 1990s, by contrast, there was no possibility of hiding or segregating destitution and want, however heatedly the city planners and the mightiest commercial actors may have wanted to do so. Wealth coexisted with poverty, inside apartment blocs as well as in the streets. In attractive locations such as Sennaia Square or Apraksin Dvor, there were cheap markets and stalls selling everything from groceries and alcohol to fake leather jackets brought in from Turkey by industrious citizens, and in the corners there were plenty of people hanging out, on the lookout for loading jobs as well as for bottles, empty or full.

The cityscape was in this sense quite welcoming to the homeless, not least because they did not stick out much. Only the most tattered ones were recognized as homeless, and I did not learn to spot would-be informants until I learned to recognize them not so much from their appearance as from the way they occupied space—where they were standing, for how long, what they were doing—and from their interaction with salespeople and the like. Sometimes they were revealed by the contents of their obligatory bags—a miscellany of clothes, empty bottles, and foodstuffs—although this was not a foolproof method either. Poor people who were not homeless also poked about in dustbins or added deposit bottles to their meager incomes, and most groups of drinkers in parks and backyards were ordinary workers or pensioners relaxing from their own attempts to make a living (Caldwell 2004, 39ff.). A second feature that made life easier for homeless loiterers and bottle collectors was the generous amount of refuse space. Even those who looked undeniably like stereotype bomzhi always had odd sites nearby where they were out of the way of others. In many Western metropolises there are only pavements and parks left for the homeless, but my informants spent their days in an environment infused by sites for withdrawal: empty plots scattered between houses, the network of interconnected backyards so characteristic of St. Petersburg, or seemingly forgotten backstairs and attics inside apartment blocs.

There were certainly places in the city where the presence of homeless people was not accepted. The Soviet state may not have recognized the commercial value of city space, but it definitely attached symbolic value to sites of historical or ideological importance. Tsarist Russia as well as the Soviet state designed the metropolitan centers with the primary aim of displaying power and facilitating political festivities, parades, and other forms of propaganda (Neidhart 2003, 128ff.). The center of Moscow and many other Russian cities are entirely dominated by huge monumental buildings purportedly proving the victory of Socialism, while central St. Petersburg is relatively free of them. Thanks to the imperial grandeur and the (early) modernist ambitions of Peter the Great, Nevsky Prospekt and Admiral Square by the Winter Palace were lavishly spacious to begin with, and the grand pre-Revolutionary heritage inhibited further monumental buildings in the city center. At least this is the official story; according to one homeless man, St. Petersburg was spared the architectural megalomania that befell for instance central Moscow, simply because Stalin never bothered to go there. If he had, the man said, he would not have hesitated to take down the Hermitage and replace it with some wedding-cake like construction dedicated to his own glory, as he did with the skyscrapers defining the skyline of Moscow.

There were plenty of beggars of non-Russian origin outside the major tourist attractions, but such sites lack petty commerce of the kind that the homeless usually live off and are thus not of much interest to them. I had only one opportunity to observe how the presence of presumed bomzhi affected the guardians of the national heritage. It was on Vova's birthday in September, when he persuaded me to take him and a mate of his to the Peter Paul Fortress to look at the tombs of the tsars. They were both interested in history, he said, and he had not been to the fortress since a school excursion in his childhood when, moreover, the ashes of the last Romanovs were not yet buried there. At the time, Vova and his friend looked quite disheveled, nor were they sober, but I agreed, so we went there. We were asked to leave the cathedral after fifteen minutes, when a female guard caught sight of Vova and ran up to us with a startled face. He gleefully pointed at me, and I confirmed that we were there together. The perplexed woman took me to be some kind of chaperone and said breathlessly: "But you must understand—you have chosen the *wrong place!*" We left (they had already seen the tombs) and went to the prison museum beside the cathedral instead. This site was apparently not equally "wrong," because the guards there only seemed entertained by the loud comparisons that the two "tramps" made between the cells of the famous revolutionaries and the conditions at the contemporary prison of the city, Kresty.[4]

The shock caused by our visit to the guard in the cathedral reveals that bomzhi were unthinkable in a place like the Peter Paul Fortress, in particular in the pristine church. I assume that the royal heritage was the problem and not the presence of tourists, because homeless hangouts were tolerated in other places densely populated by foreigners. Aleksandr Nevsky Square, next to which the mammoth Hotel Moscow and the famous Aleksandr Nevsky Monastery are situated, was an established homeless hangout at the time, and the busloads of tourists did not prevent its regulars from gathering bottles by the kiosks sprinkled around the entrance to the metro, nor a number of more or less regular vendors of *Na Dne* from selling street papers (Nochlezhka is situated less than a kilometer away). The homeless people there were older than for instance the station crowd and looked more harried and worn, but they were less rowdy and were apparently perceived as harmless. Concealed behind an adjacent building there was, moreover, a vacant lot (I took it to be a prospective building site) where they went if they wanted to drink or urinate.

The frequent comment "they chase us and they beat us" did not primarily apply to streets and squares. More often, it referred to experiences on public transport, a prime space to which everybody who can pay has access and not only the homeless have difficulty affording (Caldwell 2004, 46–48). Transport was a dilemma of varying proportions depending on the habits of the homeless person. Chronic station dwellers such as Vova rarely used it, in contrast to people who worked, employed the services of charities, or went *po instantsiiam,* "along the offices." Traveling was usually a time-wasting endeavor since the subway, the only reliable and fast public transport, is difficult to sneak into without paying. The surveillance of buses, trolleybuses, or streetcars is generally slacker, and the conductor often seems to take it for granted that anybody who answers her request to produce a ticket (most conductors are women) with a distracted glance in another direction is carrying a pensioner or disability pass entitling them to free travel. In the subway there are several ticket collectors observing each other, as well as frequent security guards, and only distinctly old people can get by without a ticket or a document. Thus the graying Galia at Nochlezhka's shelter always hid her relatively youthful face behind a pair of hideous spectacles when she was traveling. That she could hardly see anything only helped her, since her disorientation made her look even older. According to Vova's mate Gena, whose weather-beaten face entitled him to free travel everywhere but in the subway, the permissiveness of the conductors stems from the fact that their wages are independent of the number of tickets sold, so they have no personal reason to make anybody pay. The real threat, he said, came from the irregular ticket patrols, young men who were allegedly paid a percentage of the fines they collected from free-riders and who seldom hesitated to physically wring the money from their prey. Their existence prevented few from trying, however; after all, you have traveled at least part of the way when they get at you, as Gena stoically remarked.

Certain people slept on the local trains, although the ones I knew could thwart the ticket controllers with more or less authentic pension certificates. Others found it too inconvenient to be worth the effort. Vova and a pal of his attempted it in the autumn, but it took the last train about two and a half hours to reach the terminal in some small town or village in the oblast', where they had to wait at the local station (which is not always open at night) until the first morning train left for St. Petersburg some three hours later. In one week they were beaten up twice: first by policemen at a village station, and another night the ticket controllers used physical force to make them leave the train. In the end they were too exhausted to go on with it, and retired to the chilly staircases in the city.

Indoor Sleeping Places: "Good Relations" and Violence

To avoid the words "homeless" and "homelessness" appearing in every single sentence, I sometimes write "street people" or "the streets." In English and Swedish such allusions are conventional, but in this context they are in fact misleading. In Russia, the homeless people I met referred to attics and basements, never "streets": "So there I was, and all that remained for me was the basements," or "I took to the attics when the flat was gone." Stairways were more common as sleeping places, but indoor refuse space was nonetheless pivotal both metaphorically and materially, while at the same time it harbored the most bestial violence and dehumanization that the homeless were subjected to.

In early October I was invited to dinner by Sasha, a man in his late forties who had been staying in an attic near Sennaia Square for four months, together with Pasha, an old friend from the Zone, and Pasha's girlfriend Natasha. The last two met me at the square and took me through a network of adjacent backyards to an almost invisible door behind some garbage bins. It led to a *chёrnaia lestnitsa* (literally "black stairway"), a remnant of pre-Revolutionary times when masters reached their apartments via the street entrance and the main stairway (the *paradnaia*), while servants used the kitchen door and the backstairs leading from the backyard. The kitchen doors were usually sealed when the Revolution erased the difference between nobility and servants, but the backstairs remain as an empty passage leading only to the attic. Visited only occasionally by residents or *dvorniki,* they are coveted sleeping places, and in this one there were traces of human habitation on each of the four landings: stained mattresses, old newspapers (a few layers of these are said to protect a body quite well from the cold), food leftovers, improvised stoves, and countless discarded bottles of Bomi and Ldinka. The filth and the smell were overwhelming, and I almost stepped in some human feces. Pasha laughed when he saw my face. "Yes, this is a real *bomzhovka* (a place where bomzhi sleep), but these bomzhi are not that bad," he said, "just down-and-out old men who come here once in a while. If they're sober enough to make it all the way, that is, there are new ones all the time. They don't care about the place more than they care about themselves—you should *see* them!" He took up an old newspaper from the floor and lit it, to light the last steps up to the attic that were not reached by the light trickling through the barely transparent windowpanes on the last landing.

Like all attics, this one consisted of a large open space with a dirt floor. There were two mattresses with blankets, some clothes were hanging from the rafters, and at the very back of the attic, at an appropriate distance, a piece of cloth screened off the spot they used as a lavatory. (Stairway dwellers usually use the attic for this purpose, but the bomzhi downstairs had had to do without it, as this one was occupied.) On a makeshift stove, Sasha was cooking a vegetable stew, which turned out to be quite tasty, and for the first and only time I also tried Ldinka (it tastes like cheap vodka), which they used as "petrol," as they put it, not to get drunk but to keep themselves going.

The three of them were quite proud of their attic. Finding and keeping a good sleeping place was generally considered equivalent to having a good job: it proved one's capacity to organize oneself in "this life," to create a tolerable environment in spite of seemingly insurmountable obstacles. People who boasted about their industriousness and their capacity to make a living rarely failed to emphasize that they slept comparatively well too, and I had heard about this attic for a long time before I eventually visited it. It was a nice calm place, Sasha and Pasha assured me. During four months they had not even

FIGURE 4. Sasha's attic. Photograph by the author.

had their possessions stolen or thrown away, a fate that befalls most home-less people who sleep in apartment blocs. Irritated neighbors (as they call the apartment residents) or zealous dvorniki frequently harass unwelcome night lodgers by throwing away their belongings even if they do not "evict" them, or other bomzhi appropriate the things instead. In this apartment bloc, the residents never set foot in the attic, and the dvornik had evidently given up any pretense of cleaning the backstairs long ago. The bomzhi on the landings were, moreover, basically decent people who left their neighbors upstairs alone.

Unfortunately they would have to move soon. The weather was getting cold, they explained, and attics are good sleeping places only in the warm season. At other times, stairways are considered to be better. If there are no backstairs (not all apartment blocs were constructed to separate masters from servants), people use the uppermost landing where the doors lead only to the attic. Tenants seldom have any business there, and it is comparatively warm. But Sasha wanted something better than that, like a good boiler room. Since St. Petersburg is built on a marsh, basements are often flooded, but certain basement localities such as furnace rooms or bomb shelters are relatively fit for human habitation because they provide central heating, a blessing to lungs infected by every kind of evil that evaporates from the raw swamps beneath the city.

Sasha, Pasha, and Natasha had another good reason to move. A few nights earlier, a group of policemen had unexpectedly appeared in the attic and given all three of them a long and thorough thrashing. Natasha came out of it less injured than the men. "I'm lucky to have such a big belly," she said and patted herself on her indeed quite voluminous midsection, "they stopped kicking me around when I screamed that I was pregnant. Which I'm not, I'm just fat." They did not know if the police would come back. The explosions in a number of apartment blocs in Moscow in September were suspected of being terrorist attacks, which gave the city authorities in St. Petersburg a reason to seal off attics and basements. The police visit could mean that they were checking up on places that ought to be locked up, Sasha said, and since policemen are incurable sadists and there were people in the bomzhovka, they simply took the opportunity to have some fun as well.

Basically, the residents or the dvornik may have called in the police to get them to evict the uninvited night lodgers, but these three attic-dwellers found this unlikely. It certainly happens, but in Russia the police are as re-sented as the bomzhi, and those who live or work in houses generally prefer to deal with intruders on their own. Methods of eviction may be harsh—the easiest way to displace a person from a stairway is simply to kick him or her down the stairs. Still, most street dwellers agreed that neighbors and dvorniki were not responsible for the worst violence. I asked if they were afraid of the predatory youth gangs and drug addicts that other stairway dwellers talked about with such dread. They found this less of a problem: there were three of them after all, and such indiscriminate villains would, moreover, be satisfied with the ones who slept in the stairway if they just wanted to attack bomzhi.

Any kind of destitute bomzhovka in the city—boiler rooms, attics, black stairways, or outdoor refuse spaces—is said to be patrolled at night by groups of young men whose sole purpose is to molest or kill. This makes the choice difficult for a tired bomzh. The likelihood of being killed in an ordinary stairway is lower than in a basement or a black stairway because there are people around who do not appreciate overt physical violence outside their door. Nor do they like bomzhi being there, which increases the likelihood of being chased away. The more destitute a space is, the better option it provides for an undisturbed sleep, but it is also there that people are likelier to be mauled or even murdered. Such extreme beatings are not an everyday occurrence; only a handful of informants claimed to have received one, but I knew at least one person who died from such violence. Still, the fear of fatal attacks is certainly a part of the everyday lot of the homeless. "The first weeks were terrifying beyond words," a young man told me. "I did not know what homelessness was, I was alone, I didn't know reliable people to sleep together with. I was completely paranoid, even the sound of a cockroach paralyzed me. First I constructed a trap of empty bottles hanging from the ceiling in the attic where I slept, so that at least I would hear them coming before they got me. Later, I thought that the contrary would be better and got drunk every evening—if I was to be killed, I would at least not notice it myself." And this was, roughly, the usual way of dealing with the insecurity: to have company at night, to tranquilize oneself with Bomi or Ldinka, and to cultivate a fatalistic outlook on life.

Certain people nevertheless preferred the risk of eviction. The former pianist Irina, the woman who regarded bomzhi as "excrement of the state," stuck to her principles and slept alone. She always kept to inhabited stairways, and she was normally left alone by the few residents passing by late at night, presumably because she was alone, female, tiny, and stooped, and because she looked considerably older than her sixty years. Nor did she challenge their dominion of the space by spreading her things around; in fact, she changed her sleeping place each night so that nobody would find her intrusive. She never mentioned physical abuse or evictions, even though her things were stolen all the time, but she was certainly afraid of violence. The nights thus posed an insoluble dilemma for Irina. One hundred grams of vodka allowed her to sleep, but it also increased the likelihood that her life or her belongings would be gone in the morning. Abstaining from the one hundred grams would leave her sleepless and petrified, she concluded, so she might as well drink: if nobody robbed or killed her at night, then they would be sure to do so the next day, after she fainted from fatigue.

It adds to the fear that nobody knows exactly *who* these brutal perpetrators are, besides the fact that they do not live or work in the houses in which they prey on victims and that they are not very old. In particular elderly people talked about "drug addicts," perhaps because to them, drugs summed up all of the incomprehensible and demonic aspects of the new era that had victimized them. Moreover, drug addicts made them stand out in a favorable light by being even more of an Other to the established society than a commonplace bomzh. The same applied to "fascists," another category that was more or less implicitly indicated as possible perpetrators: "He was beaten to death by youngsters, you know, those who wear black hoods and think their mission is to 'clean up the city'... from us, that is, and from whoever else they don't like. They go to attics and such places because they know that they'll find someone to beat up there," as some regulars at the Salvation Army said about the violent death of another regular. Stephenson has interviewed such violent youth gangs in Moscow, and they do indeed display such a twisted sense of social hygiene, using an idiom of "cleansing," "pollution," and so forth (2006, 46).

Speculations about motives could stop at sheer sadism. "Three of us had this boiler room," a young man said.

We didn't drink at the time since all of us had jobs to take care of, and the basement was good—nobody came there and nobody noticed us. But nobody heard us scream either. These lads, I don't know how many they were really, just turned up and started to beat us up. They didn't go to this basement by chance, I tell you, they *knew* that there was somebody there whom they could kill without anybody poking too much into the matter. And they didn't ask us to piss off or anything—they just pulled out their sticks and got on with it. I spent three months in hospital—I survived only because my mate managed to escape and came back for me afterwards. And they were laughing, doing it only because they thought it was *fun!*

Judging from a Google search that I made and the resultant—and extremely long—list of newspaper articles, such violence may just as well be the tragic result of competition for space. Refuse space is a haven not only for homeless people but also for teenagers who have nowhere to go either (Markowitz 2000, 135ff.). Sometimes homeless people die simply because they accidentally end up in the same basement as a drunken and frustrated gang of male adolescents, whose members want to show off their purported manliness to each other. Ironically, quite a few of my male informants initiated their homeless trajectories through senseless drunken violence of a similar kind.

While the random violence of unknown predators cannot be anticipated or thwarted, neighbors and dvorniki can be appeased. A number of times I was told about occasions when residents or janitors turned up in stairways or basements with a bottle of vodka, spending several hours with the homeless "lodgers" in open-hearted conversation (or *obshchenie,* a deeper and more intimate form of communication). As we shall see, there were similar stories about the police, and I cannot tell to what extent this genre depicted actual events or dreams about an ideal world. Yet it shows that fellow humanness on the part of ostensible gatekeepers was not entirely unthinkable. However, even if the terms are rarely as friendly or soulful as these stories made them out to be, it is still possible to persuade those who live and work in houses that your presence will not cause problems or even that you are protecting the place against even more resented inhabitants. At least this was the argument of Tolik, a station regular who occupied an inhabited stairway (that is, not backstairs) not far from the station. Together with two regular "roommates" he turned it into a narrow penthouse with a sleeping room at the top and a kitchen with a brick stove on the stairs down to a makeshift dining room on the next landing. It was not particularly clean there, partly because of Tolik's dog and an adopted kitten, "but much worse before *we* came, and they're grateful for that" said Tolik, referring to the neighbors. But I wonder for how long this gratitude would have lasted, considering Tolik's habit of using odorous plastic materials as fuel when he was cooking. Unfortunately, he disappeared before I could find out.

A frequent accusation against the homeless is that they constitute a fire hazard. I cannot really disagree; Sasha's campfire was modest, but the rafters a couple of meters above it were nevertheless wooden, and no lungs benefited from Tolik's toxic fumes. Sasha and his companions did not seem to give this a thought, and Tolik acted according to the principle of trial and error: "They're used to it," he said self-confidently, "and if they've got complaints they'd tell us, wouldn't they?" People who conscientiously work on their good relations take more care, but in order to make refuse spaces in apartment blocs habitable it can be difficult *not* to constitute some sort of hazard. Armen, a deeply religious Salvation Army regular who was extremely loath

FIGURE 5. Tolik cooking in his stairway. Photograph by the author.

to be a problem to anybody, had a gas stove in the backstairs where he slept with an equally right-minded friend. In order to be able to read at night on their landing, they installed electric wires and a socket themselves. I did not think of it when they mentioned it, but later it struck me that incorrectly installed wires are also dangerous. Armen and his companion mentioned the installation in passing, as if it was something that they were used to, and perhaps it was. Professional electricians were as hard to get hold of as other craftsmen in the Soviet time (unless you knew one personally), and people often took care of their sockets and wires themselves, as they did with other domestic technicalities. There may have been far more hazardous installations inside Armen's house, but the dilemma is nevertheless the same as with camp-fires: if a place is not designed for domestic use to begin with, arrangements to make it habitable may pose a threat to everybody in the vicinity, regardless of how good the intentions are.

The dvornik did not object to the electric socket; on the contrary, he was very supportive of Armen and his companion. Before they moved in, they asked his permission, and once there they kept their landing clean in exemplary fashion, with carefully scrubbed floors and walls insulated with chipboard. The dvornik trusted them because all they did there was sleep, smoke, and read the Bible, and the closest they came to alcohol was the bottle of vodka they gave him now and then as a sign of appreciation. Later in the autumn, he even entrusted them with a key to the adjacent attic when it was sealed due to the purported terrorist attacks; Armen's and Ivan's lives improved significantly when, for the first time in years, they were able to lock their things up.

Armen and his friend had only one person to deal with, but good relations can be a complicated issue when a number of actors with divergent attitudes to bomzhi need to be appeased. Residents have internally different opinions that may differ from that of the dvornik, and often higher levels get involved too. Two acquaintances of Armen's from the Salvation Army, Nadia and Ser-gei, had to face this complication after they took over an unusually good sleeping place. They had two babies and were among the few parents I met who tried to keep their infants with them, a struggle that I describe in detail in the next chapter. Thanks to this empty commercial space, Nadia and Sergei kept their children for almost a year. It was a damp and dilapidated former dry cleaner's, like many other such businesses situated in the yard, a few steps down from ground level. A planned renovation was postponed indefinitely and the space had been vacant for years, but there was electricity and running water. The neighbors were enchanted by the babies, one one-year-old and the other newborn, and they appreciated that the former on-and-off bomzhovka was now inhabited by sober people. They even helped the little family to find furniture and bed linen, and Nadia and Sergei soon had a bed, a cradle, chairs, a table, and a cooker as well as a television set. For some time they lived an almost normal, although extremely poor, family life, until somebody—Nadia did not know if it was a grudging dvornik or a neighbor—told the local housing administration that there were permanent residents who even had a lock on the door.

Refuse space can be turned into prime space in an instant when those who have the formal authority over it discover that somebody is using it. The lock was probably extra provocative, turning the use of the supposedly vacant space into a theft of sorts rather than what might be interpreted as a more casual appropriation. One way to terminate such parasitical misuse is to turn the space into a source of profit; another is to break the lock (if there is one), evict the inhabitants, and seal the door again. That the space is now useless to everybody, tenants as well as potential intruders, is symbolically significant, since it demonstrates tangibly who is in control and who is not. In this case, the housing administration used both strategies. First they demanded rent. Nadia and Sergei tried to deal with them, which, as I understood Nadia, resulted in a strange dead-end discussion about what the locality was *not:* it was *not* a free-of-charge shelter, according to the administration, but, argued Nadia and Sergei, it was *not* anything else either, so they might as well be there until somebody figured out what it actually was. A compromise was reached that obliged Nadia to perform dvornik duties in return for use of the premises. After half a year they were nevertheless forced to leave, and then they had no choice but to give up their children to foster care. The place was locked up, in Nadia's furious words (otherwise she never used a foul language) "*only* as a way for them [the housing administration] to show their dicks." It was certainly a matter of prestige to *her* that one year later, they were still living in the same yard, albeit in another basement waiting for a purpose, but now carefully concealing their existence from everybody but a few loyal neighbors.

A number of factors make nighttime survival consistent with daytime efforts to make a living, as described in the preceding chapter. The homeless survive, thanks to refuse space in a literal sense or in a transferred economic meaning of the word, as they make use of places or tasks and objects unwanted by others. Generally inefficient or nonexistent state surveillance makes money-making and "space-carving" activities alike unprotected by the law and dependent on idiosyncratic individuals—actors with whom, as gatekeepers and channels to resources, one benefits from having "good relations," but who simultaneously pose risks, primarily deprivation of money

FIGURE 6. Sergei in the basement where he lived before he met Nadia. Photograph by the author.

and the threat of physical violence. As the following sections will show, the ubiquitous presence of purported representatives of the state does not change these basic conditions much, since in spite of an ostensible monopoly on violence, they still act primarily as disparate individuals.

The Moscow Station:
Its Policemen and Its Spaces

"The station" was an additional metaphor for homelessness, albeit used less frequently than "the attic" or "the basement." The Moscow Station and its waiting halls is still the first place in St. Petersburg that a recently dislocated person goes, and in 1999 all major railway stations were notorious for their accumulation of bomzhi, prostitutes, and petty criminals. As we shall see, extensive redevelopment schemes and the fear of terrorism have put an end to the spatial permissiveness of the 1990s. Before that, however, the Moscow Station was more of a makeshift home to its homeless regulars than the best of basements could ever be.

The station differed from the cityscape outside in the sense that the external actors determining the presence of the homeless were less disparate. The railway staff and the attendants of kiosks, cafes, and so forth remained the same from day to day, but most important was the ubiquitous presence of the police in the everyday activities of the station regulars. Homeless people are always harassed for the usual litany of reasons and with the same degree of humiliation and violence by policemen everywhere, but even if there was no qualitative difference between detentions at the station and outside it, there was definitely a difference in terms of quantity. The limited station area contained an unusually large number of policemen and homeless people, and station regulars were thus subjected to detentions and beatings by the police more than homeless persons elsewhere. These confrontations were determined by spatial categorizations, and this section scrutinizes the station area and the meanings imbued in its different parts by the homeless and their opponents. The subsequent sections take a closer look at the violence generated by the homeless misuse of space at the station.

"There are some two hundred cops at this railway station alone, and at least four types of them," Vova once explained, counting on his fingers, "or five. Most of them belong to the normal *militsia,* that's the railway cops here at the station, or to the ordinary precinct at Ligovskii Prospekt that looks after the metro station. All these beat bomzhi. Then there's OMON. They beat the militsia and us. Spetsnats beats us, the militsia, and OMON. And then there's the FSB and the military police, and they can beat whoever they want but they're sort of too important to be bothered with bomzhi."

The FSB is the former KGB, while OMON and Spetsnats are elite forces under the Ministry of the Interior. Spetsnats has, to my knowledge, exclusively military functions, and Vova's estimation was probably far from exact in other details too. As I may have mentioned, he was prone to embellishment, and the mere presence of occasional Spetsnats and OMON soldiers at the station need not mean that they were assigned particular tasks there. (The ones I saw were drinking.) To add to the confusion, the railway police come under the Ministry of Transport, whereas the other police forces belong to the Ministry of the Interior. It was not only the station regulars who had difficulties grasping the structure of surveillance. The policemen I asked refused to answer for "security reasons," but one of them explained that the disparate police forces were linked to different branches of the state apparatus and that he did not know the exact role of each of them in the particular station context.

Station regulars usually confronted the railway militia, whose task was merely to maintain order. Criminal charges were handled by another police department situated on the way to Botkin Hospital, which Vova forgot to mention. "Maintaining order" implied keeping the homeless away, since they were regarded as a public threat due to contagious illnesses and criminality. However, as the policeman I talked to added somewhat regretfully, there were no legal means to keep them away since no laws prohibited loitering at railway stations or in any other public place. The task of the police was thus doomed from the start, since they were not legally entitled to do what they were expected to do. Another obstacle was the spatial design of the station and the entrenchment of the homeless in its economy. The quite powerless law-enforcing organs thus settled for the next-best solution: a fragile compromise that was largely upheld by illicit coercion and violence, which basically aimed at letting the bomzhi know their place and, at times, profiting from them.

The implicit compromise implied that the station regulars were prohibited from entering certain places, while others were conditional and regulated by a code of conduct. There were also places that were apparently considered to be meaningless to anybody but a bomzh, so they were free from restrictions. The compromise was fragile because it matched the spatial taxonomy of the station regulars only to a certain extent: for them, different spaces at the station had different levels of usefulness. Certain sites provided neither income nor leisure, while other parts of the station were entertaining and profitable but fraught with behavioral restrictions. In addition, there were places for rest and leisure that were as devoid of surveillance as of income. Sometimes the interests of the police and the station regulars clashed, and the station area was thus at the same time differentiated in terms of contestation.

In particular, recently renovated indoor spaces were seemingly invested with similar kinds of meaning by both the authorities and the station regulars: for example, in the main ticket office, tickets were purchased. Even though it was warm in the winter, regulars had no interest in hanging out there since the crowded office offered neither deposit bottles nor options to empty other bottles. The main station hall was also uninteresting. Without benches to sit on, this spacious hall is basically a thoroughfare that travelers pass through on the way to the platforms, hanging about only briefly until their trains arrive. A complete commercialization of the walls in the form of kiosks inhibits loitering—I never saw people hanging out without anything to sit on or lean against. Smoking is prohibited, and even if drinking is allowed (I am not sure, but I never saw anyone doing it in this hall), the few kiosks selling alcohol provide no tables where it may be drunk. The adjacent cafe is of the updated kind where no regulars work. Vova's mate Raia once did, but she had to leave when it was renovated in the late 1990s. The connection between her dismissal and the makeover seemed evident to her: "They made it fancy, you know—evroremont and all that, so of course we can't work there any longer." There is also something about the "eurospace" look of the hall: this modern face of the station makes bomzh bodies out of place in a way that was not the case in the yard before the renovations, and many regulars seemed to feel this. Raia always shuddered and slumped when she walked through this hall, hurrying up as if she felt that everybody was staring at her, and station regulars never went there unless they had to pass through. There were comparatively few policemen in this hall; discipline was, to frame it in Foucauldian terms, internalized through sheer design. Other types of surveillance were redundant since the purpose of the space was so unambiguous that nobody attempted to use it in ways not intended by the planners and architects.

Such an internalized discipline works only when there are less disciplined spaces nearby. Otherwise the undesired "dirt" would trickle in anyway, lacking other places to go, as in the case of hypermodern city centers, as mentioned above. If station regulars passed through the Main Hall, it was only to reach the tunnel leading to the subway, which was joined up by another tunnel, quite long, that began somewhere near the police station. The passage to the subway was as busy then as now, but in the junction of the two tunnels, just before the entrance to the subway, there was enough space by the wall for a bottle gang to hang out, fully visible to passersby. For some reason, the attitude of the police was quite slack precisely in this spot: they chased the drinkers away if they passed through, but this occurred so infrequently that some acquaintances of Vova's spent a few winter months here relatively undisturbed. The adjacent tunnel leading to the police station was frequented by neither travelers nor (strangely enough) the police, and the hot water pipes running along the walls made it a popular sleeping place. It was also as dangerous as any refuse space; in the spring a dead body was found here. The police forced Vova to assist in moving it, and he said that it was an unknown bomzh whose head had apparently been smashed against the wall a number of times.[5]

He and many others believed that the police murdered the man, but such suggestions were quite unusual. In general, station regulars did not expect to be *killed* by the police, not because they believed them to be unwilling to murder a bomzh but because corpses attract undesired attention. In this case, however, the talk did not concern the station police but the squad situated at nearby Ligovskii Prospekt that was responsible for the subway. Beyond their own territory and in a secluded place like the tunnel, I was told, there is no difference between the police and the monstrous villains that made the attics unsafe. The murder was never solved, and it did not take long before people were sleeping next to the warm pipes again; the fatalism with regard to unexpected and extreme violence was the same at the station as everywhere else.

Next to the Main Hall is "Cold Hall," as the free-of-charge waiting hall used to be called. In the daytime it was relatively free of station regulars, who were busy elsewhere, and the people who shuddered on the benches were, with occasional exceptions, travelers. In the late evening, particularly in the cold season, it was, on the contrary, a contested space. Station regulars persisted in resting here for a few hours before the station closed at two a.m. in spite of being regularly chased away by the police. The latter were said to use their batons quite brutally on the legs of those whom they recognized as homeless; more than once I was shown bruises from such late evenings.

On the second floor of the main building is the *platnyi zal,* which literally means the "chargeable waiting hall." While the rest of the station is closed for a few hours every night, this hall remains open for transit travelers. (Many long-distance trains depart only once or twice a week, so changing trains may be a lengthy business.) Its original purpose was certainly not to provide makeshift housing for dozens of homeless people, but the entrance fee (three rubles per night in the first half of 1999) converted a bomzh into a paying guest with the same rights as everybody else. To the station regulars, the modesty of the fee made money less important for admittance than physical appearance and relative temperance, but Vova said that certain attendants could be bribed. They preferred alcohol to money and did not cause much trouble, and since they were too drunk themselves during the night to be alert to the drinking inside the hall, only very provocative debauchery would lead to eviction.[6] Vova liked to exaggerate, and I am not sure that the parties in this hall were as wild as he liked to picture them. In the daytime, the code of conduct was observed to the extent that I once found the usually hard-boiled Katia the Colonel squatting between the rows of chairs, anxiously hiding her cigarette inside her jacket so as not to be thrown out for the rest of the day from the non-smoking hall. The same flight of stairs leads to the men's room one floor below ground level. It seems to play a role similar to the ladies' room I described in the preceding chapter, although Vova gave a more dramatic picture. There, he claimed, the men consumed the same amounts of liquid as they disposed of, and he loved to deliver sensational stories about drinking sprees, ruthless fights, and bloody revenge in the urinal.

On the ground level by this staircase there is an exit from the main building to the yard. Outside it, the prostitutes used to wait for clients, and this spot was generally the most eventful part of the station, in the opinion of the regulars. In front of this exit, on the other side of the yard, is the so-called Military Ticket Hall (*Voennaia kassa*), a special ticket office for soldiers. In contrast to the ordinary ticket office, this place was heavily contested. The panorama view over the yard provided by the large windows and the broad flight of stairs leading to the entrance made this a very popular drinking place. In contrast to the subway, the police did their best to keep the drinkers out of this hall. Some policemen only chased them out into the yard, while others dragged them out of the entire station area; sometimes they were taken to the police station. As soon as the police turned their backs, the drinkers returned and continued where they had been interrupted, and a conspicuous minority of mainly younger women and men sometimes seemed to tease the police on purpose. As their drunkenness increased, they became more and more daring, like coy, giggling schoolchildren outmaneuvering disrespected but insistent teachers. Their persistence sometimes endowed the futile efforts of the police with the character of a bizarre cat-and-mouse game, an impression that was strengthened by the short distance between this hall and other types of space.

Only a few feet away, there were during this period refuse spaces where drinkers could take refuge. Neither the police nor anybody else bothered much about their presence behind the kiosks or in a little green lot at the far end of the yard (commonly called *Piannyi sad,* the Drunken Garden), and in the immediate proximity of the actual station area there are still plenty of backyards connected to residential buildings. Behind the Drunken Garden there was an abandoned building site where the regulars Liuba and her boy-friend Dima occupied a ruined bunker. In the summer there were usually groups of people gathered around bottles or sleeping their drunkenness off on the ground. Another dead body was found here in the autumn. Like the corpse in the tunnel, it was male, mutilated, unknown to the station regulars, and apparently homeless, but this time the station regulars believed the villains to be violent youth gangs. Liuba and Dima did not find this a reason to move from their bunker, however, and others continued to rest here as before.

Drinkers on the run from the police often halted in the yard, where their presence was negotiable and a matter of conduct. One could hang out here "as long as one behaves," as the homeless put it, which means avoiding attention through visible drunkenness, large crowds, a lot of noise, or aggression. Usually, regulars were aware of the conditions, hushing and reproaching each other for attracting attention, and if clusters became too large they usually dispersed voluntarily, before a police officer appeared and ordered them to do so. The police were subject to continuous attention, and any station regular entering the station for the first time during the day knew within minutes which "cops" were on duty and how alert and angry they seemed to be. Exceptionally ill-reputed officers rarely made people leave the station area as such, but some might retire to a calmer place while others adapted their noise and visibility to the perceived mood of the police. During the day, the drinkers who were chased out of the Military Ticket Hall tended to comply with the code of conduct, and many police officers appeared to reevaluate the situation once they were outside, deciding whether or not the delinquents were challenging the rules of the yard as well. If so, the pursuit would go further, to the precinct or the main gates of the station; otherwise they were left where they were. It was particularly toward the end of the day that certain bold drinkers seem to think "to hell with it" and continue the party out in the open, not caring in the least about the consequences.

Detentions, Abuse, and Unpredictability

Station regulars who were brought to the precinct did not always know the grounds for the detention until they were inside the police station; indeed, often it was an open question if the police knew it either. At least they were free to decide later whether the detention should concern drunkenness or lack of ID documents. Violations of the passport laws (having no ID papers) always have to be charged; if a suspect cannot produce the required documents on the spot, he or she is taken to the police station. Most such detentions were thus correct from a legal point of view, even if an inconvenience to the regulars who were arbitrarily interrupted and delayed in their own affairs. Certain police squads fulfilled this duty with such zeal that they charged the same person several times within a very short period of time, for reasons unknown to the delinquents. At the station, moreover, the police knew beforehand which station regulars possessed documents and which did not, but this did not affect the random detentions. An acquaintance of Vova's was charged three times in the same afternoon by the same squad; he supposed that there were census purposes behind it. Vova instead connected it to a theory about a planned economy of arrests that I frequently heard also from non-homeless people. Allegedly, a police squad is obliged to meet a quota, a particular number of arrests for different crimes within a certain period of time. From eavesdropping on policemen at the Moscow Station, Vova calculated their local plan as nine bomzhi per policeman per day, recounting certain phrases: "Are you done with the quota yet?" or "Only eight so far, one more to go!" His friend then recalled a police precinct in Moscow that was said to offer one hundred grams of vodka to "violators of the passport laws" who turned up voluntarily. "They fulfilled the plan within minutes each morning," he laughed, "without even leaving their chairs!"

Such detentions were frequently confused with detentions for drunkenness, because drunken people without ID papers were charged with a violation, while people taken in for ID checks could be detained for longer if they were perceived to be excessively drunk. A detention for drunkenness did not necessarily imply anything more than having to sit for three hours on a bench at the police station, judging from the assorted comments from people leaving the precinct. If it was a good day, there would be people to talk to and perhaps the guard would also be talkative. If it was a bad day, the guard would be irritable and there would be nobody to talk to; on such days, boredom and an accelerating hangover made the three hours feel like three days.

A common opinion among station regulars was that as long as you do not put up any resistance once they get you, nothing worse will happen. "The *menty* [cops] took him in only minutes ago," Papik said about Vova one time I came to the station, "but he's calm, so he'll come out all right. He's smart enough not to provoke them." Now and then, Papik was taken in for checkups of his always nonexistent ID papers, and he never had any problems as long as he hid his money. To Papik and many other regulars, the police were merely public servants: corrupt, stupid, and with a high-strung tendency to overreact, but nevertheless acting on a rational basis. The police at this station were in fact better than in many other places, I was told, such as the Finland Station and, in particular, all of Moscow.

To Papik it was self-evident that, since the police are not well paid and a bomzh is a nobody, it is perfectly rational that they would steal from the homeless. He protected his money under a long strip of gauze bandage wrapped around his chest, well aware that anybody who is detained is subject to confiscations of money without legal grounds. Any detention—not only at the station, and not only of the homeless—gives the police the opportunity to steal, in particular if drunkenness is the reason for the detention. Homeless people also told me about policemen who demanded bribes to accept the ID papers that they were actually able to produce or who destroyed ID papers, although this was said to be more common in Moscow than in St. Petersburg. Some station regulars with relatively regular incomes also accused the police of demanding tribute—substantial quantities of cigarettes and beer (according to the wagon cleaner Liudmila) or cash, as when Dima, who worked for the regular cleaners, was forced to hand over his entire weekly wage. Vova said that the prostitutes had to pay tribute in kind, but I never heard that from the girls themselves. According to many others, however, they had to pay large sums to policemen on a random basis, a form of extortion that is the plight of sex-workers all over Russia and not particular to the station.

Papik and many others argued that the police do not gain anything from physical abuse (unless it is necessary to get hold of money), so they do not engage in it unless they have just cause. Resisting a detention is asking for trouble (or even just speaking back, considering their nervous temperament), and nobody needs to do that. Nor does anybody need to reel around openly in the yard, when there are so many hideouts available. Papik was not alone in finding the behavior of bold drinkers detestable. Railway travelers often seemed uneasy at the sight of extremely drunken gangs, and on a few occasions I saw station regulars pick fights with each other. I never heard about travelers being assaulted, but it nevertheless looked menacing. Two of these brawls were initiated by Vova's mate Fyodor, notorious for his drunken bad temper, who was a living proof of Papik's theory: he fought when he could, always resisted detention, and as a result he always had a broken rib or two, either by the police or by somebody else. Otherwise I rarely heard about fights between homeless people, although the drinking habits of many suggest that this was not uncommon. As we shall see, however, the risk of conflict is reduced since one can always leave people one does not like. In addition, I believe that such fights do not really count as violence. As an assumed and commonplace facet of drinking, tragic perhaps but fully explicable and occurring among people one knows, such fights might have been quickly forgotten, unlike the gratuitous violence inflicted by state representatives or roving packs of teens.

Those who argued as Papik did thought that the same logic applied to the deportations: only very drunken and provocative people were gathered into large vans at night and driven to the forests, nobody else. These incidents first became known to the public in late 1998, and according to *Na Dne,* the order came straight from the governor of St. Petersburg. The street paper successfully created a media uproar about these events, and for a while they ceased. From the station regulars, however, I heard about such measures in connection with major official visits to the city during the following years too. Needless to say, the deported people returned within hours, but I was told by a couple of victims that certain old and ill people never made it back. Late November is cold, and people were dumped without any clear idea where they were. The police have fiercely denied the existence of such deportations throughout, and it helps them that they indeed seem to pick only people who are quite drunk (nobody who claims to have been deported denies this), since this means a paucity of reliable witnesses.[7]

The view of police violence as something predictable and rationally motivated was far from uncontested, however, and few people maintained it for long. Masha was a woman in her early forties who conscientiously kept herself cheerful by being constantly drunk. Jovial, humorous, and generous, she was liked by most people, and she was completely confident in her own ability to charm the policemen. Regardless of how drunk she was, she used to say, they never considered *her* to be troublesome. On the contrary, they brought out the vodka as soon as they saw her, greeting her as a friend and treating her to drinks as long as she kept their boredom at bay with jokes and stories—in fact, she was often detained *because* they wanted entertainment. One day, however, Masha left the precinct with a huge black eye. She was laughing as always, but this time she held tears back as well: "They told me to choose between a rape and a thrashing, so I chose the thrashing and that's what I got. . . . And they hit my *face,* I can hardly believe it—you know, this is the first black eye of my life! I almost feel selected, why such an extraordinary treatment of *me?*"

Masha had no idea why they suddenly changed their benevolent attitude towards her, or why they chose to hit her in the face. Since police violence ostensibly occurs only in situations of justified self-defense, they purportedly avoid blows in the face and choose less conspicuous places instead: the legs or the torso, in particular on the back where the kidneys are located. But at the station, I learned, unpredictability was seen as a hallmark of the police, in spite of all of the efforts people made (and took great pride in) to foresee their moves and moods. The notions of "behaving well" and "excessively drunk" that ostensibly regulated detentions were at best opaque, and according to many regulars the same uncertainty concerned the three hours in the precinct. People known to be calm and compliant, like Masha, left with bruises, while at other times well-known bullies such as Fyodor were not touched, in spite of violently resisting detention. Elderly people, in particular *babushki*, were less likely to be beaten (they were deprived of their money instead), and if Pasha's girlfriend Natasha was right, the same was true of pregnant women, but otherwise most men and women seemed to have been subjected to gratuitous physical abuse at some point or other.

The police demonstrated their unpredictability to me too. Most of them ignored me, but some were curious, and a few times Vova made sure that we were seen talking to each other, since he thought this might protect him. Some were, if not friendly, at least proper, while others liked to end jovial conversations abruptly with concealed threats such as: "Well, we'll see what trouble we can cause this lady, now that she's here." A few indulged in nitpicking and faultfinding with my visa, which was never considered to be in order. At some point I overheard them saying to each other: "She's here only to poke her nose into the work of the [law-enforcing] organs," which suggested that at least some of them were as paranoid towards me as I sometimes felt towards them.

I do not know if this arbitrariness was a conscious strategy on the part of the police. One way to exercise power is to deliberately confound the subjects and undermine their referential frames (Taussig 1992), and in Russia the technique of "confuse and rule" was fundamental to Stalin's terror regime, among others. The question is, however, if the police at the station or in the upper hierarchies actually made the effort to formulate a policy against subjects deemed as worthless as a bunch of drunken bomzhi. In fact, of course, the same state of confusion may be achieved by a complete *lack* of a systematic strategy. Generally, it seems as if the treatment of bomzhi is largely left to the idiosyncratic temperaments of individual policemen, who are implicitly authorized to act according to their personal and contingent whims. Regardless of how intentional the inconsistencies were, they certainly undermined the sense of control that station regulars tried to establish.[8]

Getting Back, Physically or Verbally

Most station regulars—even those who believed that only troublemakers were beaten—liked to get back at the police in some way or another, that is, to counter the dehumanization with some sort of manifestation of their personal agency. I am tempted to use the concept of resistance in a wider sense, although with the precaution that it is fraught with controversy and obscurity (Abu-Lughod 1990; Ortner 1995). To *constitute* a resistance (which the homeless do since they are always considered to be in the way) is not the same as resist*ing,* that is, acting with the intention of being an obstacle to power. In recent years the concept largely appears to be abandoned in favor of De Certeau's term tactics: attempts to thwart the panoptic strategies of a power that controls a certain space by manipulating time instead (De Certeau 1984, 36ff.). Tactics are in themselves obstructive to power, but the concept says nothing about intentionality. Sasha's campfire was a tactic: he lit it beyond the gaze of power, and he thereby defied its intentions. Perhaps he was aware of this fact and liked it. Nevertheless, he did it because he had no choice if he wanted to eat and keep himself warm. When, in contrast, the young bon vivant Zina, her brother, and their bottle gang had been chased away from the Military Ticket Hall and the police had turned their backs, there was always a decisive moment when Zina looked first at the calm Drunken Garden and then back at the stairs, only to head off toward the latter, full of energy and with a malicious smile on her lips. There was no doubt that she was a thorn in the police's side and that this was precisely what she wanted, but her choice was not motivated by a conscious struggle for liberation so much as a simple desire to have fun: she actually seemed to like the chasing to and fro, as if the game temporarily relieved her of boredom and monotony. This resistive play (for want of a better expression) was, as I see it, focused on risk and control, an adventure sport in which one risked a thrashing for the sensation of being more in control of the situation than the police were (just as others risk their lives to conquer Mount Everest).

The easiest way to get back is obviously to hit back. To fight with a police squad in Russia is generally regarded as akin to suicide, but regardless of the futility of such a bold venture, there were people at the station who were tempted. Not everybody who was dragged to the precinct complied peacefully, almost as if helped by the knowledge that one cannot win: if you will be beaten in any case, why not try to hurt at least one of them? Even Vova, who was known to be calm even when very drunk, sometimes gave it a try. Once he blamed a black eye on the police, even though only minutes before, he had argued that they left him in peace now that he was working with me. I asked him how he wanted me to understand this contradiction. *"They* didn't beat *me,"* he laughed. *"We* were *fighting!"*

More often, Vova's way of getting back was to make sure that they knew that he was working with the "Swedish correspondent." Having them know that somebody would bear testimony if he was hurt was obviously a tactical means of control, a form of insurance, but there was indeed a glint of malicious delight in his eyes every time he introduced me to a policeman. I have no idea how often it was practically possible for people to put the police in their place with the help of more powerful allies, but it was a recurring theme in their stories. The intervening and protecting agents were usually human, even though Olga, who together with her boyfriend Kostia worked for a kiosk, at one point actually referred to the law as such and not a powerful person. Once she scared a violent policeman by threatening to file charges on him, she said, and after that he became nicer and she was never beaten again. (Others claimed the contrary, however—if anybody knew what a baton felt like, it was Olga.) The homeless often mentioned violations of human rights when talking about their situation in general, but Olga's comment surprised me. I rarely if ever heard anybody use a similar notion of law as a potential instrument for changing one's own inferior position with respect to a source of power as local as this one.

Hitting back or threatening the police with powerful allies was most probably motivated by desperation more than a desire to play, but when people retold events, they always did it with sarcasm and, as in Vova's comment about the fight with the police, a good portion of humor. Getting back is a matter of reversing power relations, and this can be effected by narratives as well. Few means are more efficient than irony and scorn, and even if a good sense of humor hardly cures pain entirely, it can at least alleviate it. People whose money was stolen by the police were in fact more seriously upset than those who talked about beatings—savings are difficult to recover, whereas pain passes. A beating may even become a good story. After all, "One shouldn't allow them to destroy one's good mood too," as Masha argued. The common distrust and disdain toward the police make jokes and laughter particularly rewarding. The slang term *musor* (crap) refers to the police and not to bomzhi, in all other respects *the* human refuse, and it is commonly assumed that the only ones who take this low-paid and disdained job are uncultured and badly educated boys from the countryside who, in addition to the opportunities to extort bribes, do it for a place to live and a propiska in the city. In this case bomzhi have the same enemy as any other citizen, and at some symbolic level they include themselves in mainstream society when talking about the victimization.

A common way of talking about friendly and drunken encounters with individual policemen (as well as other representatives of the powers that be) was what I call pacification stories. They were similar to the aforementioned stories about generous janitors treating homeless stairway dwellers to vodka, but in a more distinct way they blended the theme of fellow humanness with an often subtle but spiteful irony. Vova reveled in them, and his best one goes as follows:

> There was this cop, neither good nor bad really, just an ordinary officer but of high rank. I was in for drunkenness when he called me into his office and offered me a liter of vodka if I allowed him to screw me in the ass. I said no, of course, as politely as I could, and he didn't insist. Instead we shared the bottle and talked about this and that all night, and afterwards he was always good to me and helped me a great deal when other cops were troublesome. It was a long time ago, though. He doesn't work here any more.

A good pacification story restores individual policemen to mankind by picturing them as essentially and unconditionally human, but simultaneously it augments the repulsiveness of the policeman *persona* by emphasizing that not even the police can endure it in the long run. In Vova's story, a well-mannered refusal of a degrading form of sexual intercourse proves him to be a man with self-esteem, not just a bomzh who will do anything for a sip of vodka. Thus he gains the respect of the policeman who thereby simultaneously loses his official facade and his homoerotic desire.[9] The further drinking confirms the transformation of a potentially unequal, exploitative, and humiliating situation into mutual respect and intimate friendship. In most such stories, human hearts are enticed from underneath coarse uniforms only by witty comments from the bomzh's side or by his or her good spirits and capacity to cheer people up. Masha commented on each detention (before they hit her, that is) as follows: "And as soon as I entered they pulled out the bottle and said 'and *where* have you been for so long, it's been so *dull* here,' so I took up a song and they wouldn't let me out before midnight."

Shifting Positions

When Masha left the precinct with a black eye, I wondered if she had gone too far this time, if they wanted her to know that their occasional approval of her company did not put her on an equal footing with them. Masha did not seem to reflect on this at all, however, as if it had always been obvious to her that the jovial relationship was only for that brief moment. Nor did others, whose hopes of immunity through personal tranquility or charm proved unexpectedly to be wrong. Rather than analyzing their interpretative framework and trying to adjust the factors that did not work out, most people simply changed

perspective: the cops turned out not to be semi-reasonable state officials or potential fellow humans, as a matter of fact they are nothing but the same sadistic,
unpredictable predators that hunt through the attics at night. *Neliudi* means
"monsters" but literally means "non-people." Or, on the contrary, the purported monsters were swiftly redefined as humans, as contradictory experiences mounted in rapid succession. In addition, the experiences of others may
color personal outlooks, and as a result many station regulars seemed to hold a
set of internally contradictory positions regarding the police, seemingly at the
same time. Vova, whose empathetic capacities were inexhaustible, could thus
only by listening to others move between idioms of "unpredictable sadism,"
"it's OK as long as you behave," and "they're humans too" within minutes,
which was not paradoxical at all since all these frameworks were available and
well-known, and always strictly connected to his immediate here and now.

Masha, Vova, and the others seemed to understand that their own models
of explanation regarding police violence could never be more than makeshift attempts to make sense of a reality that was beyond their control. Their
interpretations about the organization and behavior of the police, why one
is beaten and how to avoid it, where on the body one should expect the
blow and for what reason, were attempts to establish a measure of coherence.
Coherence in the form of enduring opinions and lasting models of reality, on the other hand, are a luxury relegated to privileged people, who are
able to exercise enough influence on their existence to thwart contradictory
impressions. Station regulars had to compromise; they grabbed a new truth
after each shock and cared little about consistency and permanence. Every
link in their coherent interpretative chain was weak, and when one broke, it
took a great effort to keep the entire chain intact. Because of the everpresent
risk of exceptions, ruptures, and disturbances, and because tomorrow for the
station regulars was indeed another day, no coherent way of conceptualizing
violence was likely to last long, so it was more practical to change between
certain fixed frames when the situation so demanded. What works here and
now is good enough; views of reality need not be less situational and contingent than life itself. After all, what is at stake is *an* explanation for the time
being, not *the* purportedly true explanation for all days to come.

The constant shifts of attitude toward the police confused me in the very
beginning of my fieldwork, until I understood that this adaptability was an
important survival strategy. I was considerably more disturbed by other inconsistencies that I thought questioned the credibility of my informants. When
Vova introduced me to Fyodor, he had a black eye, for which he blamed the
police. A couple of days later, Fyodor said that he got it when angry neighbors in an apartment bloc threw him down the stairs. A couple of days after

that, Fyodor's former girlfriend turned up with a black eye, which she had received from Fyodor, and as time passed it became evident that Fyodor had a terrible temper under the influence of alcohol and rarely sobered up *without* a black eye, since he persisted in attacking people much bigger than himself (which most people were, as Fyodor was very short). I commented on this to Vova, who could not see the problem. Fyodor obviously had a bad memory, he said without much concern, which was not strange considering how much he drank, and if he did not get the black eye from the police *then,* it would have happened some other time instead. Somewhat later Vova turned up with a bruised face and told me that the police had done it. An hour later another station regular made a remark about his looks, and Vova said that he had fallen when he was drunk. I asked him what actually happened, but he only shrugged indifferently and said: "So what?"

I felt manipulated and angry at unwittingly being used by my informants for *their* purposes (getting back at the police, gaining sympathy from me, or whatever) when I wanted to use their innocent reflections for *my* purposes (increasing the body of anthropological knowledge, helping the homeless, making a career of my own). There and then my aim felt completely irrelevant. In the end I decided that our mutual use of each other was fair play, and as time passed, the relevance of the concept of credibility decreased. Perhaps Fyodor was too drunk to remember, perhaps Vova did not want the other station regular to know that he blamed the police. Perhaps they were manipulating me, or seducing me, as Robben (1995) has called less conscious attempts by informants to win the favor of the anthropologist. Their message was nevertheless clear: the police beat the homeless, and if they did not beat a particular person this time, they would do it some other time or beat somebody else.

I sensed the same thing when people mentioned the notorious deportations to the forest. The most convincing stories were casual comments that merely contextualized other events: "Once when I came back to the station—this was after they drove us away, the second time I think, because I remember getting a lift back to town after walking only seven kilometers, and the guy who drove me had this trouble with his wife.... Anyway, they [the cops] caught sight of me, and Ivanov laughed and said: 'The Mafia is immortal!'" (Olga, asserting that, as an old-timer at the station, she was so familiar to the police that none of them believed that they could get rid of her, any more than they thought that the Mafia could be eliminated.) Direct accounts were not only devoid of data on exact times, locations, policemen, or vehicles, they were also generally emptied of personal reflections and observations: "They gathered us quite late in the evening and drove us for some time and dumped us somewhere beyond the train station X and I walked for Y hours and took the train back." Even if the victims were drunk when they were deported, I always got a vague impression that they were telling somebody else's story, indeed a generic version of the story, as if the important thing was that I knew that deportations occurred *as such,* and the most effective means of making me understand this was to tell it as a narrative in the first person structured in the simplest of ways. As in the case of Fyodor's black eye, conventional conditions for veracity were not relevant to them. What they wanted to convey was not a scientific, objective truth so much as a thoroughly social experience that permeated and shaped their lives at the station: "They chase us and they beat us, this is how we live!"

The Advent of a New Discipline

The station was effectively purged of the homeless in the end, but not by beatings or secret deportations so much as by major refurbishments and a more effective use of station space. It had already begun before my fieldwork; Raia did not remember exactly when she lost her job at the restaurant next to the Main Hall, but that was when it started. In the summer of 1999, the waiting hall upstairs closed for renovation, and when it opened after a couple of months, the fee was raised to ten rubles per night. In effect, everybody except for pensioners (who had a discount) moved.[10] During the years after 1999 the redevelopment escalated, and each time I returned to the station, another refuse spot had been eliminated. The Drunken Garden turned into a fenced-off parking lot where an apartment bloc later appeared, at the same time that the building site behind the station was settled with new luxurious apartment buildings. The tunnels beneath the station were closed or bestowed with kiosks along the walls, and the ladies' room was rebuilt with new toilet booths, too small even for Raia's diminutive body. The final blow came with the impending three-hundred-year jubilee of the city in 2003, after which the Moscow Station looked like any hypermodern metropolitan transport facility: sterile fast-food restaurants in the Western style, shops rather than kiosks (with the exception of some impeccably clean fast-food places), and, in addition, a thorough reorganization of the police surveillance that enabled the evidently enlarged police force to check the ID papers of every traveler who appears to originate in the Caucasus. There are no bomzhi to be seen, with the exception of a couple of very old babushki who apparently still enjoy an immunity of sorts.

Violence and illicit methods were nonetheless necessary to get rid of the regulars, I was told by a former station regular whom I happened to meet in the station yard in 2004. Just released after a year and a half of incarceration, he was himself quite confused about the changes. "Half the crowd you knew is dead," he told me, "and the rest are on the inside. Before the jubilee they [the police] planted bags around the station with something inside that would lead to at least a year or two in prison. So I found this suitcase, and obviously I kept it, and they came down on me and dragged up this old camera, and there I was." He may have exaggerated—at least I hope so, especially with regard to the deaths—but I have no reason to doubt the cleansing method as such, rational and effective as it seems. He said that one bomzh or another still hung around in the vicinity, but during our brief talk we were thrown out twice, and I never found him again.

The fate of the Moscow Station (and all the other railway stations) supports my suggestion about the 1990s as a liminal phase between systems of spatial regulation. It was succeeded by a mode of surveillance based on urban design complemented by increased policing, although the latter in the Russian case is justified by the battle against terrorism rather than against homeless behavior. As for the city at large, the facades of the central city, its main boulevards and most conspicuous areas, are indeed entirely "eurospaced" Although the winding maze of backyards unfolds only meters from the station, its archways are increasingly barred by locked gates. Keypad door locks proliferate, and the old (and easily outwitted) mechanical model is gradually replaced with electronic door locks. Gentrification gradually turns empty attics into fashionable penthouses, and with this the last landings in the stairways disappear as well. Homeless people are thus deprived of the only sleeping places available, while at the same time their options to make an income have been drastically reduced. The commercial landscape of St. Petersburg is changing rapidly, as outdoor markets and small kiosks, so characteristic of the transformation years, are redeveloped into shopping centers and proper restaurants (see Axenov 2002). "Refuse incomes" are directly determined by refuse space and a permissive atmosphere toward poverty in prime space, but as evroremont and eurospace eliminate the links with the Soviet past, its perceived human legacy is squeezed out of the picture as well. The management of the renovated restaurant where Raia no longer works may still rely on labor unknown to the tax authorities, but even though Raia dresses better than many others, they cannot have a stooped, half-sober, and toothless person like her wiping the tables. There is absolutely nothing "renovated" about Raia, and as such she doesn't match the new design, the new ambitions, or the new, purportedly democratic, Russia.

I do not mean to be cynical when I claim that the St. Petersburg homeless never had, and probably never will regain, the position that they had in 1999.

Power is the wrong word, but their presence as a collective body was undeniably unthreatened for a long time. The regularly recurring abuse against their individual bodies was a heavy price, but I doubt that they are beaten any less today, wherever they are. My evident nostalgia turns this chapter into a requiem of sorts, already halfway through the book, but it is the end of one of its main stories. Hitherto addressing the functioning of a social system and the unintended niches it provides, I will now proceed to a discussion of intimate social relationships and questions of self-perception. These issues may appear to be less vulnerable to fluctuating political and economic trends, but they are still inseparable from the social structure in which they are embedded. Like this first sub-story, the following part constitutes a whole on its own: it begins with stories about origins, continues with the homeless here and now, and concludes with conceptualizations about the final end, death.

CHAPTER 4

No Close Ones

About (Absent) Families and Friends

When the homeless told me about the events that finally brought them to basements and attics, they frequently omitted all circumstances apart from those relating to family. Details about housing conditions, registrations, migration, and so forth I had to extract retroactively, whenever I happened to meet them again, and in a way this was logical. The first thing that had to be explained was how one became alone in the world. Loneliness is, in turn, an invitation to all sorts of dangers, and the disasters that it later led to were thus merely derivative. *Blizkikh net,* "no close ones," was the curt summary of everything essential: whoever could have helped—if there was anyone in the first place—was not there any longer, whether dead or disappeared or simply unwilling or unable to help.

"Close ones" refers to family and close friends, the core of *svoi* (emphasis on the *i*), "one's own," a wider circle of trusted friends, friends of friends, and so on (Yurchak 2006, 102–18). The contrasting categories, "strangers," *chuzhye,* or "they," *oni,* differ from each other in the sense that strangers are persons, albeit unfamiliar ones, while "they" may refer also to less fathomable social entities (see Paxon 2005, 77–85). In the late 1990s, the mightiest "they" was a vaguely defined alliance between those in charge of the state and powerful constellations such as oligarchs, the criminal elite, and New Russians (Klimova 2002; Nazpary 2002, 33ff.). "They" were no different from any clique of "one's own" insofar that they guarded their own common interests, but their network was by far more powerful, ruthless, and egotistic than those of ordinary mortals. To the majority of people, close social ties do not render wealth and power inasmuch as a humble compensation for a state that persistently fails to meet its obligations. In the Soviet time, svoi were thus the prime channels for access to deficit goods and services, and in the chaotic post-Soviet period they constituted the only functioning social safety net for the penniless. Svoi were also—and remain—one's primary locus of social belonging, the people one trusts, confides in, and experiences intimacy with, the ones among whom one is needed. As the soil in which human beings are cultivated, close ones and one's own are thus more "home" than any four walls or a permanent propiska can ever be. The crucial role of one's own is often explained with reference to the split between public and private that was characteristic of not only the Soviet system but also the Eastern bloc in general (Borneman 1991, 79–81). This separation should not, as Yurchak (2006) has convincingly argued, be interpreted as a relationship of opposition and resistance, or even as split subjectivities. The state became the ultimate "they" only after the downfall, while the average Soviet citizen was not particularly critical to the system. Rather, there were different kinds of interaction and purposes in the spheres of one's own and "officialdom" respectively, but the two were nonetheless interdependent and mutually productive. In effect it was the *lack* of opposition and contradiction and not the contrary that, as I take it, enabled people to live two parallel lives with very few mutual matches with regard to thoughts, values, and behaviors (Shlapentokh 1989).

This social safety net has ruptures too, however, for every person in Russia is not, and never was, from the outset endowed with a crowd of loving relatives and friends. Moreover, the capacity of the existing ones to help has always been determined by structural constraints. Already in the Soviet era, poverty and state residence regulations affected the options of near and dear ones to support each other, and the transition aggravated this ability further, while at the same time these networks were being decimated and reshuffled by poverty and new economic inequalities. Social conventions about the meaning of social ties did not crumble as fast as the economic structure did, so many people faced a chronic dilemma of how to negotiate the mismatch between ingrained ideals and practical options with regard to loyalty and helpfulness (Nazpary 2002, 85–88; Caldwell 2004; Davidova 2004). Nonetheless, "normal" people were generally assumed to have kin and friends with at least a minimum of supportive capacity, and a lack of such close social ties was perceived as a very persuasive measure of poverty (Caldwell 2004). Loneliness was pitied, but it could also suggest a one-sided failure from the side of the loner to fulfill the expectations that the mutual neededness of near and dear ones implies. The latter scenario is part and parcel of the popular etiology of the stereotype of the bomzh, who is assumed to have renounced burdensome duties by abandoning family and friends, or whose kin is thought to have cut the ties first, exhausted by the bomzh's antisocial tendencies. I shall show a somewhat more nuanced version of the state of matters. Though it is mostly a bleak story about deprivation and loss, it still conveys the makeshift ways in which many women and men try to remain needed as friends, relatives, and parents.

Bereavement and Loss

Homeless careers frequently began with the loss of a crucial close one, and in many cases the purported social safety net was so small from the beginning that one or two deaths were enough to eliminate it entirely. It is not unusual for metropolitan residents to have relatively limited family networks (Caldwell 2004, 167). A fair proportion of them have migrated from other parts of the country where their relatives may remain, but the parties are nonetheless separated by considerable distances and, in particular, perpetually increasing travel expenses, mostly in the form of higher ticket prices. In addition, contemporary Russian families tend to be small, with one or two children at the most, which obviously means the number of close ones is not likely to expand.

Most vulnerable in this sense were ex-cons, many of whom even structured their life stories around the dates of their terms of imprisonment and of the deaths of their family members: "My grandparents died in 1974 and 1980, I was on the inside between 1977 and 1988, my father died in 1985, then I was back in the Zone between 1989 and 1995. While I was there my brother died in 1991 and then my mother, in 1994." The criminal conviction itself and the sentence already shrink whatever social networks the prisoner used to have as he or she is rejected by friends, family members, or spouses. (Judging from these stories, men are far less tolerant than women of long-term incarcerations of their partners.) Quite often I received only three words in reply when I inquired about their past: "*Sidel, umerla mama.*" (Literally: "I sat and my mother died," "sit" being the colloquial expression for spending time in prison.) This is enough to convey the essentials: mama was the only one left who cared, and when she died there was nobody to whom the prisoner could return after the sentence.

Without a supportive family waiting on the outside, there are virtually no pathways back to established society, and the vast majority of old-timers lost such ties many years before finishing their last sentence. Entering freedom after decades behind barbed wire is an ambiguous blessing for most of them. An entire "life-world" is gone, one that involves material support and social ties as well as personal identity and, most probably, some sort of existential purpose in life too. These aspects are intertwined, since mama's death eliminates other social contexts that otherwise could cover up the loss somewhat: a workplace, a neighborhood, or a home that might serve as a base for developing a future social life. "Nobody even cared to keep the photo albums for me," said one man bitterly. "They even stole my memory!"

Ex-cons are usually more occupied with the loss of family members than with the fact that they are homeless because of straight state intervention. Article 60 deprived them of their residential rights when they were imprisoned, so mama's flat was returned to the municipality after her death—unless it was taken over by relatives less devoted to the prisoner than mama. In addition, I met a few ex-cons who were subjected to the infamous 101-kilometer rule that prohibited certain categories of ex-cons from settling in a number of large cities. The rule applied to political prisoners and to perpetrators of serious crimes of violence, but *tuneiadstvo* (parasitism, in practice prolonged unemployment) could lead to forced exile too. The state should provide these people with jobs and places to live, but the system was not very satisfactory, as is evident from the story of the shelter resident Galia:

> I returned to Piter after three years for theft, intending to register with my mother who lived with my son. My husband had already divorced me. But at the registration office they told me that I had to go and live somewhere north in the oblast', because besides paragraph 144 [theft] I was also sentenced for paragraph 209 [tuneiadstvo], because I had not been working for some time before the conviction. I went to that place—one bus went there per *week!*—but there were no jobs, nothing. Not even the cops understood why I was sent there. I was bomzh [unregistered] there too, and prohibited from returning to Piter, the only place where I *could* register.

Galia was soon imprisoned again for theft. Upon her release a few years later, precisely the same story repeated itself and she was once again dispatched to a distant village where no arrangements were made for her. In order to obtain a propiska and a job, she married a local man, but he was violent, so she left him and slept in secret at her place of work. A male acquaintance offered to put her up, but it turned out that he wanted sex in return for the favor, and in the resulting struggle he was killed. When Galia was released after six years in 1994, the 101-kilometer rule was history. So was her family, however, as both her mother and her son had died during this sentence.

To everybody, not only to ex-cons, the loss of close ones—in particular bereavement, but also divorce or having to abandon a child—was often the source of other evils that finally resulted in homelessness. Loneliness is, to begin with, dangerous in itself. Victims of fraud and extortion were often targeted *because* they were lonely and defenseless, and bereavement was frequently another relevant element. In certain cases the loss of close ones gave full rein to reckless drinking that, in turn, paved the way for deceit and fraud or even prison. When I first met Vova, he summarized his past as follows: "My mother committed suicide and I drank from grief, drank away everything I had. Before me, she did the same—she never tasted a drop until my father died, but then nobody could stop her, and in the end she hanged herself." "Drinking from grief," *pit'ot goria,* is an idiom that nobody elaborated upon: they added it with a shrug after mentioning the bereavement and took it for granted that I understood. To Vova this was the only thing that mattered; only long afterwards did he bother to tell me about his fatal imprudence with the forged health certificate (which he did to get money for alcohol) and the subsequent prison sentence.

Alcoholism in the wake of bereavement or separation was regarded as tragic, but nobody seemed to find it shameful. Suffering tends to be associated with inner worlds and deep feelings, although excess proportions of it also may kill the soul (Ries 1997; Pesmen 2000, 39). Hence, drinking from grief confirms that one has profound emotions that must be soothed when life gets too hard, in the same way that unbearable working conditions can legitimate drinking "for the sake of the soul." In this sense, it alludes to the same notions of martyrdom and virtuous weakness that are evident in descriptions of bomzhi as *weak* people or in the reminiscences of many a victim of estate fraud. Vova and the others related to the disastrous effects of their heedless drinking merely as an unavoidable cross that a true human being must bear if he or she is endowed with a soul in a cruel world, although only Vova explicitly claimed to be a Christian.

Children of the State

"It was the orphanage," the station regular Nina stated firmly. "We weren't given enough to eat, so we learned how to steal instead. Nobody looked after us really, so we ran about in bands looking for food like stray dogs—first it was forage, like turnips and oil cakes, later valuable things. And that brought most of us to *maloletka* [youth prison] and the Zone, and that's where I've spent twenty-two years, nine times in all."

Many of my informants are former *detdomovtsy,* inmates of orphanages. As such, they have had no families from the beginning or families that for some reason or other could not take care of them. Children may be abandoned on a supposedly temporary basis to an *internat* (boarding school), which theoretically is a provisional form of child care. "Full-scale orphans" live in orphanages, *detdomy,* but in practice the categories are blurred, and detdom and internat tend to refer to institutions for small and older children respectively. Children who cannot return to their parents when they finish school should be given a place to live, but the deficient supply of low-budget (or easy-access) housing frequently creates problems. Usually, they go on to *professionalno-tehnicheskoye uchilische* (vocational school), which in the Soviet period provided them with *obshchezhitie* (dormitories) until they received a proper place (usually a *kommunalka* room), thanks to their promotion in the waiting list for housing. The system was far from perfect even then, but the situation became considerably aggravated during the transition, when the shrinking municipal housing stock and the disappearance of the obshchezhitie often resulted in a place in the waiting list that never led to a real place to live. This did not affect Nina, I should add, as she was already imprisoned for the first time before the state was obliged to provide for her.

Deficient state provision of housing is nonetheless not the paramount problem when former detdomovtsy and others relate homelessness to orphanages. The issue is rather the quality of the institution as a surrogate parent. The orphanage system was created on the Soviet assumption that the state is the best entity to foster future model citizens, in possession of rational, scientific competence to form ideal citizens (Ball 1994; Stryker 2000). Accordingly, parents who could not provide for their children were not assisted by the state but simply replaced. The popular image of orphans has nonetheless always depicted them as starved, imbecile non-persons, and today nobody regards state care as anything but a necessary evil. Orphanages are criticized for not feeding the children properly, as Nina's statement shows, and also for not providing adequate education, which Nina touches upon only indirectly: the children had to learn to survive on their own, since nobody else taught them how to live in a "proper" way. Many contributors to the "Tell Us Your Life" writing competition point the finger at bad schooling and the general lack of civic knowledge conveyed to the children: "Those who were with me at the orphanage did not even try for VUZ [higher education]—there they raise you so that you become a nobody who is not even eligible to apply," "At the age of 15 I left the internat . . . and became homeless straightaway, because

I could not move to an obshchezhitie, as I did not know which documents to get,... because I had no experience of an independent life," "Nobody told me that I was entitled to housing" (*Na Dne* 1999, 213, 121, 90). Nor are det-domovtsy encouraged to make personal decisions and to engage themselves in the outside world, which is an additional handicap once they enter it (Creutziger 1996). A manager of an NGO-based shelter for former orphanage children told me that most of his charges received places to live after school but lost them because they were not informed and, in the capacity of detdomovtsy, selected targets for organized real estate criminality. Generally, these insufficiencies and the assumed neglect of psychological needs in the orphanages result in a stigma depicting them as more or less mentally retarded throwaways (Creutziger 1996; Stryker 2000). This stigma is, moreover, neatly stamped into their passports for future employers to see.

An orphan is not by definition deprived of close ones. Most detdomovtsy are taken care of on a temporary basis, and many of them return to their families of origin after school.[1] A reunion does not in itself necessarily mean support, however, in particular not if the problems that originally caused the abandonment remain. Instead, the peer community of the orphanage may be conceived of as a family of sorts—powerless and poor perhaps, but still better than no family at all or a dysfunctional family. "The only good thing about being brought up in an internat is that you have lots of old schoolmates," said twenty-nine-year-old Viktoria, who lived in Nochlezhka's shelter:

> My alcoholic mother abandoned me when I was a baby, as she did with most of my ten siblings. They're of no help now either, we're not even friends. She was even deprived of her parental rights,[2] but I had to return to her; I got pregnant and was kicked out of the obshchezhitie where I lived after the internat. And in spite of my condition she allowed my stepfather to throw me out! I spent half a year in basements, then a schoolmate put me up. I had to hand the baby over to an orphanage, couldn't take him back until I got a room from the municipality two years later, but all this time I could rely on old schoolmates, and they are still there for me.

Detdomovtsy are encouraged to form their own peer networks by staff, and to a certain extent these networks replace their dependence on adults (Stryker 2000). Viktoria's mates remained supportive in adulthood too, but I am not sure how common such continuous loyalty is. The precondition for her friends' capacity to help her was, after all, that they in spite of everything had access to the antithesis of an orphanage: supportive families. And Nina would probably not agree with Viktoria at all. It was the older children who taught her to steal, and they were hardly of much help to her later, since they ended up in the Zone too.

Domestic Conflicts and Fractured Ties

"Happy families are all alike, but every unhappy family is unhappy in its own way," reads the first line of Tolstoy's novel *Anna Karenina*. The quotation well illustrates the wide variety of disastrous family frictions that I was told about. In all, about a quarter of my informants considered themselves to be homeless because of some sort of conflict with their close kin. As a cause of homelessness, this one is readily recognized by public consciousness in Russia as well as in Western countries. The "worn-out welcome thesis" contends that the incapacity of certain individuals to conform to a normal family life makes them abandon hearth and home voluntarily, unless exhausted and disillusioned family members initiate the eviction instead (Snow and Anderson 1993, 260). Critics of this stance prefer to locate the problems in the nuclear family as an institution: its inherently oppressive hierarchies of gender and age may expel nonconformists (Wagner 1993; Passaro 1996), but its supportive capacity is also easily eroded by macroeconomic factors (Snow and Anderson 2003, 259–65). I have no empirical evidence to suggest anything about the presumed oppressiveness (or lack thereof) of the family as an institution, nor do I have any personal opinions on the issue. I do know, however, that poverty, crammed living, and minimal chances to find a place of one's own exert immense pressure on families, whether or not they are unhappy in the first place.

The stories that were told to me involved all sorts of kinship ties: elders escaping/evicted by adult children; adult children escaping/evicted by parents; teenagers escaping/evicted by parents; lateral kin and, in particular, spouses escaping/evicted by each other. (Spouses are more likely than other relatives to swindle their relations out of the propiska and the formal right to the living space.) It was often difficult to grasp these stories in full: bitterness, confusion, and sometimes self-blame tended to muddle accounts that were more focused on the troublesome relationship as such than on the series of events. The most detailed account I have is from Viktoria, who became homeless again as an adult due to a conflict in the family of her common-law husband.

At the age of twenty, after four years in basements or with former schoolmates, Viktoria eventually obtained a room from the municipality. In 1990 she moved in with her boyfriend Zhenya, who was an old schoolmate from the internat. Zhenya and his twin brother had been left there at the age of eleven by their mother Oksana when her husband died, after which her parents fell sick and her economic situation fell apart in the early 1980s. The relinquishment was supposed to be temporary, but Oksana's life did not improve, and the boys returned only after finishing school at the age of sixteen. While Zhenya lived with Viktoria, his brother married another schoolmate from the internat, Lena, who moved in with him in Oksana's apartment. Zhenya's brother and his wife soon had two children. In 1993 Zhenya and Viktoria decided to improve their housing conditions by selling her dilapidated little room and moving to the much better four-room apartment where Zhenya's family already lived. Once the deal was completed, Oksana unexpectedly refused Viktoria a propiska on the grounds that Viktoria's sale of her room was irresponsible and her pretensions to a propiska presumptuous. In addition, she thoroughly disliked both of her daughters-in-law who, she claimed, drank and abused her physically.[3] (Viktoria says that Lena was alone in this.) The two daughters-in-law did not get on well together either, and the conflicts were further aggravated when Zhenya prosecuted his mother for refusing to register Viktoria. As the situation worsened, Oksana periodically escaped to the streets, living nowhere and spending the days working in a church.

In 1995 they decided to solve the problem without involving the courts by exchanging the four-room apartment for two smaller ones. The exchange turned out to be a fraud, and the only result was a ramshackle single-room summer house far out in the oblast' for Oksana and nothing at all for the others. Oksana blames her sons and their wives for a careless choice of partners, and the others blame Oksana for urging them to act too hastily. During the next three years, Oksana moved among her workmates, the others between friends. In 1998 Zhenya's brother tragically drowned only weeks before the entire family—Viktoria, Zhenya, Lena, three young children, and Oksana—obtained a twelve square meter room with four beds at Nochlezhka's shelter. When Lena brought a new fiancé to live there ("almost immediately," said Viktoria), Oksana decided that she had had enough and went back to her former wanderings between acquaintances and her dilapidated country house.

This particular family conflict was probably aggravated by the fact that the mother, Oksana, and her sons were separated when the boys were growing up. The main factors in this conflict are nevertheless commonplace in other stories about problematic families: crowded housing and extended households with two or more adult generations, plus lateral kin (usually siblings) with their own families who want to live separately but are unable to find apartments. Even though the nuclear family is the ideal composition of a Russian household (with the possible addition of a kind live-in babushka), extended households of Viktoria's kind are just as common in practice. Most people seem to adapt and put up with things relatively peacefully, and cohabitation has obvious advantages due to the possibility of sharing and pooling resources. However, in my own experience, such households nevertheless try to segment themselves according to the nuclear norm if they possibly can. Viktoria would have preferred it, but everybody's problems with Oksana had priority over her own dislike of Lena.

Oksana was subjected to physical abuse. She is far from the only elderly person I met who was beaten up by their children or children-in-law. Had I included street children in this study, violence between generations would probably be the most common cause of homelessness. Some of these children are simply rejected by their parents (as Viktoria was in her late teens), but most of them are on the run from physically abusive adults in the household (Stephenson 2000b). Twenty-nine-year-old Nadia, mentioned in chapter 3 as living in a basement with her husband Sergei and two babies, faced this as a teenager: "My stepfather and my mother used to beat me all the time, and when I was sixteen he raped me. I ran away and lived in the streets for more than a year. I got pregnant with someone I hung out with, but returned only after the baby was born. Then they left me alone, perhaps they respected my motherhood or something, I don't know." However, a few years later Nadia's mother and stepfather forged her signature on an authorization, sold the apartment without her consent, and moved to Ukraine, leaving her and the baby behind. Nadia had to give up her son to an orphanage and found herself homeless again.

Women seem more vulnerable to domestic conflicts than men. The majority of those who claimed to be homeless due to some sort of family conflict were women, most of whom were expelled by, or left, male partners. Western studies of homeless women often argue that they frequently have a history involving marital violence (Järvinen 1993; Wagner 1993, 52; Passaro 1996, 62). Logically, there is no reason why Russia should be any different in this regard, considering the recognized scope of violence against women, the housing shortage, and a police force that generally treats domestic violence as a private matter (Zabelina 1996; Attwood 1997; Johnson 2001). However, marital violence is not much reflected in the stories of my own female informants, in contrast to violence between generations, which was stated in a very straightforward way. I knew four women who left male partners in connection with some sort of disagreement. Three of them denied having been beaten but avoided other details: "That's not interesting to you!"—in spite of my affirmations that it certainly was—"He doesn't understand me," "He offended me so that I don't want to see him ever again." The fourth one turned the violence into an accidental and humorous banality: "This time I ran off because he tried to slaughter me instead of this rabbit we were going to cook!" I knew that this was not the woman's first stay at the station and asked if he used to beat her often. She stared at me as if she did not understand and then burst into laughter. "Beat me?" she smiled, "No! He's very good with women, in fact. It's just that drinking makes the old man mad!" To her the vodka was the problem, not the aggression of her man, and their respective status as wife and husband had nothing to do with it.

If wife beating was involved in these cases, the women weren't saying anything about it. It is easy to conclude that they did so out of embarrassment, but I suspect that if this is so, the shame may concern the escape as well as the abuse. Violence between spouses is surprisingly normalized, which is reflected in proverbs such as "If he beats you, he loves you." The media, the judicial system, and state councilors assume that men are not abusive—until the women provoke them (Johnson 2001), and in my experience a moderate amount of physical violence is frequently assumed to be part and parcel of married life. A woman might thus interpret an escape from a violent husband as proof of her incapacity to cope with what she takes to be a very mundane aspect of everyday life. In contrast, elders *should* be respected and honored, and children *should* be loved and educated, and since grave violence in these cases is not equally acceptable, the victims do not hesitate to talk about it.

Being a Burden to Someone: The Homeless and the Remaining Ones

Certain homeless people were still on speaking terms with family members or close friends, but most of them nevertheless felt estranged from these old social networks and minimized their contact with them. Some felt that these purported close ones in some way or other held them responsible for their own fate, while others claimed to be ashamed of their situation or embarrassed at being a burden to dear ones who were having a hard time of their own. The different articulations of shame easily merge. It is shameful to be a burden, but it is also shameful to end up in an attic, so few of the homeless are completely free from self-blame. Perhaps the "nobody's burden" argument is the lesser of two evils; if one is ashamed anyway, why not denote the least shameful reason for being ashamed, now that there is a choice?

It is a fact, however, that the transformation to a market economy made it more difficult to live up to the imperative of always helping close ones in need. Besides increasing poverty, unemployment, and so forth, old reciprocal patterns were affected by money as a means of exchange. The Soviet "economy of favors" consisted of mutual support based on nonmonetary currencies such as influential contacts (*blat*), pilfering items at work, labor (for example at the summer house, or *dacha*), cooperation in waiting on lines, and the like (Ledeneva 1998). Moreover, since other people were the source of goods and services, the labor of this economy literally implied socializing, so as to enhance the quantity and quality of one's own network. Money was in this context considered to be uncultured, a proof of alienation and hostile vulgarity, and this sentiment lingered for quite a few years after the downfall. "Everybody wants something, but only through someone," is how Pesmen (2000, 117–45) summarizes the avoidance of money in everyday exchanges in the mid-1990s. A monetary economy, in contrast, prevents people from meeting each other by forcing them to work all the time, and even though old "currencies" still matter, the ubiquitous need for money interferes with the opportunities of the penniless to be of any help (Nazpary 2002, 85–89; Sedlenieks 2003). In effect, social circles tended to become more narrow or break up entirely, at the same time that mutual help was becoming increasingly less self-evident (Ledeneva 1998, 194–200).

Fifty-five-year-old Evgenia stayed at Nochlezhka's shelter and worked as a door guard at Caritas' soup kitchen. When the shelter closed, she began to alternate between stairways and an old and very close female friend. This was not because the friend resented Evgenia's staying there but because of the implicit reciprocal demands that Evgenia imposed on herself:

> She would never ask me to contribute anything, but I feel that I have to. She has a minimum pension, we both smoke—she even more than I do—and then there is her son, he is thirty-four but he hasn't sorted out his life really, so she has to take care of him too. So I have to find food for two or three people every day, or I'd feel that I'm using her. This is simply too difficult. In the shelter each of us was responsible for herself only. We shared things, of course, if someone ran out of tea or somebody else had some vodka, but we had no *obligations* towards each other. So while it's warm outside I sometimes tell her that somebody else will put me up for a while, and then I sleep in some stairway. It's better for her to have me out of the way and I feel better myself.

What Evgenia found especially disturbing was that even though her friend was willing to give her a propiska in her flat, she was not allowed to do so.

By a few square meters, the apartment was too small for Evgenia to receive enough space according to the sanitary norm. With a propiska she would be able to take a job, she argued, be able to bring home at least *something*, regardless of how little. Now her primary contribution to her friend was her "salary" of foodstuffs and clothes at Caritas.

The mere lack of means is, as Evgenia points out, a problem, but the change that the inequality imposes on the relationship is in itself an additional source of conflict. The ideal friendship for people like Evgenia is of the type in which "the material side of the transaction is repressed by the social," that is, generalized reciprocity (Sahlins 1984, 194). Giving is perceived as a mutual give-and-take between agents united by some commonality, the ultimate one being kinship. Debts are not explicit, and counter-obligations are considered to be relevant only when the recipients are able to reciprocate the gift, which might never happen (Sahlins 1984, 196). Judging by Evgenia, however, this principle is seriously disturbed when one of the parties is deprived of any conceivable possibility of contributing, destitute to the point that it is impossible to pretend anything else. The obvious inequality shatters the "us" by infecting it with dissimilarity. What Evgenia and others in her situation are confronting, is partly the insight that their friends are no longer their friends. The infinite duration of the extreme inequality is in itself antithetical to friendship, because the relationship itself has no room for the apparent difference in needs. It no longer hinges on mutuality and sharing but rather on pretense and the art of producing white lies.

Parental Obligations

The only close relationship that permits an enduring one-way dependence is the one between parents and children. Exchange with lateral kin such as siblings, aunts, and so on is similar to the reciprocity between old and close friends, whereas the bond between parents and children is articulated differently. "It would be different if my mother was still alive," said a middle-aged man whom I met at the station. "I've never been on good terms with my brother, and now he doesn't want to know me. It's the same with most of my old friends. My sister is OK, but she's got her own life, and she's poor too, with children, and I feel inconvenient being there. Parents are different, you can ask them for so much more, they are always there for you."

There is a deeply ingrained idea that parents should sacrifice themselves for the sake of their children and help them in all possible ways, while the reciprocal duty of adult children to care for their parents is less pronounced, a bias that is tied to the attempts of parents without hopes for themselves to advance socially by proxy (Shlapentokh 1984, 87–93; Ledeneva 1998, 102–3). "Parents" can be substituted by "mother" because most parents *are* mothers—fathers die earlier, or they disappear in divorces—and because unlimited self-sacrifice primarily is conceived of as a female and motherly quality. Nonetheless, my informants usually discussed such bonds in terms of "parents," and I met homeless men who had given up everything they had for the sake of their children—one of them found it absolutely natural that he should sell his own apartment to cover his son's heroin debts.

Homeless adults expected support from their own parents (if they had any) and openly expressed disappointment and bitterness if they were denied it. Even elderly people did so, in spite of having children with material resources exceeding those of the parents. Thus sixty-year-old Aglaia went to her mother for support, even though her daughter was married to a New Russian who certainly had the means to help her. Aglaia was cheated of her propiska and her living space by her husband, but it was the complicated relationship with her mother that occupied her. The mother had persuaded Aglaia's daughter not to support Aglaia, but Aglaia would never ask for this anyway, she said; it was the *mother* who should help, and until she did so Aglaia would not give in. She took efficient revenge for having been let down by choosing the landing outside the mother's entrance door as a regular sleeping place and by making the situation clear to any neighbor who questioned her presence.

In the same vein, many homeless parents went to great lengths to support "homed" children even though they were no longer infants. Liuba, who lived with her boyfriend Dima in a bunker near the station, supported her three teenagers with money that she made cleaning train wagons. They still lived with their father, whom Liuba had abandoned, as she said, because "he offended me." Even more dedicated was the old man who collected bottles at the station every day and gave what he could to his adult, non-homeless daughter. She was not particularly poor, but he said calmly that one *should* help one's children; as long as he did so, it was not all that important what happened to himself. Besides, he added, someone gave him a cup of tea and some bread this morning, so life was not all bad.

This man did not seem to feel reduced to a non-person. By persisting in being *nuzhen* (needed), he managed to fulfill what he considered to be the single purpose of his life, to be a decent parent, and he accordingly felt like a human being as well. Liuba had plenty of humiliations in a number of other contexts to complain about, but she seemed perfectly self-confident with regard to her value as a mother. In spite of being homeless, she contributed something important to her children's well-being, namely their pocket money, which (let's face it) from the standpoint of a teenager is often more vital than bread. (Moreover, she showed her children that she was as good a parent as her wretched husband, which I believe she thoroughly enjoyed.) However, both of them were quite unusual. Homeless parents with adult or teenage children usually have few options to make themselves needed. Loath to ask for help and lacking the means to help, they settle for second-best: avoiding being a burden by not seeing their children too much.

Hence Aleksei, a construction engineer who became homeless after August 1998, did not find the prosperity of his adult children relevant in the least. He frankly stated that his pride was the main reason for not telling them that he was homeless: "Never in my life could I imagine that I would end up like this, and of course I don't tell them. A father should take care of his children, not be a burden to them. What respect do I earn from them if they know?" Thus Aleksei said that his telephone was out of order and continued to visit his children as usual on their birthdays, when in reality he spent that winter in a waiting hall at the Moscow Station.

Homeless Parenthood: A Story of Abandonment

The ethos that you do everything for your offspring does not escape the homeless parents of young children either, even though elderly people may be more willing to sacrifice themselves than the younger generations. Needless to say, homelessness provides no opportunities for such an ideal parenthood, despite the courageous struggle of many mothers and fathers. In the end, everybody who does not solve the housing question has to abandon their children, which usually leads to estrangement from them.

In this case too, parenthood is in reality a matter of motherhood, even if parental dilemmas seemed relatively gender-neutral as I observed them during my fieldwork. Neither women nor men talked much about their children to begin with, and I could know people for months before they mentioned the subject at all. I did not find this particularly strange, since the same was true of every other subject that did not concern the here and now. (Adult close ones, in contrast, were potential sources of support and as such part and parcel of homelessness as a topic of conversation.) The subject did not seem to be emotionally charged or taboo in any way; it was simply not relevant most of the time. The only reason that I know that Katia the Colonel had five children is a comment she made about dental care. Katia showed her own, very bad, teeth and said: "That's the Soviet legacy: phobias against dentists and gynecologists. Look at me—rotten teeth and five kids!"

It was not only women who showed concern about their children. Yet men and women called attention to (or kept silent about) their children from different structural positions and with different cultural expectations of themselves. Once I went thoroughly through all the information I had about each parent, there were significant variations between women and men. Custody is perfunctorily granted the mother after a divorce, and reportedly only a minority of the fathers maintain a regular and frequent contact with their children (Prokof'eva and Valetas 2002). Accordingly, most homeless fathers had seen little or nothing of their children since the divorces or imprisonments that made them homeless in the first place. Women were more likely than men to have become homeless or incarcerated while living with their children, and they therefore had to arrange the future custody of them. Hence more women than men maintained some sort of contact with their children, however sporadic.

Mothers are perceived as the ultimate custodians of children, and they are expected to keep the family intact in all sorts of ways: to cuddle, educate, nurture, and, on top of all that, make money. Fathers are expected to satisfy emotional needs too, but once a divorce is finalized, the established gender order easily estranges them from their children. With exceptions such as the dedicated fathers mentioned above, many homeless men seemed to think that the incapacity to perform the conventional breadwinning functions justified a total abandonment of family life as such, even in cases involving motherless children. Vova's mate Gena provides a striking example. He lost his birth family during a twenty-year prison sentence, but unlike many others, he managed to settle down afterwards and lived for some years as a married factory worker with two children in a small Karelian village. Perestroika, withheld salaries, and a desperate food shortage led Gena to break into a grocery shop, which brought him, a recidivist, another six years in the Zone. On his return in 1998 he found the village deserted, the only factory closed, and his family gone. His wife had been murdered a couple of years earlier, he was told, and his children were now in an orphanage. Gena left for St. Petersburg where he assumed that survival would be easier, but he never went to see his children. "I couldn't see what on earth I could do for them now," he said with an indifferent shrug, "so what was the point of seeing them at all?" His fatherhood somehow expired when his protective and supportive capacities disappeared, as if he viewed fatherhood as a social bond that is a product of support rather than as a biological function that is expressed by it, which seemed to be the opinion of Viktoria and others who insisted on assistance from their own parents.[4] The fact that fathers easily let go of their children says nothing whatsoever about their emotions, I should add. Gena seemed quite detached, but Vova often talked about his daughter with love and sadness. Nevertheless, he considered her to be lost forever once his wife left him, and the additional grief only added some extra fuel to his relentless urge to drink.

Without speculating about feelings, which are unknowable anyway, women are supposed to be there at all times for their children, taking care of emotional as well as material needs. Since they face different pressures to stay in touch with and help their offspring, they are more likely to explain and justify their position. There is one course that needs no excuse, however, namely passing over the child to relatives, in particular to one's own mother. The arrangement is commonplace among non-homeless Russians too, and it needs no justification. It is not unusual for siblings to take care of children, but the first option to help inexpert or overburdened parents is by tradition the babushka, who might take over the rearing of her grandchildren completely while the parents deal with their own lives elsewhere.[5] For some of my informants, this arrangement worked out relatively harmoniously, but in quite a few cases the relationship with the relatives was strained, to say the least. "The condition is that I visit them *only* on my son's birthday and stay away the rest of the time," the station regular Zhanna said about the terms set by her brother for taking care of her six-year-old son. The five children of her sister, Katia the Colonel, lived with their mother in the same town, although I do not know if the mother laid down similar conditions—Katia talked about them only in the aforementioned witticism about dentists and gynecologists.

The sisters came from a small town outside Murmansk, and like many other homeless mothers, they were also prevented from seeing their children by vast geographical distances and expensive railway tickets. Zhanna was better off than many others and went back at least once a year for her son's birthday, but this year she could not afford to do so. She was not very informative about private matters either, and the only reason I learned about her son was that she took the cancellation of the journey as a good reason to get drunk. When I asked her on another (more sober) occasion, Zhanna claimed to be satisfied with the custody arrangement in spite of her brother's strict terms. He *was* a small-minded bore, she laughed, but her boy was fine there, he had no particular need of her, and the main thing was that he was growing up with the family. As I understood her, the most important thing for her was that she could provide her son with close ones. Since she had fulfilled this duty, there was nothing more she could do for him as a mother—in spite of her own longing and her anger at not being able to see him.

Orphanages: A Bed and a School,
or Neglect and Estrangement?

If there are no benevolent relatives, only the state remains. In practice, the orphanage system thus functions as a kind of recycling unit of homelessness: homeless mothers dispose of their children there, and once out of the internat the teenagers run an increased risk of becoming homeless. Theoretically, unregistered children have no formal right to state care. The orphanage needs proper documents to prove who the child is and on what grounds the parent wants it to be taken care of; if the parent lacks ID documents and is a nonlocal, this can be complicated. According to my informants, however, directors of orphanages tend to circumvent these rules and take pity on the child, and I have never heard of a homeless parent who failed to find a place in an orphanage once they tried to.

In spite of the former pretensions of the state to superior parenthood, abandoning a child to an orphanage is regarded as a serious violation of the maternal virtues. According to Isupova, the scholarly literature of the Soviet and post-Soviet era ascribed abandonment to the individual and deviant psychological characteristics of the mother, assuming that motherhood was "the foundation of the sexual identity of every 'normal' woman'" (Isupova 2004, 44). Many Russian doctors and other experts on reproduction employ the same depiction of ideal motherhood as an argument against abortions, but in my own opinion it is equally effective for the opposite purpose: if you cannot care for your child, you should avoid having one in the first place (Rivkin-Fish 2005, 103–8; see also Isupova 2004). Accordingly, the handful of women I met who had abortions during my stay justified them precisely as a maternal obligation to the unborn child, not because the child would make their own situation considerably more complicated than it already was. The authorities seemed to be of the same opinion, and abortions were easily accessible even to women without medical insurance. One has to pay for anesthesia, but to most women, these pains seemed immaterial compared with the later perils.

Isupova (2004) argues that expert discourse and popular prejudice alike reduce relinquishment to the personal pathologies of mothers, while ignoring circumstantial factors and poverty. In my opinion, however, there is an oppositional discursive strand that justifies abandonment if the material well-being of the child is at stake. It would, in fact, be very odd if it were *not* there, considering the old propaganda of the state as a surrogate parent and the fact that the abandonment of children is part of the personal experience of countless women. I do not imply that homeless women embrace such a view unanimously, but some apparently did. Others continuously negotiated the different facets of motherhood implied by the respective standpoints.

The maternal responsibilities at stake in condemnations of *otkaznitsy* (mothers who give up their children) are love, attention, and upbringing, not the provision of food or other material necessities that, in the end (that is, when the man is gone), are also a woman's responsibility. In the homeless reality, any parent must choose between material provision and attentive love. The former wins by definition, since good parents first and foremost keep their children alive. If there is no choice but an orphanage, a good mother thus accepts this option as a makeshift form of motherly care, with or without negotiations. Most homeless women with children in state care thus stated that there was no choice; that an orphanage at least provides food and clothes and a school; and that they checked for themselves that the place was clean and tidy. Some were perfectly confident, while others seemingly tried to convince themselves during our conversation that their children were all right, as if they had to do this each time they thought about them. My point, again, is not that they felt a certain thing but that the food-clothes-school argument was considered to be acceptable by many.

Some homeless parents were criticized for being irresponsible when they rejected state care of their children. Viktoria was one. She had grown up in orphanages herself and had already been compelled to give up her son once when he was an infant. To her, more desperate circumstances than Nochlezhka's shelter were needed to justify a second abandonment. She did not deny the material advantages of an internat, but her son, she argued, was a sensitive and receptive eleven-year-old in need of adult attention. At an internat he would simply disappear among the other children, and he was not assertive enough among his peers either. She cared better for him on her own, she argued, and she had found a job (albeit a very low-paying one) for her common-law husband Zhenya at the Botkin Hospital and made use of a number of charity organizations herself. The other women agreed that Viktoria was a good mother, but they were not convinced that she had done the right thing. The shelter was not a normal environment, nor were Viktoria's attempts to organize some kind of schooling enough: the boy had in fact not been to school since they had become homeless four years earlier, and the part-time evening education that she had found at a Catholic mission was no alternative.[6]

Education was indeed the factor that finally made Viktoria give in. When the shelter closed, she and her family resumed their former wanderings among former schoolmates, and finally she decided that an internat was the only solution if her son was not to end up illiterate. As her relationship with

Zhenya was falling apart, she also found it better for the boy not to be around until the separation was over. When she told me, she was disillusioned and depressed, framing it as if she had failed in the only project she had ever undertaken: keeping her family together. She also added in passing that she had lost her domestic passport (she had invested quite a lot of effort in organizing a new one), somehow underlining the extent to which she felt reduced to a failed nobody, with neither family nor documents. As it turned out, however, her son felt at ease in the internat and obtained good grades, which was more than Viktoria had ever expected. Her former roommates from the shelter said later that they had known all along that an eleven-year-old boy did not need motherly pampering so much as a school. Perhaps they were right, but the need of the mother to be needed has to be acknowledged too. And apparently Viktoria became needed again, because she soon met a new man who was not homeless and did not even drink, and a few months later her former roommates told me that they got married.

The shelter was a luxury environment in comparison with the stairways and basements where Nadia and Sergei kept their babies for more than a year. Their stubborn opposition to state care of children partly derived from negative experiences of orphanages, but to a certain extent they also resisted consistent pressure to abandon their children coming from the charities on whom they were dependent. As explained earlier, Nadia became pregnant while on the run from an abusive stepfather, and gave up her firstborn son to an orphanage when her parents cheated her of her living space in the early 1990s. Eight years later she became pregnant with Sergei, an ex-con in his mid-forties. When their daughter Sveta was born two months prematurely in August 1999, Sergei had a small salary as a caretaker at the Salvation Army, and they rented a room. A few months later he was fired and their landlady evicted them. For the next year and a half, they slept in stairways and at the Moscow Station until they finally found the former dry cleaner's described in the preceding chapter. In July 2000, Sveta received a little brother, Danila, a stout boy born in full term. The housing administration reluctantly accepted the family on condition that Nadia clean the stairways for free. Sergei suffered from bad health and took care of the children, taking occasional odd jobs. In the vicinity there were a number of churches and NGOs that provided clothes, food, and medical care. This assistance, supplemented by occasional help from acquaintances (most of them homeless too), they somehow struggled along.

After Sergei was fired in the autumn of 1999, they handed Sveta over to an orphanage on a temporary basis, but took her back in the spring when they discovered bruises on her body. She was ill, and they found her motor learning

FIGURE 7. Nadia in the basement she shared with Sergei. Photograph by the author.

unsatisfactory. After that, Nadia and Sergei became firm in the belief that orphanages are more dangerous to infants than the streets, an opinion that was bolstered by the deficient development of Nadia's older son. By this time he was ten years old, but Nadia claimed that mentally, he was at least five years behind due to institutional neglect. The orphanage doctor tried to evade the responsibility in the usual way, Nadia said, by giving a diagnosis. In this case it was Down syndrome, even though her son's slightly slanted eyes originated in her own Kazakh origins (see Hunt 1998). In spite of all this, the organizations with which they were frequently in touch were appalled by their refusal to accept an orphanage and (with the exception of one church) by their decision not to abort Danila. Nadia and Sergei hated this pressure but could do little to minimize the contact because of their dependence on them.

The more Nadia and Sergei were criticized, the more unflinching their resistance became. They argued that they could see for themselves that their children were relatively healthy, and their occasional coughs were nothing compared with how ill Sveta had gotten in the orphanage. After all, Nadia said, cold in itself harms nobody, only germs do, and germs spread in orphanages. Moreover, they argued, lack of attention does more harm than the occasional cold. Even if life in the basement was not good, it was endurable. The main problems were the same that most parents experienced: expensive Pampers (they dried and reused the ones in which there was only urine) and unreliable babysitters. Moreover, it was all only temporary. They were writing pleas to all sorts of bureaucratic offices for housing, and sooner or later this would yield results, and then the situation would be sorted out.

Ironically, the argument they used—"it is only for the time being, until the situation is sorted out"—was cribbed from the very people urging them to use an orphanage. Agents from the charity sector as well as the state administration, and also many of their own friends, gave them one and the same message: "There's food, clothes, and a school, and it is only for a while, until your problems are settled." I found this advice cynical, because they knew as well as I did that their case was hopeless. There were no offices to go to, no bureaucrats with the power to conjure up a room from nowhere, and no laws or regulations that favored people like Nadia and Sergei. They were the only ones who believed that anything at all could be worked out, and for the others the device only served to soothe their own pained consciences and silence the intolerable insight that there was absolutely nothing anybody could do.

When the family was evicted after almost a year in the basement, a state of emergency set in. At this point an NGO targeted at orphans found a solution so good that not even Nadia and Sergei could refuse it: foster care with two staff members of the organization. Nadia and Sergei yielded reluctantly, on condition that they could see Sveta and Danila as often as they wanted. How-ever, the foster parents gradually became "mama" and "papa" to the children, as a staff member at the NGO told me in private, and these new mamas and papas became less and less intent on keeping in touch with the old ones, according to Nadia and Sergei. Finally, Nadia and Sergei gave up contact completely. "We see it as if we have lost them once and for all," Nadia said, "and then there's no point in seeing them." Some gleam of hope nevertheless remained, but when they talked about the children later, it was as mere tokens of a utopian future: "So perhaps this army mate of mine can help us with an obshchezhitie, and then eventually we can take the kids back."

This seems to be the normal way in which homeless parenthood ends when the children are brought into state care. Parents end conversations about them by saying, more in hope than in certainty, "This is only for the time being—once this situation is sorted out, we'll take them back." The longer they have been separated, the hollower the statement sounds. Visits become more and more sporadic, and sometimes they cease totally. Birthdays remain obligatory occasions for the most minimal of parental obligations: a visit and a nice present. Or only a gift, if the child is living far away. Sometimes parents said that they could not afford the ticket, but in certain cases—when it was a matter of the local trains, where nobody hesitates to try for a free ride—this merely seemed to be an excuse for skipping the visit completely because they were ashamed of not being able to buy a good enough birthday gift.

Parenthood was thus subject to the same fate as the ties to adult kin or "pre-homeless" friends. The incapacity to contribute wears the closeness thin, until it withers away from shame and embarrassment. The last and only thing that the "not-needed" *can* do is manifest their concern for the well-being of the others verbally, by culturally legitimate expressions such as "being nobody's burden," "they've got their own lives," and all the possible forms of "helping one's children"—whether by supporting them, avoiding them, abandoning them, keeping them, or aborting them. Homelessness is not merely a product of fractured ties, it also creates fractured ties; spatial and social displacement are thus mere functions of each other. This might give the impression that the homeless are entirely lonely, which is most probably how they would put it themselves. The truth is rather that in spite of a lack of close ones, the homeless are nonetheless immersed in a lively social life with enough reciprocity to keep them alive. The dilemma is only that since those inhabiting this social world are classified as bomzhi, they cannot be defined as close. The next chapter explores how reciprocity, cooperation, and mutual help take place among people who by definition regard each other not as "one's own" but as "strangers" or simply "them."

CHAPTER 5

Friend or Foe?

The Ambiguity of Homeless Togetherness

Traditionally, bomzhi are depicted as belonging to a subculture in its own right. As criminals are supposed to do (in "the good old days," anyway), they are assumed to organize their secret world in a fair and egalitarian fashion, and every bomzh is allocated his own dustbin, into which nobody else is permitted to intrude. The idea is so ingrained that even the homeless believe in it—but they argue that it only pertains to bomzhi far away, in the suburbs, where they never go themselves.

I witnessed nothing of the sort, to my regret; it would have cast a glimmer of grace over an ambiguous social world that was as shallow, unreliable, and callous as it was generous, caring, and inclusive. Apparently, such a duality is characteristic of homeless togetherness in other countries too (Snow and Anderson 1993; Dordick 1997; Rosengren 2003). For the most part, this is determined by the "ecological" constraints of homelessness; the permanence and stability of the space occupied by homeless people is reflected in the continuity of their social ties (Dordick 1997). In addition, these studies suggest that the mere stigma of being homeless fosters mutual suspiciousness and disregard, and in my own field this aspect was crucial. People were aware that they had nobody else to turn to than each other, and their togetherness was indeed characterized by conviviality and mutual support. Nonetheless, the suspiciousness of bomzhi as a kind, the lack of a shared past, and the contingency of street life prevented any sense of "one's own" from appearing, and the result was an awkward type of interaction in which most people in each other's eyes were absolute Others and potential soul mates—at one and the same time.

Knowing Everybody: Conviviality, Contingency, and Contempt

At charities as well as at the Moscow Station, it was easy to believe that everybody knew each other from before. I did not quite understand how large these social networks could be until I counted through the different hangouts, and thereby the possible number of acquaintances, of Lyosha, a Salvation Army regular in his mid-thirties. After many years in the gutters of the Moscow and Vitebsk stations, Lyosha managed to sober up, in his words mainly through the intervention of the AA and, to a certain extent, of God. When I knew him he drank only occasionally, albeit hard and with disastrous effects. In Lyosha's opinion, temperance emptied life of everything that was beautiful, entertaining, and meaningful, but if he gave in to his unyielding craving for alcohol he would die, and he preferred a dull life to no life at all. His recurring relapses were, he claimed, entirely the result of a stifled need to socialize. "I don't want to go back to the railway stations," he told me once when we met at the mobile soup kitchen of the Salvation Army. "But God knows that I miss having people around me. I knew *everybody* who came here then, even by name. If they weren't hanging out at the stations, I knew them from the soup kitchen that Nochlezhka had in those years. Or from the corps [of the Salvation Army], because I went there now and then long before I seriously tried to sober up. And if there was someone I didn't know, I'd at least know somebody else who knew that person. Now I hardly recognize anybody, and I can feel sort of lonely sometimes."

He did not appear to be very lonely. While talking he greeted a dozen people, and as he elbowed his way toward the car arriving with the soup, he exchanged a few words with perhaps another dozen. Lyosha, who was a regular at the Salvation Army and at one of the Caritas soup kitchens, visited the same places as at least another two hundred people on a more or less daily basis, and he knew several outside these contexts. In the old days, when he hung out at two different railway stations, he would have confronted regularly some five hundred people in the same fluctuating manner. By the end of my first ten months of fieldwork, in comparison, I knew (or, rather, had talked to) about two hundred people.

The pool of contacts as such was always intact as long as one did not lose touch with the hangouts (which Lyosha partly had), but specific individuals were hard to keep track of. I had my share of this problem too—I always bumped into *somebody* whom I knew (or, rather, had talked to) when I came to any of my field sites, but it was very difficult to get hold of particular individuals. My informants had similar problems with each other. On the same occasion when Lyosha spoke of his loneliness, Evgenia was talking to a sullen man who was apparently waiting in vain for somebody. As a doorkeeper at the Caritas soup kitchen, she knew "everybody" too, but this man was a stranger. Nevertheless, she did her best to console him. "This is the worst thing with this life," she said empathically, "that one can't plan anything. You don't even know where you will be yourself in fifteen minutes, so how can you expect to find others?" He only shrugged and said that he had ceased to bother long ago: "I've been doing this for the past ten years—losing people, finding new ones, losing them too. . . . It is just the way things are."

The homeless reality does not favor punctuality and trustworthiness, for these qualities by definition anticipate a certain control over one's immediate future. Police checks, ticket controllers, long lines at administrative offices or charities, unexpected income opportunities, or—for those inclined to it—tempting bottles, and any number of other petty circumstances easily changed plans and caused delays. Fully aware of these obstacles, people nevertheless persisted in trying to meet up, and there was always someone who, without result, was scrutinizing passersby or impatiently asking others if they had seen this or that person. Their pursuit was complicated by the narrow repertoire of Russian first names. Katia the Colonel, Andrei Half-Finger, and some other prominent station regulars had complementary nicknames, but most others were simply standard Lenas and Seriozhas. In addition, the perpetual flux of new acquaintances made it difficult to remember names in the first place. At the station, people even addressed each other arbitrarily, disregarding the protests of those who had suddenly been endowed with new names.

A common outcome was that the neglected parties would give up on the appointment and head off with some others who perhaps shared an interest in whatever practical concerns had motivated the original rendezvous: checking out a sleeping place, finding information of some sort, exchanging items. Just as often, they went off on their own, cursing the "bloody bomzh" for letting them down—and themselves for daring to hope that it would work out. Failed commitments tended to be blamed on the personal qualities of the absent party, as if the possibility of external obstacles was considered to be somewhat less than the chance that the other party was simply inconsiderate or drunk. It was generally expected that anybody subjected to "this life" sooner or later would lose normal reference to time and place and cease to respect commitments to others, and to a certain extent this became a self-fulfilling prophecy. I often heard comments such as: "I said I would meet her there, but she's never on time anyway, so I won't bother to go."

The informal and unreserved manner of approaching others was sympathetic, at first glance. People did not hesitate to involve themselves spontaneously in the conversations of others with frank questions and comments, usually addressing each other with *ty*, the informal "you singular," and by their first names, often in the equally intimate diminutive form (Lyosha for Alexei, Galia for Galina, and so on). However, this spontaneity could also be perceived as insolent and tactless. Interrupting was a constant topic of argument and scolding in the crowded yard of the Moscow Station, where regulars spent their days with the primary purpose of finding an income and not, as in the case of charities, of finding a break, a bite, and a chat. Also, the taken-for-granted use of *ty* and of diminutives could be perceived as disrespectful, in particular by people who clung on to past identities characterized by *kul'turnost'*, meaning "culturedness" defined as intellectual refinement, higher education, or just good manners in general (Rivkin-Fish 2005, 12). The former pianist Irina's sense of self depended heavily on her past as a intellectual with a proper upbringing, and she hated every feature of what she regarded as bomzh manners: being interrupted while talking to others, having her proper name not respected, being addressed with *ty*, and all this from people she had never met before. "They weren't even *na ty* in Stalin's prison camps," she snapped, "even though they knew each other inside out. They insisted on using *Vy* to show each other respect, to remind themselves that they were still *human!*"

Ironically, I believe that the habit of using *ty* stems precisely from the Zone, albeit not the camps for educated dissidents, where Irina's relatives once perished, but the latterday ones for what she regarded as simple, uncouth criminals. Perhaps the general informality originates in the Zone too; in any case the experience of imprisonment permeated homeless hangouts. Linguistic forms, gestures, and visible tattoos as well as verbal comments and stories were signs of a past behind bars, and it was also the case that ex-convicts immersed themselves very easily in the crowds. They were used to the casualness, and many of them needed more information than others since the society they entered upon release was not quite the one they had left. "I've even been sentenced to death," an old man told me, "but they changed it to thirty years. But those six months on death row were *nothing* in comparison with what I felt when I was released. I have no relatives, no home, no friends, and I can't even have a sensible conversation because I'm so lost in *time!*" I frequently met such desperate and confused ex-cons at the station right after their arrival. Later, usually acting on advice from a sympathetic station regular, they would appear at Nochlezhka, subdued, breath tinged with the distinct smell of solvents; finally, in a state of total resignation, they would arrive at the soup kitchen, where they would be relieved, if only for a moment, to meet somebody who had been through the same thing.

Stairway Partners and Station Cliques

There were cliques or loosely defined groups of homeless people that stayed together on a more frequent basis. Contingency was a hallmark of these relationships too, partly because they were subject to external events, but also because the people involved did not regard them as anything but makeshift solutions to everyday dilemmas. The everpresent option of "voting with one's feet" had a leveling effect: relationships were always replaceable, and no person became more important than anybody else. This did not mean that there was no mutual affection between people, but it could be ruptured as easily as it arose, and people were quite aware of the intrinsic vulnerability of such attachments. This blend of tolerance and indifference was salient in all of my field sites, but the divergent physical setup, the ecology, of each place created a distinct pattern of social interaction and mobility. In particular cases a faint sense of togetherness or belonging appeared in spite of the chronic flux of individuals.

Street dwellers often tried to find regular "cohabs," since sleeping alone poses obvious risks. It seems to me that such agreements were struck quite easily; if a stairway partner disappeared, it was easy to find somebody else who was in need of company. When I first met Lyosha, he shared a large bomb shelter with some five or six men and women, but most cliques consist of two or three people, enough for a stairway landing. The degree to which such stairway partners keep together during the day varies depending on their means of survival and general interests. Lyosha saw nothing of his companions in the daytime, whereas others keep together through thick and thin. Generally, couples or cliques like these rarely lasted long. Sleeping places easily disappeared—Lyosha's group was dissolved within a month by a zealous janitor who locked the bomb shelter—and individual circumstances with respect to work, improved lodgings, or just personal preference were equally flexible.

Stairway partners parted as easily as they had met, perhaps with a terse justification such as "They're not really my kind of people," or "I'll be better off somewhere else." Even if such curt statements might conceal bitter conflicts, I never heard straightforward accounts of serious discord except in the case of outright theft (an issue to which I shall return). Instead, the decisive factor that kept people together (or not) related to lifestyle and, most important, drinking habits. Those who preferred to be restrictive could have difficulties in finding others with the same inclination, in particular since reality did not always correspond to original plans and agreements. "They said that it was a calm black stairway and that they weren't going to drink," somebody said about such a disappointment, "but then the Ldinka was there anyway and it became an all-night party, and in the end we were thrown out and I lost my new jacket." To Lyosha this was a permanent dilemma that infected every attempt he made to stay with others, homeless people or not. For a while he ingeniously solved the problem by sharing an attic with three chronic alcoholics who always ran out of Ldinka well before midnight and then fell asleep. Lyosha spent the evenings at AA or the Salvation Army and returned to his sleeping place only when he was sure that the alcohol was finished.

A night shelter is a different type of homeless environment. Researchers on shelters for the homeless often associate them with closed institutions in Goffman's sense (1968; see also Gounis 1992; Passaro 1996, 32; Wright 1997, 220), but in 1999 Nochlezhka's shelter was neither particularly institutionalized nor closed. I found the lax attitude appealing, even though it resulted in incidents of violence and a reorganization of the shelter. I spent more time in the women's section, which was relatively calm, although the women said that drinking parties in the other flats had a tendency to spread into Viktoria's room in particular (according to her because her former sister-in-law and her new fiancé were drunkards) so that the night became a welter of loud talk, singing, arguments, and brawls. This lack of safety and privacy, the women agreed, prevented the shelter from being a *home,* even if only a makeshift one. Basically, they related to it as an unusually durable, safe, and comfortable stairway, a temporary place to sleep that sooner or later would disappear, along with everybody else contained therein. Nevertheless, the comfort made "voting with one's feet" a less attractive option if conflicts arose, and the women proudly emphasized that they were managing to share the scarce space without serious disagreements. There was a considerable amount of mutual help as well, and many of them combined their subsistence efforts. When the shelter closed, most women went their own way, however, and those who stayed in touch mainly did so because they were still going to the same soup kitchen.

The Moscow Station as a "homeless social space" had a continuity that set it apart from the fragmented world of exposed attics and staircases and, for that matter, also from the shelter: in 1999, shelter residents knew that their stay would be short-lived, whereas station regulars did not expect their life world to change significantly in the near future. Vova claimed that he knew everybody at the station and was rather proud of it, even though supposedly new acquaintances sometimes claimed not to be new at all and insisted on long circular discussions about how both of them could know everybody without knowing each other. But Vova had only been there for four months when I met him, and he might have missed out people in spite of his indefatigable sociability. *Real* old-timers like Nina or Olga spent the entire 1990s in this yard (when they were not in the Zone, that is).

Regulars did not necessarily see each other every day. Encounters were determined by working hours; whether or not individuals made a living at other hangouts too; sleeping places; and their individual drinking habits. Cleaners of train wagons worked a bit off to the side of the main station yard, and some of them shared the frequently expressed resentment against station life and went to work and left without having much contact with the people in the yard. Others worked in other places, and many regulars disappeared from time to time for jobs outside the city or for other, unknown, reasons. The unpredictability fostered flexibility with regard to sleeping company. The number of familiar people at the station in the late evening made it possible to follow anybody to his or her sleeping place without a previous arrangement. Vova thus thoroughly explored the surroundings of the station together with whomever he happened to be drinking with, but his casual stays remained as contingent as the bottle gangs were.

Bottle gangs normally lasted no longer than the contents of the bottle, but at times more continuous groups of drinkers appeared. Olga and Kostia, a couple, always attached one or more people to themselves. When I met them they were often with the young rascal Zina, her brother, and some other young men and women in their mid-twenties. Sometimes others joined them for a night or two (Vova was a frequent visitor here too), but this team remained intact for a couple of months and kept together both day and night. As usual, when such a clique dissolved (I never understood why, but it rarely seemed to be a matter of conflict), the middle-aged participants, Olga and Kostia, remained at the station afterwards and continued to mingle on an ordinary individual basis. The younger ones left the station promptly for nearby Vosstaniia Square and the Vitebsk Station, where they joined up with some local regulars and a few young participants of another former clique at the Moscow Station. When these new cliques dispersed, older participants remained where they were, whereas the younger ones moved on to a new cluster somewhere else. They usually had a fair idea of the whereabouts of their former drinking mates, and new groups were often formed by people who had known each other from other gangs in the past.

FIGURE 8. Zina and her brother at the Moscow Station. Photograph by the author.

Many of the young people (not least the women) fostered a "live fast, die young" attitude that saw life as an intrinsically futile project coped with only by reckless partying. Some of them made homelessness (and a modest dose of criminality) seem a voluntary choice, a way of dodging the mundane constraints of established life. Their alcoholism exceeded the norm, even among station dwellers, and many of them died during the years following my main fieldwork. Sometimes they had experiences with other drugs than alcohol, but they related the railway stations exclusively to drinking and moved if they wanted something else. A couple of them thus finally swapped the station for Vosstaniia Square, a notorious hangout for heroin users.

In contrast to most of their elders, these youngsters seldom complained about not being needed, nor did they speak disdainfully about bomzhi in general. They seemed content with the small, fluctuating cliques within the overarching network, because they were socializing in this fashion long before they came to the station, as I understand it. Their peer community is reminiscent of those found in streets and yards, regarded as characteristic of the life of Russian teenagers, although these young women and men kept at it until their mid-twenties and modeled their lives as homeless adults according to it (Pilkington 1994, 110ff.). In addition, many of them had experienced more advanced peer communities. Zina and her brother grew up in an orphanage, and others had a past in *maloletka* (youth prison), the Zone, and, in a few cases, the army. These contexts share certain features with a railway station: the authorities are remote figures with an exclusively controlling and punishing function, whereas the others, on supposedly equal terms, share a crowded, bounded social space in which the options to select and cultivate certain relationships in favor of others are relatively restricted.[1]

During the first half of 1999, the upstairs waiting hall, the one that offered security from police purges for the fee of three rubles, constituted a kind of durable social context for many station regulars. Vova jokingly called some of its permanent inhabitants the "bomzh bourgeoisie" because they dressed better than many others. About a third of the people I knew at the station slept in the hall on a relatively regular basis, and I estimated at least half of its visitors to be such permanent night-guests. Excepting the occasional, lonely newcomer, they usually sat together in small groups, kept an eye on each other's possessions, and frequently also shared food. Katia the Colonel, her sister Zhanna, Andrei Half-Finger, and a few others used to stick together, while Vova usually joined up with the two Armenians, Papik and Synchik. People drifted from one clique to another, but at the same time a loose hierarchy made it self-evident for people like Vova never to attempt to join Boris, a man who Vova said had "authority," whereas Katia the Colonel could sit wherever she wanted. Apparently the bomzh bourgeoisie had more right to integrity than others, or at least they were less likely to be interrupted or asked for sips from their bottles, but since nobody else depended on their relative wealth, their authority in other respects was questionable. Boris's leading position mainly seemed to be the concern of his own clique, a handful of well-dressed young men with whom he continuously appeared to be *fixing* things (petty fraud such as forged concert tickets, he admitted later). They depended on him and his dealings, but Vova did not, nor had Boris any wish that he should.

Vova liked to picture the station as a self-conscious community in its own right. There, he said, a norm of internal loyalty ruled, decisions were taken by consensus, and everybody knew who had prestige, who had *status,* and who did not. He was quite alone in this, however, and my impression was rather that he was recreating an idealized image of the Zone because he personally felt at home with it. To others, the station was just a place where certain people had more than others and were stronger than others, but this concerned nobody who did not want a piece of the same pie. Perceiving yourself as part of a social whole was largely a matter of individual choice: if you desperately want one, you are free to construct it, but nothing compels you to do so. In the end it is all in the eye of the beholder.

Station regulars were nevertheless more prone than others to refer to themselves as "us," and their use of the notion was somewhat different. Outside, the homeless referred to themselves in the collective in the broadest sense, as "us who are homeless" in contrast to the general public or the state: "Everybody looks down on us," or "This is a planned genocide—they've decided that we'd better just die." At the station, the use of the term was more narrow and precise. "We" were the people who helped each other, in contrast to the ones who did not. Thus "we" rarely served to set homeless regulars apart from domestics, whereas it distinguished regulars of this particular station in contrast to in-flyers, Vova's contemptuous term for newcomers. Primarily, however, "they" referred to people who were not only unhelpful in general but who in addition oppressed, constrained, and exploited—the police, but also unpleasant railway employees. "It's *our* station," Olga once furiously said after having been refused entry to the washroom by a particularly mean attendant. "She's worked here for a few months and I've been here for *nine years,* who does she think she is?" The "they" that defined "us" was, on the other hand, never constructed in relation to travelers, a group that in the discourse of the regulars figured merely as a kind of faceless raw material out of which profit could be carved.

Dealing with Domestics:
Dependence and Drinking

Quite a few non-homeless people spent time in the same places and under similar conditions as the homeless. Many station regulars were poor pensioners and others who had places to live at their disposal, and certain visitors to the soup kitchens had more or less temporary housing. Such *domashnie,* domestics, occasionally permitted homeless acquaintances to stay with them. I do not know to what extent they deliberately used their places of residence as an exchange resource, which for instance was the case in Stephenson's Moscow study, but I assume that some did (2006, 23–25). Such cohabitations were, moreover, contractual, whereas the reciprocity among the homeless, to which I shall shortly return, was of a more generalized kind (Sahlins 1984, 194). Even though domestics frequently participated in the fuzzy give and take of the homeless (particularly in the case of alcohol), the distinct economic and social interests of the parties were apparently too evident to ignore when the deal concerned a place to stay. The social bond between the parties was not so close as to make an overt scoring of balances inappropriate, which, as noted in the preceding chapter, was often the case when the homeless stayed with relatives and old friends (Sahlins 1984, 194). The balanced reciprocity could involve straight cash payments, but more often the deal was simply a place to sleep in return for food and, frequently, drinks.

When the waiting hall at the Moscow Station closed, Vova's mate Papik and his son Synchik moved in with Uncle Vania, an impoverished, hard-drinking pensioner who lived nearby and collected bottles at the station. The explicit deal was that Papik and Synchik were to provide the old man with food, and in addition Papik gave him exactly one hundred grams of vodka every evening to keep him calm. After some time Vova joined the company, and the cohabitation ended in a very familiar fashion: due to Vova's presence, Uncle Vania received considerably more than one hundred grams every night, and after a month or so all three of them were evicted when the old man had a fit of drunken aggression.

The attitude to domestics among the homeless was ambivalent. As workmates or drinking mates, they were included in the general "us" of the station and considered on an equal footing with the homeless. These relationships were not characterized by an assumed hierarchy that imbued the interaction between homeless station regulars and employees at the station, however jovial and open-hearted these were at times. The difference between homeless and domashnie consisted exclusively of a place to stay and the right to decide who is allowed to sleep there, and the inequality thus surfaced as a relevant issue mainly when the agenda turned to cohabitation. Nonetheless, domashnie were rewarding objects of comparison when the homeless considered their own status as bomzhi. If you have a propiska and a place to stay, you have no excuses for this lifestyle, I was told, and if you persist in doing it, you are more bomzh and less human than those who have no choice: "She has a flat and everything, but she doesn't value it, she hangs around here all the same, sleeps here even" (Olga, frowning, about an acquaintance), or "He isn't a bomzh, but he lives like one" (Gena, hinting at the physical appearance and the lack of sobriety of a man passing by). Uncle Vania was regarded with more compassion, although somewhat patronizingly. Old, sick, and ill-tempered, after all, who needed somebody like him, and how would he manage without helpful lodgers?

Furthermore, the distinction between the categories domashnii and bomzh was blurred. For a few weeks, before moving in with Uncle Vania, Vova lived with an acquaintance called Roma. Roma invited Vova to share the apartment of his brother, who, in turn, had moved in with his son. Vova had money from me and paid half the rent, besides contributing his share of food and alcohol. Unfortunately the brother died quite soon, and his children claimed the apartment. As I understood it, the children were not overtly fond of Roma and so gave him no grace period. Roma obviously set the terms of the cohabitation as long as it lasted (Vova wanted to bring in Papik too but was not in a position to lobby for such a claim), but he was in a similar situation of dependence himself with respect to others. Such serial dependencies were often the case when homeless people found purported domestics to live with, and together with alcohol, this fact tended to limit the length of the stays.

"All That Is Mine Is also Yours"

The sociability among the homeless was inseparable from mutual support: the one fostered the other and vice versa. Drinking was a collective issue everywhere, at soup kitchens as well as in the station yard, but food, clothes, and other usable items were often given away *prosto tak,* "just like that," even between people who were not very familiar with each other. Sahlins's (1984) notion of generalized reciprocity was reflected in comments such as the following: "I found this fine leather jacket at Sinopskaia today so I took it with me, even though it's too small. But there's always someone who needs such stuff, and true, I just walked into the station and met this guy, I don't remember his name.... Somebody stole his coat in a stairway, so I gave him the jacket. One can't drag stuff around for long anyway, it just gets stolen in the end. And another time someone gives something to *me* for nothing."

However, this type of exchange is a result of circumstances as well as of human intentions, and the latter tend to be open-ended. The original intention of this man was probably not as philanthropic as he made it sound; if so, he might as well have left the jacket for the person who came after him in the line, thus saving himself the effort of carrying it at all. But he took it, knowing that in one way or another it would come in handy, if not as barter, then at least as a chance investment in a general morality in which he and everybody else has a vested interest. Nobody really denies that they hope to profit from the things they find, but barter must occur as an immediate face-to-face exchange or the opportunity is lost. Delayed barter presupposes a minimum of trust and reliability, which makes it a practical impossibility in the homeless reality: if people against all odds trust each other, they are still chronically subject to external circumstances that obliterate reliability (Humphrey 2000b, 259). Objects that could have served a particular purpose for a particular person through a "particularized" balanced exchange are thus easily fated to the same leveling as homeless people are: they are turned into "anything" given away "for no reason at all" to contingent "anybodies."

In spite of the common disregard in which the homeless held other homeless people, the mutual helpfulness at times surfaced as a source of pride, or at least as a redeeming trait: "You can never count on 'domestics,' but a bomzh always shares his last piece of bread," or: "We have to help each other, because if we don't, nobody will." However, only at the station were help and generosity talked about in ways that depicted them as some sort of structural foundations, or organizing principles, of "us." This was not reflected in the general valorizing of mutual helpfulness as much as in verbal assurances that sharing was a norm and that sanctions were implemented against those who violated it: "You didn't treat me to anything when I had a hangover this morning, so don't even think about a sip from my bottle now," Olga reproached a younger man one afternoon. She turned to me and repeated the familiar motto, "At this station we help each other, and if you don't you'll have problems." Those who did not abide by the norm of mutual helpfulness relieved others of *their* duty to be loyal, Olga implied, and refusing to soothe somebody else's hangover was indeed the ultimate in stinginess. The youngster was fully aware of his transgression and apologized, arguing that on the particular occasion he did not understand how bad she was feeling, but Olga was merciless and finished her bottle on her own.

However, such sanctions were often mitigated by time itself since neither accusations nor disagreements lasted for very long. A short and selective memory was quite characteristic of station regulars. States of consciousness were as fleeting as the social environment, and as events replaced each other the importance of earlier incidents was gradually overshadowed. Antagonists were easily reconciled by drinks offered by third parties, unless they were united as joint victims of yet fiercer Others—the police, or aggressive railway employees. Olga restored the young man to favor only a few hours later, when she was tipsy and happy again and when a conscientious shift of policemen had spent a couple of hours futilely chasing her, her antagonist, and everybody else away from the stairs of the Military Ticket Hall.

Even if small incidents were easily forgotten, the continuous interaction among the same people enabled them to distinguish singular accidental failures to contribute from repeated and calculated ones. Egor, a young man from Moldavia, faced this very tangibly. During his stay in the waiting hall, he worked very hard for a long time—at what he did not say—to save money for a ticket back home. One day a woman called Inna disappeared with all his money, by then a few thousand rubles. This seemed quite ruthless, considering that they had belonged to the same clique for a couple of months, but nobody showed much sympathy for Egor, which is interesting insofar as theft almost always elicits sympathy. But this time, many of the listeners just smirked at his laments and walked away. According to Vova, Egor had earned himself an unflattering reputation as stingy during his stay, and not only Inna was tired of feeding him for nothing in return. But Inna was scum too, Vova added. She took the cash without sharing it with the others, and if she were ever to return to the station, nobody would hesitate to steal from her.

I seldom or never heard homeless people other than station regulars talk in terms of rules and sanctions, nor was the greed of others a recurring topic of laments. The mobility made such problems redundant: if the current partners turned out to be egotistic, one simply left them before the moral flaw became a source of conflict. The quality of consideration or helpfulness was in this sense not a norm, because norms are expected to regulate social relationships that already exist, to create peaceful conditions among people who are connected *a priori*—be they relatives, neighbors, or workmates. Station regulars, for instance, had to put up with each other whether or not they shared their resources, and helpfulness was a way of making this involuntary coexistence tolerable. Stairway dwellers, however, had far fewer involuntary links to the flow of replaceable anybodies. Since mutual support was the only reason for them to socialize in the first place, no particular rule was needed to make such support obligatory—the simple fact of the matter was that if there was no help, there was no relationship either.

Makeshift Neededness
but No Place for Friends

A paradox that permeated most aspects of homeless togetherness was that people without doubt needed and cared for each other, but they did not count these dependencies as social relationships in a proper sense. Since they did not match taken-for-granted conceptualizations of social bonds, they had no names. Accordingly, people did not refer to each other with a classification of the kind of relationship they were embedded in (friend, buddy) but with a description of how, functionally, they made themselves needed by each other: "we help each other out," or "it's easier to survive if you're not alone." Sometimes the trust in the other party was emphasized, but always in terms of what the parties *did* (or did not do) together: "We've known each other for a while," "we're sort of used to each other," "neither of us drinks."

I often heard sad accounts of the pain of not having somebody to be close to, somebody who would listen and understand, a true friend. Friendship can in Russian imply an exceptionally high degree of intimacy and trust, as *the* sole refuge and protection from a menacing external world (Shlapentokh 1984, 218–28; Markowitz 1991, 638–40; Lindquist 2005, 208–10). Judging by what I was told, however, homeless social ties do not include such a profound sharing of personal issues. There was an implicit agreement not to ask too much that surfaced as brief statements, even curter in Russian, that "everybody got here in his own way" (*vsem po svoiemu*) or "that's his/her private business" (*eto ego/ee lichnogo*). Some referred this cautiousness to distrust and suspicion: "We've all done something we're not proud of, and therefore we don't talk about ourselves with each other. If we do, we lie. Only outsiders like you believe it."

Certain people went to great lengths to help and keep in touch with each other, but nonetheless old and faithful stairway partners hesitated to define their relationship in terms of nouns. An old woman at the Salvation Army went to the tuberculosis hospital in Pavlovsk several times a week to provide her former "attic mate," another elderly woman, with supplementary food, and she was quite concerned about the condition of the patient. Nonetheless she never gave the motivation for her efforts by simply stating that they were friends; on the contrary, she emphasized the loneliness and defenselessness of the other woman: "She's all alone in the world, there's nobody to care for her, and so I do as much as I can." When people explained why they kept together, the implicit assumption was that, basically, they were only "anybodies" to each other, but they helped each other because of mutual need or out of pity for one's coincidental neighbor. This did not exclude tender feelings for the other party, but the emotional aspect was consistently downplayed.

The word *drug* (friend), in fact referred more often to the particularly sympathetic stray dogs that were occasionally adopted than to homeless humans, as an implicit hint that the difference between a dog and a bomzh is that you can trust the dog. Not only homeless people prefer the faithfulness of dogs to the capriciousness of humans, but the choice still says something about the limits of homeless togetherness. Friendship implies reliability, trust, and unconditional love, enduring qualities expected only in the intimate social context that homelessness by definition lacks. However supportive and kind another homeless person is, the context in which the relationship is situated is not one of those culturally approved hothouses in which friendship may thrive. The stairway clique or the group of drinking partners provide a neededness of sorts, but they are rarely or never conceptualized as more than a makeshift solution for everyday dilemmas: the risk of sleeping alone, the burden of gathering alone, the shame of drinking alone, and the boredom of just being alone.

When people *did* talk about friends, they referred to relationships that in some way or other were grounded in a social life before and beyond homelessness. Usually it was non-homeless people who were still available for more or less lopsided and problematic exchanges of help. In a couple of cases, the parties were friends before both of them became homeless, but these relationships were entirely dependent on a domestic third party who helped them to keep track of each other. Sasha and Pasha (mentioned in chapter 3) once became the closest of friends in an extraordinarily cruel prison camp, but once released and homeless, they lost touch for the simple reason that they could not find each other. Fate brought them together again when Sasha a couple of months after his release just happened to spot Pasha in the street, but after some five months, their paths parted again when Sasha was arrested for a knife assault committed half a year earlier. If they ever meet again, it will only be by an act of providence, for they still have no non-homeless base from which to transfer letters and messages so as to bring them together again.

Malkki (1997) coined the phrase "accidental communities of memory" for people who have endured the same wars, fled the same revolutions, or spent time in the same refugee or internment camps. To Sasha and Pasha, their time together in the Zone was fundamental to their friendship, but it mattered that it was a special camp involving even more suffering than the ordinary lot of homelessness—their friendship began with a month of written correspondence through a hole that they secretly made in the wall between their respective isolation cells. Otherwise the experience of incarceration was simply too commonplace among the homeless to serve as a non-homeless basis for friendship. It happened now and then that ex-cons who once shared the same

FIGURE 9. Pasha and Sasha. Photograph by the author.

cell or even cell block suddenly bumped into each other, but they tended to relate to each other more as old classmates than as close friends, and they rarely joined up on a long-term basis.

"All That Is Yours Is also Mine"

One cold spring day, Sveta, a handsome prostitute in her early thirties, staggered up the station yard, barefoot and dressed only in slacks and a shirt. Furious and tortured by a hangover, she came up to me and some others and yelled: "And these bastards were supposed to be my *mates!* We drank together in an attic and I passed out, and when I woke up they were gone together with my handbag, all my money, my new expensive coat—they even took my shoes! And I *worked* to get this stuff," she moaned, "I even paid for the booze we drank! All bomzhi are like that, they steal only from their own [people] because they know that the cops don't care about it!"

The objection that always came up when somebody extolled internal loyalty and mutual helpfulness among the homeless was that it was a mere chimera, a thin curtain of hypocrisy that in no way concealed the bleak fact that bomzhi steal from each other and use each other as much as they support each other, if not more. Theft provoked strong reactions as an obvious and tangible breach of the ideals of helpfulness and generosity, but even more common were laments focused on petty manipulation and abuse of these values. "They talk a lot about giving, but most people here disappear when it is their turn," said Andrei Half-Finger, echoing many others. It was as if the altruistic motto "since things cannot belong to me anyway, I might as well give them away" came with a cynical obverse: "since things cannot belong to anybody else anyway, I might as well take them." Being deprived of things or money is always an infringement of one's personal integrity, even if the lost items were found only recently and had no particular monetary or emotional value. Theft is particularly painful when the perpetrators are people who should have the potential to feel and show empathy. It is all the more upsetting if, as in Sveta's case, they are old acquaintances who previously have benefited from one's own empathy and loyalty.

There was a widespread ambivalence concerning one's brethren in misfortune not only at the station, although it tended to be openly stated more often there. When sharing was perceived to work as it should, and when the more mighty "them" were discussed, other homeless people were referred to as part of "us." At other times they were seen as potential predators and are referred to as "they," or just "bomzhi," because in spite of occasional assurances that

"bomzhi always share their last crust of bread with each other," the word
bomzhi was rarely used as "us." In particular this concerned constructions
such as the above, "it is typical for bomzhi...." When for instance sharing
was praised, the more vague "us" was more common as a referent, as if the
notions of generosity and typical bomzh were oxymoronic. Nor did the
homeless apply the term *svoi,* "one's own," to themselves in positively charged
contexts such as sharing or support. It was always "we help each other," never
"we help our own," as if they thought that the latter formulation would be a
gross exaggeration. They used svoi only in negatively charged situations, such
as when Sveta said: "it is typical for bomzhi to steal from their own [*krast'
u svoikh*]." It is intriguing that a word that highlights solidarity and (almost)
community was only used in contexts in which loyalty was betrayed, whereas
much more modest expressions were employed when unity actually existed.

The ambivalence was not ubiquitous. Papik never had anything positive
to say about the station regulars as a collective, and certain others were even
more consistent in defining other homeless people as an Other with whom
they had no relationship whatsoever. To Irina, the former pianist, even the
notion that the homeless *should* help each other was totally emptied of meaning since, in her opinion, bomzhi by definition are incapable of helping. She
spent the nights alone, arguing that homeless companions were more likely
to steal from her than non-homeless strangers were likely to beat her. Each
time I met her, Irina had different bags, different walking sticks, and different
clothes. Each time she also had new stories about being robbed by unknown
bomzhi, and her possessions disappeared when she was awake as well; it was
enough to put her bag down for a moment to fetch a bottle or buy something, and it would be gone. Her favorite story was of when she bought
hamburgers for some bomzhi, and in return they disappeared with her bag
in which for once she had both money and cigarettes. I had a feeling that she
repeated the same incident a few different times and that it somehow served
as a metaphor for all infringements of her integrity taken together, conveying
one single message: "They have stolen my life!"

In practice, exploitation and loyalty were often the prerequisite of each
other. Generosity sometimes displayed wealth that provoked theft, but, on
the other hand, the misery caused by theft awakened compassion and generosity. Those "who had" risked being deprived of what they had, but the have-
nots were taken care of. Sveta was, for example, not only drunk again for
free within the hour after her first outburst—she was also dressed in a new
(although less fashionable) outfit that another station regular just happened
to have handy. This is an example of how the mere situation of homelessness fosters equality. Besides the obvious poverty of everybody, the mobility

and the paucity of space for storage prevent the accumulation of wealth. The seemingly opposite generalized and negative reciprocities that prevail result in one and the same thing: a leveling of wealth that is accumulated against all odds. The common characterization of the above-mentioned forms of exchange as indicators, or constituents, of ties that are different in terms of closeness does not quite work out in a context where also relationships tend to be leveled: most of them are equally distant, or close, from the viewpoint of the subject (Sahlins 1984, 196–204). Giving and stealing are thus different sides of a general tendency to even things out, and the difference lies only in the degree of volition on the part of those whose wealth is transferred.

A significant minority did not accept the equality implied by poverty and ecological circumstances, and they tried to save up the means for future, individual purposes. They were constantly prey to the leveling activities of the others. Egor made the mistake of indebting himself in the system of generalized reciprocity, which gave Inna an acceptable legitimacy for stealing his savings. Papik, who also saved up in order to go home, never talked about his earnings and hid his money from bomzhi and from the police alike under the bandage wrapped round his chest. He stayed out of all kinds of exchange with the exception for Vova, whose salary from me was an assurance that their cooperation would not cause Papik any loss. "It's better not to accept gifts if they are offered," Papik argued. "If you take, you have to give back, or else they think you're stingy and steal from you, and they'll always make sure that they give less than you do." Those who like him had serious plans for their own future preferred the exchange to be balanced, that is, for both parties to recognize each other as separate entities reckoning the balance between themselves (Sahlins 1984, 195). The leveling approach might have suited the bomzhi who preferred to remain where they are, distanced from each other as individuals but nonetheless immersed in a larger wholeness that by its own logic permits nobody to be different in terms of ownership.

"Every Man for Himself"

To change one's situation for the better in a serious way, even to the point of exiting homelessness for good, one needs to be alone. There seemed to be an implicit consensus that other homeless people can only obstruct individual ambitions, even if this was rarely stated quite so explicitly. It was quite common for those who found paid jobs to discard stairway partners and, in a few cases, station cliques, and not only for the sake of geographical convenience.

While certain subsistence activities benefit from cooperation, others clearly do not, and while the boring and unprofitable gathering may well be a joint venture, "proper" jobs were largely regarded as individual enterprises. It indeed happened that a number of men were hired together by the same employer for agricultural work or certain risky assignments (such as the Armenian and the telephone cables), but in general job hunting was a lonely venture. Other homeless people may hamper one's own options if they turn out to be less ambitious and serious than oneself, and a drunken, dishonest, or simply absent work partner can destroy one's own important relationship with an employer.

Alcohol was another, albeit infrequent, justification for avoiding involvement with others. Not all stairway dwellers drank heavily, but even a small amount of Bomi for the mere sake of sleeping is dangerous to a sober alcoholic who wants to work the next day. Hence many AA regulars preferred AA groups with as few homeless people as possible. Lyosha went to a group in a different part of the city where he did not know the local bomzhi, and this made him less vulnerable to tempting bottles on the way to and from the meeting. Another advantage, he claimed, was that most of the other participants were wealthy, some even driving Mercedes. The difference in social position prevented interaction outside of the meetings, which saved him from the risk of relapsing into drinking in the company of his AA acquaintances—a scenario that according to him was not uncommon in groups consisting of people of his own sort.

The necessity to battle one's situation individually was framed as a necessity provoked by the deficient characters of bomzh Others, rather than as an intrinsically unavoidable result of poverty, alcoholism, sharing as a survival strategy, or a wish to be helpful and needed: "With people like *these* [bomzhi] around you, you can only trust yourself." The same trope often cropped up in discussions about life in society at large, as a bitter lesson taught by the changes during the past decade. If society were truly in order, there would be neither egotism nor homelessness in the first place, and it would not be necessary to go through life like a singular fortress expecting nothing but trouble from others. However resolutely the value of independence was put forward, it was not really considered to be fully human, *po chelovecheski*. Accordingly, pessimistic proclamations about the necessity of keeping others at a distance were frequently followed by sad statements about one's own incapacity to live up to it and the resulting necessity to drink in order to make life and other people bearable.

To other, less nostalgic, people, "trust only yourself" was on the contrary a fully fledged "every man for himself" ideology. As long as you *want* to, the credo went, and as long as you *work,* there are no problems, but bomzhi lack the will and incentive to work, and they instead become parasitic, so keep away from them. The most consistent champions of this individualistic worldview were men, usually not very old, who liked to intertwine an element of voluntary choice in their explanations of how they ended up in the street. "Circumstances" made it favorable for them to be tramps for a while, but the situation was only of a temporary nature; following the motto "if my individual willpower could take me to the street, it can also take me away from it," the way back was open. "Sure, I was ruined after [the] August 17th [crash in 1998]," said Boris, formerly a kiosk owner, later a purported authority at the Moscow Station. "There were debts and creditors, but this is not why I took off, I left because of my mother-in-law." The wretched woman, he explained, bluntly refused to end a presumed one-month visit that ended up lasting more than a year, and in the end Boris left instead. There *were* other circumstances, he indicated, but basically he could go back to his old life at any time. There was simply no reason to do so yet; he was not afraid of working, he managed reasonably well at the station, he knew what he wanted and was used to getting it, and he trusted himself. In the summer the time was evidently ripe, and Boris disappeared without telling anybody where he was going.

Just before I finished my main fieldwork and left, Papik dropped an ironic comment to me in private: "I'll be back home before the end of this year—now I've started to steal too, like everybody else here." There was no doubt that he meant stealing from homeless people. Papik was not stupid—Sveta was right when she said that no policeman bothers to investigate thefts among the homeless, whereas stealing from others is taken seriously. Nor was he alone in trying to find such a final solution to his dilemma; to me it seemed as if many people contemplated the same idea from time to time. After particularly spectacular thefts, bystanders usually condemned the deed and consoled the desperate victim, but they could also express a certain understanding for the perpetrator who was assumed to have sorted his or her situation out by the theft. "She rented a room," the rumor went about Inna after she stole Egor's money, "and they say that she brought her little daughter from Riga to have this expensive eye operation." There was even a trace of envy in these remarks.

Such events reveal the profound ambivalence in the attitude of the homeless to each other and to their mutual togetherness. On the one hand, they know that they need each other both to survive and to feel needed, and this sense of unity turns other homeless people into equal parts of an implicit "us" that should be treated accordingly. On the other hand, they do not consider this neededness to be more than a makeshift solution in view of the lack of a *real* "us," and in addition, the leveling tendencies of the homeless life and the inescapable drinking obstruct the way back to an established life of sorts. People are torn between disparate subjectivities; at one point they adopt the position of a homeless person among equals in the same situation, only to transform themselves into whoever they were, or believe themselves about to become, in an existence beyond homelessness, on in which bomzhi are indisputably Others. The shifts are as swift and situational as attitudes toward the police. It is not so much that people move between subjectivities—they always do—but that they are incommensurable; they are, in a manner of speaking, polarized self-representations. I believe that Inna and others exploited this lack of convertibility: as homeless, you can do things that your domiciled incarnation would never consider, and once safe on the other side, back home, the misdeed is not a burden on your conscience for the simple reason that the perpetrator was not you—it was a different person.

Roofless Lovers

If friendship cannot be conceived of in "this life," is romantic love then possible? To the extent that men and women talked about this matter at all, the answer is no. Judging by what I observed, it *is* possible, but only under quite particular conditions. Love was not a big issue in my conversations with informants, although the desire to meet somebody to one's liking (*po dushe*, literally "in line with one's soul"), was voiced occasionally, for some reason by men more than by women. Nobody really seemed to believe that his wish would ever be granted. "You're not strong enough to satisfy a woman if you live in the street," Lyosha explained, adding that the remaining preconditions for romance were not exactly thrilling either if you sleep in an attic, not least because Bomi is a sedative, not an aphrodisiac. From others I understood that the main problem was not sexual desire but the ordinary dilemmas of flux, distrust, and prejudice against bomzhi as a kind. It is telling that love usually cropped up in the context of hopes and plans of exiting homelessness, not when the homeless present was still on the agenda, as an implicit confirmation of the fact that the way out is individual and that other homeless people, whether lovers or not, cannot be anything but a burden.

Nevertheless, I knew several couples, and some of these affairs lasted for quite a long time. In contrast to faithful stairway partners, these men and women were very explicit about their affection for each other. They usually referred to each other as "my wife/husband" (the common-law status was taken for granted), "my sweetheart" (*moi milii/moia milaia*), or just "mine" (*moi/moia*), often with a satisfied look in their eyes. I have argued that other relationships remain unnamed, masked as mere survival strategies, because they are situated outside the intimate social context that is constitutive of friendship and other relationships. Basically, the same should apply to love relationships, but apparently it does not: on the contrary, love has the potential power to make a relationship "real" simply by being what it is—love. In itself it constitutes a legitimate reason for two persons to declare to themselves and to others that they belong to each other and intend to stay together.

I believe that these relationships were relatively lasting for two reasons: firstly, neither the man nor the woman had serious ambitions to get back into the "homed" world. Olga and Kostia, Pasha and Natasha, Liuba and Dima, and some other couples I knew were quite resigned in this matter and accommodated themselves to the present situation as well as they could. Nadia and Sergei did not, as they fought for the future of their babies, but their joint struggles led nowhere, and as the story in fact ends, her homelessness came to an end only after she left him. A second characteristic was that none of these couples constructed their mutual needs and support in terms of the traditional division between men as breadwinners and women as caretakers of hearth and home (or, at least, a makeshift hearth). Another way of framing this division is in terms of material and emotional provision respectively, or as an economy of complementary needs. Russians often describe the woman's part of the deal as to understand, love, and be attentive to the emotional needs of the man, tired as he is from his warlike struggle to protect and provide for his woman and his offspring (Sinelnikov 2000, Novikova 2000). Roofless lovers, however, did most things together and in relatively equal shares, working as well as socializing, drinking, and taking care of each other after a hard day's work. Nadia worked as a *dvornik* while Sergei took care of the babies; Natasha had equal responsibility in loading vegetables and lifting wallets together with Pasha (and Sasha too); and Olga and Kostia appeared to be equal partners in the work for the kiosk. More important is that they never commented on themselves or their partners in ways that juxtaposed them as women in contrast to men, nor did people who knew them. There was no occasional "one needs to provide for one's woman" or "he needs someone who *understands* him," in contrast to couples with makeshift housing, who had a different need to define themselves *qua* men and women in relation to each other.

The few Western studies of homelessness that take love affairs into account describe them as based on female submission in return for protection and/or as frequently violent (Toth 1993, 189ff.; Wagner 1993, 63ff.; Rosengren 2003,

Figure 10. Liuba in her bunker, and a glimpse of Dima behind her. Photograph by the author.

189ff.). I met a few women who had left homeless boyfriends because of
violence, but I never heard about physical violence between these long-term
partners, not even as ill-willed gossip. Also, the men apparently appreciated
tough women. Kostia, who was quite silent and withdrawn in comparison
with his loud and extroverted woman, used to joke that if people irritated
him he just threatened them with Olga, and the enemies would drop off. I
doubt that he or the other men would accept as readily being the distinctly
weaker party, but they liked women who could fend for themselves and share
a rough life. A few couples with criminal backgrounds even talked about
themselves in a way that gave a slightly romanticized image of partnerships
à la Bonnie and Clyde. The most extreme was a tattered couple that I met
at the station. They had been together for fifteen years, most of the time
through correspondence from different Zones. He had served twenty-four
years altogether and she eighteen, but they always met up between sentences,
only to be arrested again: "Burglaries, usually," the man said, "except for
this armed robbery—she had the pistol and I ripped off their jewels. . . . She
got twelve years because she refused to tell them where she hid the gun.
I received only seven." He gave her an admiring glance—she had an infection in the jaw that prevented her from speaking—and said tenderly that this
time they had been together for as long as a month.

Pasha and Natasha played with similar notions when they talked about
themselves. They met in the TB hospital in Pavlovsk, where Pasha was sent
after his last sentence. His co-patient Natasha, twenty years younger, promptly
abandoned a husband and a dull domestic life for his sake, and once out of
hospital they spent two years wandering among acquaintances, stairways, and
rented rooms, surviving on occasional jobs and petty thefts. They liked to
emphasize their equal partnership in everything, and Pasha talked with particular delight about a period when his TB was bad and *she* sold potatoes in
the market while *he* thoroughly enjoyed being a "housewife," *domokhoziaika,*
in their rented room. When I met them, they were living with Sasha, Pasha's
old Zone mate. As they told it, he was simply incorporated into their equal
partnership and now they all lived for each other, combining the passionate
friendship between Sasha and Pasha with the passionate love between Pasha
and Natasha.

I have no idea about the reality concealed behind these stories; my point
here is merely how couples—not least the men—like to *represent* themselves
as equal partners. Pasha made his housewife period sound like a nihilistically
inverted gender order, but far from everybody would see a woman supporting her unemployed and sick man as particularly rebellious. I am not sure if
the equal partnership openly stated by some, and implicitly acted by others,

can be seen as some sort of alternative model according to which lovers may interpret their mutual needs and responsibilities. In order to do so, I would prefer it to be more explicitly elaborated upon by social scientists. According to Lindquist (1994), the breadwinner model was not ubiquitous in the Soviet period, but she gives an account of egalitarian practices in the context of educated, intellectual professionals. The admiration for tough women that I observed seems on the contrary to be connected with a life on the margins of the law and established society, even if the criminal subculture provides no cultural idioms of gender equality—in fact, it is genuinely sexist (Chalidze 1977, 51–53).

When Olga understood that she was pregnant, she and Kostia abandoned their former equal partnership for dreams about a more conventional gender order. Earlier, Kostia did not mind being in the background behind Olga, but now he became obsessed with the future responsibility of fatherhood, repeatedly reassuring everybody around that "no matter what, even if *I* perish, I'll provide for Olga and the baby." Olga loved being pregnant and boasted delightfully about her craving for tomatoes and kefir. An elderly mate of theirs, *Dedushka* (Grandpa), took over Olga's work when she felt tired, and more and more frequently she would sit quietly on her own (nobody at the station had hitherto heard of Olga being silent) just caressing Grandpa's puppy, "the little one" as she called it. Options of future habitation were discussed, such as rented rooms or heated basement localities where one could live in exchange for work. Olga eagerly and vividly described how the men would go to work in the mornings and how she would take care of the home, the baby, and the puppy, and Kostia confidently vowed that he would give her this future.

In the autumn Grandpa disappeared mysteriously and was replaced by Kostia's younger brother, recently returned from the Zone. Olga's moods took a turn for the worse. Kostia drank too much, she complained, and he was inattentive to her growing need of support. A month later the romance was over. The last time I saw Olga she was not talking much. She had had an abortion, she said (in the fifth month, by my reckoning), and was sleeping in the washroom again. A strange nausea prevented her from both eating and drinking, and she had lost more than twenty pounds. Kostia did not make any comment at all, but Vova said that he had grown tired of Olga's nagging. Perhaps he realized that the entire thing was *real* and not just a daydream—which Olga had probably discovered earlier, and so she nagged—and that the impending parental and matrimonial responsibilities were an impossible burden. And once his brother was there, he had family anyway. I always wondered what happened to Olga, whom I liked very much but never saw again. I could never get myself to ask Kostia, whom I saw repeatedly over the years but never managed to like after that.

In Kostia and Olga's case, the emergent need of a home was enough to ruin the relationship. Before they even got access to a makeshift place to stay, they began to perceive their mutual needs in accordance with the traditional economy of complementary needs that was impossible to realize in their lived reality. One may object that this model is in fact impossible to realize in *any* reality besides that of the very wealthy, a scarce category anywhere and even more so in Russia at the time. Nevertheless, a home (or the expectation of one) implies the basic division between waged work and domestic life on which this model rests, and this seems to be enough for it to prevail as a general ideal. In my own field it seemed as if the roofless couples were not even trying to construct their mutual needs in terms of separate duties of providing, as if the idea as such does not appear without at least an imaginary division of life into public versus private spheres.

Semi-Domestic Love

In contrast to roofless lovers, semi-domestic couples readily accepted the economy of complementary needs. Homeless people who found makeshift accommodation and brought their partners there, as well as those who had affairs with domestics, embraced it as readily as any other Russian. However, this economy applied only when the man and not the woman provided the place to stay. The few men I knew who suddenly had access both to housing and to a dependent woman were perfectly enchanted, at least initially, and so were the women. A soup kitchen patron called Foma was positively beaming with bliss when he burst out: "She's got *nobody* but me! She's all *alone!*" In his early forties, Foma was officially a Pavlovsk patient after a decade or so in the Zone, but in practice he was living in the apartment of a recently deceased friend. He had a minimum tuberculosis pension as well.[2] His beloved was a younger Russian woman who had arrived on her own from the Far East and whose immensely thick spectacles did indeed make her look somewhat lost. They were madly in love, and when I left for Sweden in late 1999, Foma was still exuding an aura of pride and self-confidence. Unfortunately his responsibility as a provider evidently became too much for him. I saw him again only in the spring of 2002, tattered and harried, and he told me that he had just left the Zone: "I broke into a *dacha,* but it belonged to a cop so they actually investigated the case and I was put away." He bluntly turned down all questions about the woman, but I assume that he would not have attempted a burglary had he been able to support two persons on his minimal pension.

I never heard men staying with women complain about unmanly dependence, but they tended to frame it as a temporary necessity. Ostensibly, Pasha emphasized Natasha's potency when he talked about his time as a housewife, but he nevertheless described this period as a contingency caused by his TB. When Sergei was still supporting Nadia and the baby and providing them with a room, he happily boasted about his responsibilities, but later, when he was ill and she got a dvornik job and he did not, he was quite content to be at home changing diapers. As long as the inversion was short-lived, the man was able to view his dependence as temporary, without experiencing the frustration of being superfluous that other researchers observe among unemployed or low-paid Russian men (Khukhterin 2000). In general, it seemed that when circumstances permitted a traditional enactment of gender, most men and women appreciated it, but when the stage was undoubtedly homeless, they accepted a template based on equality and partnership. If circumstances forced them to, they even reversed established gender orders without much lament—at least temporarily. The issue was, with reference to Olga's and Kostia's sad love story, never to mix the different dimensions up.

A few younger women and men claimed to have had affairs with *established* domestics, the kind that have propiski and places of their own and who thus may become a way out of homelessness, but these prospective partners rarely manifested themselves in practice. Marriages with such domestics were, moreover, the central theme of a category to explain disappearances, at least of young and attractive people. (People like Vova were usually supposed to be dead or imprisoned if they failed to turn up for a long time.) "He married some rich woman and moved to the east somewhere," said the station regulars after Boris's mysterious disappearance. "I'm getting married and he'll register me, so I'm out of here soon," said a woman at the shelter whose lover remained unknown and unseen by the others. "He's a sportsman and doesn't drink and he has proposed," said Viktoria in September 2001. "She got married and everything is fine," said Viktoria's former shelter mates about Viktoria three months later. Viktoria apparently made it, but to what extent the subjects in other stories actually got married, received a propiska, and lived happily ever after, I obviously cannot tell since the ones who did by definition disappeared from my field.

A less idealized way of expressing an affair with a domestic is "sex for a place to stay." General differences in wealth between men and women, as well as gendered differences in the willingness to support and be supported materially by one's partner, suggest that women survive this way more often than men. Sustenance strategies of the sort are also more stigmatizing to women, since the label of "prostitute" is generally attached to males with less ease than to females. The only one who frankly stated situations in such terms was, accordingly, Lyosha. As he was relatively attractive and skilled in flirting, his housing arrangements from time to time involved stays with domestic women. Disillusioned or just afraid of boasting too soon, he always summed up his affairs as balanced exchanges in which both parties contributed alcohol—the main raison d'être—whereas his unique contribution was sex, and hers a roof over his head. In this sense these affairs were akin to his similar frequent stays with domestic alcoholics (replace "sex" with "food"). They ended when Lyosha departed of his own accord, either because the alcohol was about to kill him or because the woman had replaced him with a man who was better equipped both in terms of alcohol provision and sex. As he concluded his last affair: "I found her and this stranger unconscious in bed, and on one side there was a heap of bottles and on the other a pile of used condoms. I understood that we didn't need each other any longer, so I left."

Lyosha was quite alone in stating things in this blunt fashion. The economy of complementary needs includes much subtler emotional cravings than sexual satisfaction. "He is mean, stupid, and conceited," forty-eight-year-old Ksenia summed up the character of her then boyfriend and cohab. He was an ex-con, "only a silly little twenty-five-year-old" (Ksenia is very youthful in appearance), who had a job unloading trucks and was renting a flat. "But I sort of got hooked on him," Ksenia said, "I guess I feel sorry for him. He would be all on his own without me—who on earth needs such a wretched bore?" After a rhetorical pause, she added ironically: "And who on earth needs to sleep in a stairway?" Ksenia did not like being "kept," but the view of the relationship as an exchange of complementary needs legitimated her side of the deal. She justified their cohabitation by the coincidence of her need of a roof over her head and his need of her care and attention; as she saw it, his needs were more urgent than hers, which gave her an advantage. As I interpreted her, however, the main need that her man satisfied was not a place to stay but Ksenia's need to be useful to someone else: to be a "somebody" rather than an "anybody" in an infinite mass of "everybodies."

I assume that her volunteer job at the Caritas soup kitchen (before she left in a fury because of the corrupt staff, that is) served the same purpose, but without her pitiful boyfriend it would nonetheless have been difficult for her to feel needed to the same extent. Love affairs provided a unique niche in which particular relationships to "significant others" were allowed to flourish, while homeless togetherness at large was subject to natural laws and unspoken rules that effectively prevented people from becoming "some-bodies" to each other. It is admittedly easier to become friends with people whom one can find in the first place, but trust and intimacy, the social quali-ties for which everyone so longed, were not inhibited only by the contin-gency and unpredictability of homeless everyday life. They were effectively prevented also by the near-universal distrust and suspicion against those who cannot be determined territorially and genealogically, an anxiety from which not even the uprooted themselves are exempt when they confront each other. I suppose that infatuated couples escaped this logic because human roots quite literally originate in erotic desire; because a man and a woman are conceptualized as a nascent family, the beginning of "close ones." Still, there was a togetherness of sorts available even to the outcasts, because in spite of distrust and disregard they all knew that survival hinged on mutual help. This makeshift neededness took everybody's inescapable replaceability into ac-count: it invited each and everybody without reservation, and with an equal lack of discrimination it stripped each and everybody of anything that could set them apart from others.

I will continue to elaborate on the issues of anonymity and sameness, as these products of the leveling force of homelessness affect not only the re-lationships between people but individual human bodies as well. The next chapter discusses the struggle for a decent physical appearance, a crucial fac-tor in homeless perceptions of humanness that determines not only who is a "somebody" but who is alive or not as well. In this context, I will also bring up a question that has been implicit throughout this book—how does one get used to it all?

CHAPTER 6

Dirt, Degradation, and Death

One day Raia introduced me to a man of her own age, a good fellow, she said, whom she had known for ages. They resembled each other enough that I spontaneously asked if he was her brother. I knew that Raia had grown up in an orphanage, but some orphans stay in touch with their siblings when they were adults (for instance Zina and her brother). I was wrong, of course, and the two of them were quite amused by my mistake. "Of *course* we resemble each other," the man laughed, "*all* bomzhi look the same!" I told them that this likeness had to do with their eyes and eyebrows, not bad teeth or lack of teeth, swollen faces or hollow faces, broken noses or misplaced noses, or all the other physiognomic effects of street life. Raia shook her head. No, she insisted, what I was seeing was merely the capacity of "this life" to turn all faces into one and the same bomzh. "I was beautiful when I was young," she said with a nostalgic smile, "and very photogenic too. And now I'm wrinkled, graying, and toothless. Just like everybody else." But, she added, this was not a justification for allowing oneself to ignore one's looks. For *her* part, she always kept herself clean and took care to look decent. I could not object: alert for new clothes and willing to work for them, Raia was usually rewarded for her efforts, and this day she was wearing not only a pair of new, striped trousers but a nice leather jacket too. Far from all bomzhi at the station, Raia concluded, made an effort to look like human beings, as if it was the same to them whether they were dead or alive.

"Looking human" was a perennial concern that Raia shared with most other homeless people. As they saw it, a decent appearance was the most manifest proof of one's willingness and capacity to work, which in turn separated human beings from typical bomzhi. Underlying themes in these negotiations were death and life and the boundary separating the two; sameness, the one face that all bomzhi sooner or later acquire; and adaptation and resistance. To Raia and the others, a decent physical appearance was directly linked to the capacity to withstand the destructive impact of homelessness, a centripetal force that forcefully strips humans and their bodies of individual differences until nothing remains of their former humanity—not even life. The crux of the matter is that survival requires the ability to endure and cope with dehumanization— but too much adaptation is dangerous. The homeless understanding of human appearance has the potential to resolve this dilemma, for while being modified in accordance with the homeless reality, it draws a manifest boundary against excess adaptation, and thereby between life and death.

Parts of this chapter are closely related to the discussion in chapter 3 about space and its misuse. After all, filth spreads to human bodies from the floors and walls of sleeping places and from garbage bins and puddles in daytime hangouts, and nobody becomes cleaner by receiving a violent thrashing. The *understandings* related to filth are an intra-bomzh concern, however, created and maintained in the social interaction between homeless people. In this sense, dirt continues the discussion about social relationships in the preceding chapter. Dirt is, in addition, a suitable conclusion to this book, for in the opinion of its principal actors, death is merely the ultimate immersion in dirt, and as such the end of the story.

Letting Oneself Go

When Raia said that *she* kept herself clean while others did not bother to do so, she nodded towards Vova, who was talking to somebody else not far away from us. It was early September, and I had hardly seen him for almost three months. Some time in mid-May, his drinking had increased sharply, and he began to miss our appointments at the station. When I finally bumped into him, he was drunk and unshaven, with soiled and shabby clothes, and the remaining tufts on his balding head were growing over his ears. Unconcerned by his looks and as assertive as ever, he promptly insisted that we resume our work together. During the next month and a half, we did so occasionally. Sometimes I refused because he was too drunk, other times he did not turn up at all, and once in a while everything worked out as well as ever before.

Throughout this time, other station regulars conscientiously informed me about his doings and, in particular, about his appearance, and they were jubilant rather than merely emphatic. Apparently they socialized and drank with him as much as ever, but in his absence they never failed to make assertive juxtapositions of the same kind as Raia had: "*I* keep myself clean, but look at *him,* hardly human any longer!" I knew this genre of talk already quite thoroughly. Shabby ragamuffins were always pointed out as "typical" bomzhi by people who wanted to underline their own capacity to keep themselves afloat. It did not necessarily imply dissociation in practice; more than once, I saw morally enraged critics drinking together with the objects of their censure only hours after the repudiation.

Sometimes the juxtapositions that constituted bomzh talk, as I called it in my field notes, highlighted other qualities than cleanliness, such as diligence and decency to others: "OK, perhaps I'm a bomzh, but I'm still *human*—at least I'm working," or "at least I don't steal from people I know, just look at X, never accepts a hard day's work, he is a parasite on everybody else." Physical appearance trumped all other virtues, however, and someone who elevated his or her own goodness or inclination to work but did not meet the standards with regard to looks was easily dismissed by others with the sarcastic words: "So what if he's making money and helps others, if he can't even keep himself clean!"

The hierarchy is logical. Hygiene is one of the life-sustaining essences for which human beings work in the first place, and a decent appearance is one of the fruits of a particular form of labor, besides food and a place to sleep. As Shilling puts it, "Body work is the most immediate and most important form of labor that humans engage in" (1993, 118). In extreme situations hygiene does not necessarily take precedence, but it was nonetheless considered absurd to boast about *success* in material matters if one cannot keep oneself clean—as bizarre as making a fortune but denying oneself food and sleep. Kindness, in turn, is not inherently dependent on hygiene, but physical appearance is still a form of communication, and dirtiness implies some sort of disrespect to those who have to look at you or put up with your bodily odors. As one woman said about Vova: "And he came up to me, all greasy and soiled, and wanted a cigarette, but I told him off...." Her indignation was concerned with his appearance, not his request: somehow the former turned the latter into an insult. Such comments were common, but they rarely resulted in practical ostracism—this woman happily shared the content of a bottle *and* her tobacco with Vova not long after she refused him the cigarette.

Vova reveled in bomzh talk previously, and quite a few people probably enjoyed getting back at him because he used to be so boastful. Nevertheless, a handful of people seemed genuinely anxious about him. Papik told me that he did his best to take care of Vova. He fed him and tried to lure him to the washrooms for a shave and a wash, but Vova showed no interest. "I've tried everything," Papik said with exasperation, "but that bloody bomzh just doesn't *want* to! Perhaps I've lost my passport, but I still have my legs, my hands, and my head—and I'm still able to *shave*! I tried to give him these new razors, but he didn't even look at them—he's completely let himself go!"

That was what everybody else said too, and they all used the same verb, *opustit'sia*, which means to sink, the way a ship sinks. I could translate it as "giving up" since this is what people do who let themselves go, but opustit'sia also stresses a downward direction and suggests a subsequent immersion in something. Not only the homeless use it; it is a general expression for going down the drain. *Opushchennyi* is Zone jargon for the lowest stratum in the internal hierarchy of male prisoners. The grammatical form indicates that the unfortunate was cast out by the others, in this case most likely frozen out or gratuitously raped by his co-prisoners because he violated some point of accepted Zone conduct. A corresponding form, *opustivshii,* suggests that the person let himself or herself go of his or her own accord.[1] In common parlance the opustivshie still *did* something to wreck their lives, usually with the help of bottles or syringes. Papik and the others did not use the word any differently, but the connotation with passivity was particularly evident in their discussions. Bomzhi do not let themselves go because anybody—they or others—*does* anything. They are already drinking, and they are humiliated and excluded from the start. Bomzhi let themselves go because they *stop* acting, in the same way that any living creature sinks when it ceases treading water. There are no external reasons for this capitulation. The process is often framed as a loss of will, as when Papik stated that Vova no longer *wanted* to be clean. The hygienic concerns are just the tip of the iceberg; it is the desire to belong to the world of humans, and ultimately to live, that those who no longer *want* to have lost. "Letting oneself go" is also perceived as a lack of strength, although I heard this more often when the capacity *not* to let oneself go was explained: "Some people are just stronger than others, *I'll* never end up like that." The two are, as I take it, seen as interdependent, even synonymous: you need strength to desire, and desire strengthens. In this context I therefore refer to the combination as willpower.

Willpower was seen as inseparable from self-respect, *samouvazhenie.* "You don't respect yourself if you live in filth," one man at the station explained, "and if you lose your self-esteem, you've lost everything else too, you just don't care any more. In this situation [being homeless], you must be strong.

You can't allow yourself to accept dirt, for if you do, it takes over—your mind goes the same way, it'll be filled with dirt too. You'll end up letting yourself go like that bomzh over there—he doesn't even care about lice any more!" (He was pointing at an extremely ragged old man not far from us who was busy scratching himself.) As I understood him and many others, self-respect means to persist in the claim that, after all, in spite of being excluded and needed by nobody, one is a human being and thereby by definition entitled to inclusion in the social world of humans. This assurance is the source of willpower, the task of which is to justify the claim to humanness. Humanness can manifest in other ways too, but the primary core of willpower is nonetheless a never-ending combat against the aggressive attacks of dirt on the most immediate battlefield—the surface of the human body.

Physical appearance is always paramount in social personhood and in the ways in which human subjects understand themselves. The outside is always taken to reflect, or even constitute, an inside, and an unapproved appearance tends to have the power to put other humanizing traits in question—be it the wrong kind of clothes or dirtiness and physical decay. Physical appearance gains importance, I suggest, in circumstances when there is nothing *else* left that may tell yourself and others who you are, and when an acceptable look cannot be taken for granted. I have shown how the homeless negotiated capacities and values that conventionally are seen to distinguish humans from bomzhi, how they adapted them to their own reality. Merits such as readiness to work, sobriety, adherence to the law, and trustworthiness are, as I have emphasized, difficult to realize in the homeless practice, and even loyalty to "one's own" is an ambiguous virtue in a social environment where everybody involved knows that sociability has a price and that one must guard one's integrity at all times. In a similar way, a number of other assets that are conventionally significant to social personhood were deemed irrelevant when humanness and "bomzh-ness" were discussed at railway stations and soup kitchens.

Some of my informants argued that they were not bomzhi in the first place because they actually had a propiska, although they could not live at the address in question. In a similar way, certain nonlocals claimed to have a place to live somewhere, which in their view disqualified them as bomzhi. Others argued that they were not *real* bomzhi thanks to non-homeless lovers who would marry them and give them a propiska as soon as various obstacles were overcome. A handful of people set themselves apart as intellectuals, and this cultured and educated background was to them an antidote to bomzh-ness. They put forward these assets as if they were some sort of capital in Bourdieu's (1986) sense—be it economic (a house), social (lovers), or cultural (education)—that could potentially insure them against the stigma of being bomzh.

On the other hand, they did not seem to expect other homeless people to take this implicit claim seriously; references of the kind were generally made to me personally, like some initial justification that "between the two of us, you know, *I* shouldn't really be here." When I asked others if they believed it, they just shrugged and said that of course, *everything* is possible, but who cares? Since the houses were somewhere else, the lovers had not yet intervened, and the past was behind once and for all, the capital was helplessly misplaced, spatially or temporarily. What cannot be displayed here and now was completely extraneous to the present situation and even more irrelevant with regard to humanness than half-attainable traits such as sobriety, diligence, or loyalty to one's mates. I think of this selectiveness as some sort of economy, or hierarchy, of relevance. Traits that conventionally turn samples of *Homo sapiens* into social persons in established society were reduced by rationalization according to their relevance in "this life," homelessness, or cut down to an absolute minimum within reach of everybody. The core of that minimum was the surface of one's body, the one thing of which not even a homeless person can be deprived.

Public Baths, Discarded Clothes, and Modified Norms

A reasonable question is to what extent cleanliness can actually be attained by people whose access to bathrooms, toilets, and laundries is by definition impaired. The general opinion among the homeless was that, in spite of abundant obstacles, relative hygiene was within the reach of everybody. Hence, Vova had no excuses in the opinion of Papik, Raia, and the others. As a station regular, he was even privileged, because railway stations are designed for travelers, a temporarily displaced category with needs similar to those of the homeless. The only criterion at the station was good relations with the washroom attendants. Raia had problems with many of them, and as an emergency solution she kept in touch with a number of domestics merely for the sake of their bathrooms. Vova, however, was a born diplomat without any inclination to become troublesome when drunk, and he was admitted regardless of his looks or his state of intoxication. There are no showers in the washrooms, but the facilities nonetheless seemed to satisfy the basic hygienic needs, and station regulars as well as travelers used them with great inventiveness. Katia the Colonel washed her hair in the sinks every day, after which she rolled it up on curlers and blow-dried it before setting off to work. The men's room was an informal barbershop: according to Andrei Half-Finger, there was always someone hanging out there who knew how to cut hair, because most men who have ever been incarcerated for a substantial length of time learn this in prison.

In the late 1990s, cleanliness was not unattainable to people who shunned the station either, thanks to the generous amount of refuse space all over the city. Certain basements had running water, sometimes even heated, and attics at least offered privacy to those with the energy to carry water all the way up the stairs. The most important support was (and remains) the public bath, a sanctuary for many housed citizens as well. The early Soviet state did not fully include hygiene in its housing plans, and I know people who to this day live in kommunalki without bathrooms or who prefer the *bania* because they share the bathroom with too many neighbors or certain intolerable neighbors. Most public bani have reduced fees once a week, in 1999 a few rubles only, which even the homeless could afford. People who are excessively dirty, look ill, or seem to have lice, are not likely to be let in, but there are public *prozharki,* a form of delousing or disinfection centers. Before he let himself go, Vova was a keen supporter of this alternative. *Pro* means "through," and *zhar* ("heat") is the root of *zharit',* "fry"; according to him, this is what the prozharka does: it heats all clothes until the vermin die, and in the meantime the client takes a shower and receives treatment for head lice. They even provided new underwear, Vova said enthusiastically.

Davis notes that in Los Angeles, a particularly sadistic method of keeping homeless people and similar misfits out of the upscale city center is to close the public toilets (1998, 233). Instead, the public are encouraged to use the services of restaurants and other places that have the legal right to turn away people they do not like. From my experience as a traveler, I assume that throbbing bladders and bursting rectums are one of the most mortifying aspects of being homeless in hypermodern metropolises, although scientific works on homelessness rarely if ever comment on it. Even if public toilets do exist, they cost money, and refuse spaces are perpetually on the retreat. St. Petersburg is no exception from the latter tendency, but the maze of interconnected yards that constitute the central part of the city is so immense that secluded but accessible spots will remain plentiful for many years to come. In 1999, neither homeless people nor tipsy night walkers faced any problems in relieving themselves in some out-of-the-way corner even in the central parts of the city.

Keeping one's *body* clean was thus not the main dilemma. "The problem is to wash *clothes,*" an elderly woman told me. "There's just no way to solve this—it's prohibited to do it in the bania, so I try to get away with it behind their [the bania attendants'] backs. They scold you if they discover you, and the bad ones even force you to leave. But even if it works, I still have to dry the laundry, and one doesn't really display one's knickers in a stairway, right? So one tries the attic, and in the summer it might dry in a night, but otherwise it takes at least three days, and by then someone is bound to have stolen it, because you can't really hang around for days like a watchdog, can you?" Laundromats are an unknown phenomenon in Russia, and the charities do not provide such services to the homeless (which would be far more useful to them than soup or powdered milk). "So I've given up the laundry totally," the woman concluded, "and now I just get rid of my old clothes on the spot if I find new ones." This was a common solution—people were often busy changing clothes behind Nochlezhka's office, discarding the old ones in a permanent heap of constantly changing contents. Visitors who did not find anything in the office sometimes took a look in this pile as well, seemingly trying to judge whether the things in it were worse than whatever they happened to be wearing.

"Rough sleepers" thus changed outfits very often, unless they had access to places where items could be washed or stored. Vova was wearing different clothes each time I met him, usually about every second or third day. At times the frayed sleeves and soiled collars of his coats were as striking as the apparent disintegration of his shoes, and two days later he might turn up with boots of good quality, spotless pants, and a presentable trenchcoat. His lavish drinking habits accelerated the pace of the eternal "find-use-lose-find-use-ruin" cycle, but others would cherish good outdoor clothes and shoes for considerable periods of time. I do not know if Vova swapped his good things for alcohol, if they were stolen from him, or if he simply ruined them due to the frequent and close contact with terra firma that drunkenness implies. He destroyed a nice leather jacket I gave him for his birthday by passing out next to a wall that, as it turned out, was covered with a fresh coat of white paint. I stopped investing money or labor in his looks after that; he found new things with astounding speed anyway, even if the replacements did not always match what he had lost.

The appearance of charities in the late 1990s improved the supply of clothes. Before, somebody assured me, everybody wore *vatniki*, felted coats that are generally associated with the Zone or with peasants. In 1999 men wore jackets in the summer, and it was even possible to get hold of leather jackets, the coat that both men and women were most fond of. Shoes were a chronic problem for everybody, in particular with the onset of winter, and people with odd sizes always had a hard time. Viktoria shuffled between

Figure 11. Vova on a good day. Photograph by the author.

charities in a pair of worn-down slippers for almost a month that summer, because her feet were larger than those of the average female charity donor. I was surprised myself that not more people wore *valen'ki,* felted boots, but the winter of 1999 was mild, and this footgear—cheap, the warmest one can find, and worn with galoshes—is more suited to a considerably colder climate.

Besides being changed frequently, clothes were of widely varying quality and came in odd sizes and combinations as well. Men's clothes have the advantage of being easier to combine—in general. *Most* trousers can usually be paired with *most* jackets or sweaters to give a relatively coherent overall impression. Disparate women's clothes are more difficult to put together without running into oddities: a coat that in itself is elegant may be seriously at odds with one's old boots and a plain pair of trousers. If the weather permits a skirt, it may be a disaster combined with the training suit jacket that was the best haul of yesterday. At Nochlezhka and the Salvation Army, quite a few available garments were, moreover, without doubt donated by babushki (or their heirs) and looked parodic on younger women. There was plenty of feminine women's clothing—skirts, thin blouses, dresses—which was neither very hardwearing nor suited for permanent outdoor use (which was, I assume, why it tended to remain where it was). The logic of the donors was sometimes bewildering: one October day, about thirty female swimsuits were bequeathed to Nochlezhka, and in the late winter somebody brought in a large sack full of bright white nylon stockings, the kind requiring suspenders. (In the end they were braided into an intricate stage decoration at a charity ball.)

Women related differently to this plurality. Most female stairway dwellers kept to the same basic outfit that men used: sweaters, trousers, and in the winter large coats, the warmest boots available, and some sort of woolen headgear. They did not necessarily wear men's clothes, but the kind of leisure wear that is most practical and easiest to combine is for that very reason not very gender-specific in the first place. For women who resented looking like a babushka, the choice was basically to settle for this variant or to look distinctly weird. Supply, weather, and mood allowed for exceptions, but a relatively unisex look appeared to be the basic point of departure, from which variations might or might not emerge. One sunny but cold spring morning, Kostia's Olga staggered up to me on high heels, dressed in a pleated skirt and nylons. "Just a whim," she laughed, "and damned idiotic too—I thought I'd celebrate spring, but I'm bloody freezing to death in this outfit!" Otherwise Olga always wore baggy pants and heavy coats, but this time favorable external circumstances evidently coincided with a good mood. She certainly took delight in the change, but as I understood her, this single excursion into femininity had nothing to do with the serious issue of looking human. It seemed more like a welcome chance for pleasure and play, for the sake of the weather, a good mood, or just for the hell of it.

Somebodies Rather than Anybodies: Gender and Class

"Looking like a human" was not so much an expression of how one ideally wanted to look as an indication of what one could get away with among other homeless people without being upbraided. Most people settled for this minimum level, while some worked hard to exceed it—men to the same extent as women, although the quest for a respectable appearance was more time-consuming to women for the reasons mentioned above. Usually, these people had access to comparatively good sleeping quarters; if not the shelter or the waiting hall at the station, then at least a good basement, unless—as in Raia's case—they had domestic contacts where they could store and wash things. To many of them, good clothes were merely part and parcel of a broader set of ambitions to exit homelessness or, failing that, to endure it in a less miserable fashion than an average bomzh. Neat or fashionable looks were instrumental to those looking for jobs or going *po instantsiiam* (visiting administrative offices) or working to improve their material standard in other ways. Shelter resident Marina, an ambitious job hunter, was thus always dressed for a job interview, matching neat slacks and cardigans with white blouses, and with a thorough application of makeup and a chic scarf around her neck. At the station, the prices of the prostitutes rose in direct proportion to how well-dressed they were. According to their male friends, "crafts" like picking pockets and petty fraud were equally benefited by a respectable appearance. As a simultaneous proof of success, clothes were also the first thing that Katia the Colonel and Boris and his gang brought up when boasting about their relative prosperity. (It is telling that few if any of the prostitutes at the Moscow Station appealed to overtly sexualized images of femininity; rather, they tried to be trendy and expensive.)

Even to those who did *not* succeed, a decent look apparently served as a token of one's imperviousness to disappointments and hardships. Marina's interviews never resulted in anything, but she still persisted, even though her gear suited neither the occasional jobs that she actually found nor the endless days of gathering bottles. In spite of the bleak reality, Marina put on her lipstick each morning and patiently endured the colds she caught due to the failure of her fashionable boots to resist puddles, mud, and slush. To her, dressing well appeared to be the last way of remaining "somebody," of keeping out of the ranks of the anybodies and everybodies who basically accepted their homelessness and made the best of it, without hope of a solution. These mere humans struggled against letting themselves go and against death, while most well-dressed people fought their battle a step or two up the ladder.

People like Marina and the bomzh bourgeoisie at the station constituted a minority, and most women and men—even those who enjoyed the privilege of a shelter bed—adhered to a "merely human" look without complaint or comment. In reality, however, male standards applied to women but not the other way around, and I was somewhat puzzled by the readiness with which women seemingly accepted this imputed masculinity. Bodies are not neutered to begin with, and in Russian mainstream culture, gender differences are quite salient in everyday talk and symbolic petty practices. Ideas about the different and complementary nature of the masculine and the feminine are equally distinct (Attwood 1990; Ries 1994; Sperling 1999). A concern for one's physical appearance is seen as essential for femininity, and most women would agree that an female and attractive appearance is crucial for their sense of self (Roudakova and Ballard-Reisch 1994; Vainshtein 1996; Azhgikhina and Goscilo 1996). I therefore dwell somewhat on the masculinized sameness of homelessness and the efforts of certain people to avoid it, as this casts some additional light on the ways in which the most ingrained of cultural ideals may be negotiated in a reality in which concessions are always inescapable.

Among the homeless, gender appeared to be a non-issue with regard not only to physical appearance but also to life in general (or, rather, to "this life"). Aside from the sphere of work, which some women found more promising for men (but which some male station regulars considered to be more favorable to women), nothing was ever talked about in terms of gender—neither the capacity to survive nor the experience of not being needed. Men did not even emphasize their own humanness at the expense of women's purported lack of femininity, which I initially thought they would; neither men nor women expressed any concern about transgressions of female gender norms, regardless of how blatant they were. Raia was one of a handful of female cross-dressers at the station, but nobody seemed to be bothered neither by her masculine looks (a smart crew cut and leather jacket), nor by her explicit sexual preferences for women, nor by the fact that she considered herself to be "born in the wrong body altogether."[2] (None of this, I should add, prevented her from regretting that she had never had children—Raia never seemed to find motherhood incompatible with being a man.) She and a few other cross-dressers flirted incessantly with me, but I know nothing of the sexual orientation of many others. A number of younger women had occasional boyfriends but consistently dressed in men's clothes (a popular variant was shiny sport suits and brand-name sneakers) with short, boyish haircuts. All these women were as integrated as anybody else in the homeless crowds at the station or the charities. I do not know if Raia could have introduced a woman as her sweetheart and showed her affection openly—perhaps that would have been too much—but judging from the usual interactions, nobody seemed to find her personal inclinations in this respect in the least noteworthy. *Homeless* people did not care, that is. One Salvationist told me about her futile attempts to get a couple of the girls who favored men's clothes to dress in a more feminine way, "or else they will become lesbians, which is a disgrace against God." Against her expectations, one of them became pregnant, and she gave up her efforts, seemingly with a blend of relief, anxiety, and confusion.

One explanation to this apparent gender oblivion—if not aborted femininity—was provided to me indirectly by the former pianist Irina, and it had to do with social and cultural class.[3] She rarely brought up gender and femininity explicitly, but the categories nonetheless emerged when she talked about "culturedness," *kul'turnost'*, a central trope in everything she said about her life, "before" as well as "now." Irina was born in an intellectual family in the late 1930s and spent her youth working at the ballet and socializing with the cream of the creative intelligentsia. This cultured background, she always emphasized, with its sophisticated criteria with regard to hygiene and good taste, made her particularly unfit for life in the streets. Other homeless people, Irina sniffed with disdain, originated in social strata that the Soviet state had more or less trained to become bomzhi, and as such they would not be able recognize a decent physical appearance even if they did see one. "Ill-fitting clothes are the worst of it all," she used to grumble, "to be forced to look like a *caricature* all the time! I'm not *used* to this, you know!" Since her own inveterate standards were simply unattainable, further efforts on her part were likewise futile, and rather than actually trying to find good clothes, she limited herself to ironic comments about whatever she happened to be wearing. Nonetheless, Irina refused to give in on one point. Every month, right after picking up her minimum pension, she bought a manicure set and a pair of fancy knickers. The things were usually stolen within a few days, but for a week or so, at least, her fingernails would be evenly filed and brightly polished.

Irina displayed kul'turnost' not with a book but with nail polish, a token as feminine as any, and to her, I take it, there was no difference. Women are assumed to have a natural propensity for the associated capacities of refinement and moral elevation (cf. Peterson 1996:186f; Kay 1997, 93–97), as an articulation of the middle-class respectability that moulds conceptions of femininity in the modern world at large (c.f. Skeggs 1997). In Russia, however, "culture" has for a long time been perceived to be under siege from a ruthless and rough society, and it is largely a female mission to defend it— simply by insisting on being feminine. During the violent transition years, the antithesis of kul'turnost' was, in my own experience, largely articulated in terms of moral collapse and nihilistic brutality, while social research of the Soviet period rather tends to emphasize the homogenizing capacities of the system in contrast to individual expression. The limited range of unfashionable clothes and low-quality makeup somehow epitomized the simultaneous suffocation of culture, individuality, and femininity, and to many female intellectuals, the beauty parlor was not only a sanctuary from the subjugations of everyday life, *byt,* but also a site of resistance of sorts (Azhgikhina and Goscilo 1996, 107ff.).

To Irina, ugliness and sameness were thus the same thing as Sovietness, and those who once upon a time accepted the latter—that is, everybody but dissidents such as herself—therefore lacked culturedness and any feeling for distinction, femininity, and beauty. These uncultured masses were thus, according to Irina, typical bomzhi from the very beginning, and in effect they had lost nothing and missed nothing once they ended up at the Moscow Station. As a further emphasis, she always used the term *sovok,* literally "dustpan," a derogatory nickname for the Soviet society as well as a typically Soviet person. Regardless of sex, bomzhi as well as *sovki* looked the same, behaved the same, and smelled the same.

Irina's argument is a (very crude) blueprint of Bourdieu's elaborations on good taste and the imprints of class on bodies, and I do not object to the idea that it would have been easier to negotiate with ideal notions of physical appearance for those who originated in social strata where such compromises had always been a necessity (Bourdieu 1984). However, the "cultured classes" had never been immune to concessions either, and Irina had in fact spent most of her adult life doing things that she was not used to doing. After a disastrous divorce, she had to leave a large, well-appointed apartment for a tiny room in a kommunalka full of what she considered to be a bunch of uncouth sovki. She had to accept a physically demanding job in an industrial kitchen, which forced her to abandon her six-year-old son to an orphanage. At the age of sixteen he returned as a crude ruffian with whom she quarreled for fifteen more years—years that she survived by selling newspapers in the street—until he literally threw her down the stairs, after which she decided never to return home. When I met her, the cultured life that she always referred to had thus been history for a quarter of a century, and her incapacity to adapt was not, as she would have it, merely a matter of ingrained habits. Rather, it was the only remainder of an identity to which she still desperately clung, and her nail polish served the same purpose as the Soviet beauty parlor, as the only available way to refuse publicly her immersion in "this life" and its people.

As I see it, the categories worked in a similar way for everybody who took pains to dress well. Gender was not primary, it was merely embedded in, and inseparable from, whichever "not bomzh" identity they opted for, be it some sort of mainstream respectability or a more sophisticated kul'turnost'. Femininity was particularly at stake, and not only because of the meager supply of decent women's clothes. On a conceptual level, homeless women are a contradiction in terms (Wardhaugh 2000, 75), which can been seen in the telling official silence about their existence; it's not too much to say that those who, against all odds, can be said to exist are considered to have forfeited their womanhood. Of the many remarks I received about bomzhi in general, only a handful specifically concerned women, and they all included the precise phrase: "they're no longer women. . . ." However, homelessness is not exactly fertile soil for the cultivation of socially accepted males either. The stereotype bomzh is a powerless, emasculated figure analogous to the refuse spaces he inhabits, far from what Connell (1995) calls hegemonic masculinity. As the stage is set, homeless men and women alike live in a second-rate man's world. Men who want to dissociate themselves from this marginality can only upgrade their maleness socially, and they do this the same way that women do, by attending to their physical appearance. So, moreover, do female cross-dressers like Raia.

I do not doubt that the homeless took for granted that "this life" was emptied of anything associated with femininity, but I believe that they primarily perceived it as sameness, as an extinguishing of differences as such. After all, homeless women and men survive or die under comparatively similar conditions. Without a home and a family, the most basic divisions of labor disappear. Sustenance strategies are less gender-differentiated than the conventional labor market. The same weather compels both sexes to wear similar clothes, without which women and men are equally cold. Bodies—as Raia said—become more and more alike as "this life" takes its toll. Women and men take comfort in, or celebrate with, the same solvents, and they risk their lives in the same sleeping places and at the hands of the same policemen. And once the process of letting oneself go has reached its conclusion, men and women are equally dead.

Not *all* distinctions are extinguished. One significant divergence concerns sexuality and reproduction: differentiated bodies sometimes have sex, but only women need to go through excruciating abortions, and few if any men

take the responsibility for having an infant accepted at an orphanage. Nor do
I imply that homeless women and men are entirely oblivious to gender. Once
a year it is even celebrated in style, for not even homelessness can kill the an-
nual cycle of festivities. On March 8, Women's Day, there was thus a grand
drinking spree at the station, and the male regulars duly presented flowers to
the ladies (always mimosas) and paid for their Bomi. Nonetheless, conventional gender distinctions in the homeless reality are reduced to an absolute
minimum. The relative sameness with regard to everyday life and, not least,
everyday death makes, I suggest, men as well as women generally conceive of
humanness rather than male and female performances. At the same time, it is
implicitly acknowledged that it is impossible to be, act, or look like a woman
if you are homeless. In practice, this means that females cannot be repudiated
for transgressing conventional gender boundaries, any more than anybody
can be blamed for not having a home. Womanhood is as low in the homeless
hierarchy of relevance as distant houses, absent lovers, or the capacity to play
the piano, which is why the loudest protest against the de-gendering capacities of homelessness is the dull scrape of Irina filing her nails.

Things That Do Not Count

Besides women's lack of femininity, there were other conventionally stigmatizing features that amounted to little or nothing when humanness was
discussed. Street life, as well as the imprisonments that often precede it, leaves
imprints on the body, and a worn and haggard face is part and parcel of the
stereotype bomzh. Traces of violence (scars, broken noses, bruises), negli-
gent dental work, or, in the case of men, previous incarcerations (tattoos on
hands and fingers, very occasionally on eyelids) are, after all, far more common in a drinking gang at the station or at a soup kitchen than elsewhere
(Mil'ianenkov 1992; Condee 1999). Bad teeth were the norm: Vova's were
worn down to about half their original size, and Nadia and Sergei used to
joke that together they had five (one was his, the others hers). Marina lost
her original set of teeth in prison, and she forgot the replacements at a party
after she took them out to show the other guests how well-made they were.[4]
Certain physiognomies were bloated, the result of hard drinking and cold
sleeping places, whereas others were emaciated for identical reasons. Faces
react differently to the drinking habits of their owners: Vova's merely im-
ploded, while others inflated into purple balloons.

   In the opinion of the homeless, however, permanent marks on the body
had nothing to do with *self-neglect,* and accordingly, physiognomic characteristics

were never mentioned in the context of letting oneself go. Raia regretted her toothless and wrinkled appearance, but it was perfectly irrelevant to her feeling that she was capable of keeping herself afloat. It was a result not of her own actions but of the imprints of a hard life, and no human is truly responsible for the difficulty of finding nutritional food, for a violent world, for the pace of time itself, or even for the ravages of alcoholism. Raia defined herself as an incurable drunkard, but drinking was, to her and to most of the others, not a matter of choice but a facet of homelessness as inescapable as sleeping in attics or being beaten up. Vova was not criticized for the alcohol he consumed or for not being able to walk straight for most of the day. The only thing that mattered was that he failed to keep himself clean.

Accordingly, illness is not relevant to letting oneself go either, in spite of being one of the most feared traits of bomzhi, by the lights of the non-homeless world. The most stigmatizing disease, tuberculosis, is generally a result of the Zone, which in the shared idiom of the homeless more often appears as an unintended consequence of thoughtless and precipitate actions than as a justified punishment for a morally deplorable act. The proverb "*ot sumy i ot tiurmy ne zarekaisia*" is frequently quoted, which roughly means that nobody can safeguard himself from the beggar's bag or from prison. In the same way, wounds, upset stomachs, kidney problems, and so forth are inescapable effects of street life as such, and they indicate that someone is letting himself or herself go only if they are conspicuous *and* remain untended. Sometimes I even had the impression that people (in particular the elderly) felt *less* estranged from the non-homeless world when they complained about certain ailments. Diabetes, heart conditions, asthma, and a number of other illnesses befall bomzhi and others alike (even if homelessness does considerably aggravate them), as one of the few remaining aspects of existence that a bomzh shares with everybody else. The chronically ill cannot be blamed for their suffering, and the unfairness that makes up their daily lot is beyond doubt because they are deprived of their disability pension, a privilege that the state ought to bestow on any weak and exhausted citizen.

The understanding of letting oneself go is also adjusted in light of the inescapable reality that everyday homeless life implies exposure to contingencies. A drinking session, a beating, or just bad weather may destroy the best appearance in an instant, and it always takes some effort to get back in shape after such an ordeal. This pertains even to people whose contacts with domestics (and their bathrooms) or whose advantageous sleeping places make it possible for them to maintain a tidier appearance than that of the average stairway dweller. Several people in the "bomzh bourgeoisie" at the Moscow Station were real snobs, but even Katia the Colonel, Zhanna, and the purported boss Boris and his crew were subjected to incidents that compelled them to wear stained, torn, or soaked clothes for a day or so because they could not instantly get in touch with their domestic support. Stairway dwellers without such social capital could be compelled to wear dirty clothes for considerably longer periods of time, but people were not accused of letting themselves go until it was quite obvious that they no longer cared.

Notions such as "contingent" or "temporary" are relative, which implies room for negotiation. Vova tried to thwart the reproaches directed at him, but he was not very convincing. After he destroyed the leather jacket (I was angry) I told him directly that we all thought that he was letting himself go. Vova took a self-assured and relativistic stance and argued that he was as aware about tidiness and hygiene as ever. But the weather would be to the disadvantage of his looks for another couple of months, so he preferred to wait until the end of the autumn mudbath before acquiring new clothes, and *then* he would make sure to keep them clean. Papik and someone else who heard our conversation smirked behind his back. Vova had not cared about his looks for months, and the summer weather had been splendid. If he had looked so disheveled for only a few weeks, his arguments might have retained a surface plausibility, but by this time the expiration date for contingency was long overdue.

Vova tried to imply that he still had some self-respect, but that for the time being, he found it meaningless to manifest it corporeally. The labor would, as it were, not be a very lasting investment. According to the local ontology of letting oneself go, however, such a statement is simply oxymoronic. As this logic goes, neither self-respect nor its vehicle, willpower, really exists unless manifested externally. Even if these categories are talked about as innate capacities that it is theoretically possible to *have,* nobody else will believe in their existence unless they assume some tangible form. One has to *do* self-respect and willpower, and this implies labor. It was telling that Papik emphasized the limbs and organs used for working—arms, legs, head (implying brains)—in his outburst at Vova's refusal to accept the razors. The durability of the product—that is, a decent appearance—is immaterial, for it is the doing, the work itself, that confirms self-respect, not the result.

Lice—the Great Divide

The final exit from humanness, the ultimate symbol of going downhill and of the "typical" bomzh, is lice. One reason may be that they are in no way ambiguous or open to debate: they either bite or they do not, while dirtiness and cleanliness are always the outcome of some sort of negotiation. Moreover, lice itch and crawl and spread themselves, as living embodiments of the entire world of filth that incessantly attacks the homeless body and threatens to take it over. To put it in classical structuralist terms, as a physical environment that eats human beings instead of the other way around, they invert an established relationship between nature and culture. Conventionally, mankind wants to transform its habitat, and being bitten by this purported domain of human intervention is quite a tangible proof of failure.

To *get* lice was considered to be forgivable: at the station it might be enough to fall asleep near one of the warm pipes in the tunnels beneath the station. However, it was *not* forgivable not to take immediate measures. Ragged people scratching themselves provoked strong reactions among on-lookers. Loud curses were tossed around about "bloody inconsiderate bom-zhi" who do not seem to understand that lice are a collective matter, not only a personal issue. They were supposed to jump from person to person, but they could also provoke reactions directed against the wrong person. "The cops won't arrest someone who they think has lice even if he's completely plastered," Raia said once, with reference to an old man near us who was fervently rubbing his scalp. "So they grab the ones *next to him* instead," she said, furiously adding in his direction, "now, go away you dirty bomzh, we're not going to suffer for your sake!"

Most people said that they went to the prozharka if they were infected, but there were other cures. "I had a nap down in the tunnel," admitted Anna, a middle-aged station regular. "I should have known better, but I was drunk. Of course some bomzh had slept there just before I came, and his vermin were just waiting for a new host." Her usual way to get rid of lice was, she explained, to bleach her brown hair, a method that left it carrot-colored. Usually she did not mind: once a window-dresser, she had still connections in the art world, and the stark ginger tone matched her long, wide skirts and colorful berets perfectly. When I met her now, however, she had a rather unbecoming short haircut. This time the remedy worked a bit too well—not only did the lice die, but most of Anna's hair fell off too.

Another reason why lice are *the* end is that they give the authorities a reason to punish and brand. As I understood it, the prozharka uses some sort of shampoo. There are also mixtures available at the pharmacies. Neverthe-less, most other state institutions save the cost by simply shaving the head of the infected person. Street children of both sexes often have cropped hair, as the centers where the police drop them off tend to practice this method of disinfection. The pre-trial jails shave only when they discover lice, although there are frequent reports that they routinely make money on the side by stealing the long hair from females in custody (Alpern 2000b, 159ff.). In the Zone, men's heads are shaved on a routine basis which, I assume, serves to brand them rather than to keep them clean, because the hygienic conditions are far worse in the overcrowded jails than in the labor camps. Nor are heads shaven in the female Zone.

Among the St. Petersburg homeless, shaved heads appeared only toward the end of my main fieldwork, due to a change in the reception procedures at Botkin Hospital. In early October Vova and I went to see Vova's mate Nina, who was hospitalized there. Vova wanted Nina to use her good relations with one particular doctor to get him admitted too, because his digestive system had recently collapsed and he was suffering from relentless diarrhea. Nina used to have short hair, but when she received us she was bald. "So—I've got a new hairdo," she said in a curt tone. "*I* didn't have lice when I arrived, but a while ago *one* single bomzh managed to infect an entire ward, and now they shave the heads of all bomzhi, no matter if there's lice or not." Nina was upset and bitter, even though she habitually dressed in men's clothes and never took much interest in her physical appearance. Her scalp looked even worse, as they had apparently used a pair of very blunt scissors instead of clippers.

Vova's plan worked out, and a week later he was hospitalized too. He did not seem to mind having his head shaved. He knew what would happen, he did not have much hair in the first place. But more than anything else, he was male. There is one stark instance when male parameters for physical appearance cannot apply to women, and that is shaven heads. To a man, a shaven head may be a way of dealing with the baldness of old age, unless it implies fondness for a current fashion or allegiance to a particular lifestyle. (Close-cropped heads were rather popular among men at the time, while only a few years earlier the same hairstyle was associated with criminals.) To a woman, however, a shaven head can only signal degradation and punishment: there is no current fashion to appeal to, and no other plausible explanation to blame it on, aside from one's own inability to get rid of vermin. The only way out is to swear yourself innocent, as Nina did, and furiously attack prejudices and humiliation. Otherwise you just keep silent and tie the scarf tighter around your head.

Acclimatization, or Getting Used to It All

At some point I was sitting on a stone in the Drunken Garden together with Andrei Half-Finger. We were entirely engrossed in a profound philosophical discussion about Love, Faith, and Existence. Andrei had lost himself in a long elaboration on the relief in accepting the truth of Nothingness when one is doing twenty-five years in Mordovia.[5] As his thoughts meandered in increasingly elliptical curves, I zoned out. Something smelled, and right in front of us, not even a foot away, I suddenly saw a very large, unevenly colored, and rampantly odorous heap of human feces. We had been sitting there for at least half an hour without even noticing it. Through my head flew one thought: "At last I seem to be getting used to it all."

"Podlets chelovek k vsemu privykaet," Dostoevsky wrote somewhere. "The bloody human gets used to anything." Not all homeless people would agree (or fail to see a conspicuous turd). On the contrary, the issue of "getting used to it" was discussed heatedly and frequently, and the same dilemma was implicitly negotiated in the talk about "letting oneself go" and the need for self-respect. Practical compromises to accommodate non-homeless parameters of a decent physical appearance—and resentment of same—were in the same way unspoken statements about acceptance or refusal of "this life," at least in its more tangible aspects. In this last section I shall extend the theme of adaptation beyond the surface of human bodies, although my main focus still rests on issues that affect physical appearance, without for that reason being body work in a straightforward sense: homeless togetherness and its unavoidable lubricant, alcohol.

Vova tried to explain away his deplorable physical appearance as an adaptive tactic, an deferral of vital concerns until circumstances were more auspicious. In the eyes of others, this went too far. Like other people who have let themselves go, he took a tacit agreement to negotiate insuperable standards for permission to abandon human norms and values altogether. Nobody said this straight out, but I understood the thought from the frequent statements people made about their own incapacity to adapt when we were discussing Vova. On the other hand, "getting used to this life" was a virtue when they boasted about decent incomes, good sleeping places, and other facets of getting oneself organized in the homeless reality. Inventiveness and ability to act are, after all, part and parcel of adaptation, and I realized quite early on that Irina's refusal to get used to a bomzh life, however admirable, was as disastrous as Vova's exorbitant flexibility. The problem for both of them an ability to find the right level of adjustment.

Adaptation, or *akklimatizatsia,* implies a number of disparate aspects, with various implications for what a homeless person should actually get used to and in which respects he or she should remain intractably rigid. Some of them surfaced in a conversation at Nochlezhka's office between two men in their fifties, both homeless since the early 1990s and faithful stairway partners throughout. "I'll never get used to it," one of them said thoughtfully, "it's not *life,* it's hardly existence." The other one shrugged. "I've adapted," he said, "I wouldn't live otherwise, would I? Nor would you, and we've known each other for years." After conferring for a few minutes, they agreed that "getting used to" homelessness means many different things. You have to learn to overlook cold and hunger at times and accept boring or hazardous ways of making a living. You must always bear in mind, however, that this is not *normal,* that neither you nor anybody else is supposed to live in this way. And you must guard your self-respect thoroughly, which means that, even if you need a little extra tolerance toward dirt, you must try to keep yourself clean. Which too many bomzhi forget, they said as they nodded at a man in the yard outside the window who had obviously let himself go some time ago.

They could have added two more significant things that people usually mentioned in the context of adaptation. First, one has to get used to people, to recognize that they are as indispensable as they are potentially treacherous. This concerns non-homeless actors who may be merciful as well as deceitful or violent, but in particular it pertains to homeless others. It is from these people that you learn the means of survival, and these people are, in the end, the only haven (safe or not) from loneliness and depression. The second factor they omitted was alcohol. Getting used to the homeless reality is tough, and nobody can, as Irina did, simply dismiss one's own appearance, whereabouts, or income strategies as hopeless and leave it there, trapped by feelings of shame and resignation. A common description of the effects of alcohol, among homeless as well as non-homeless Russians, is that it "takes off the pressure," *snimaet davlenie,* which implies both the inhuman demands of oneself and others and the feelings of isolation and vulnerability. It is a shortcut to instant humanness in both the senses outlined in the introduction: a catalyst to social agency as well as a conjurer of fellow humanness, but it also has an inherent tendency to backfire and eliminate what it was originally expected to achieve.

The agentive properties of drinking were put forward by many a man or woman who claimed that without it, they would never be able to endure situations or accomplish tasks that in a sober state, they would find boring, humiliating, morally deplorable, dangerous, or simply nerve-racking. The tendency of alcohol to debilitate and incapacitate was equally recognized, and any homage to alcohol tended to be rounded off with a moralizing remark about the importance of self-restraint. In contrast, I heard few arguments for moderation when the other function of alcohol was on the agenda, namely its capacity to befriend and create alliances. Drinking is not merely a way to endure dirt, cold, pain, and hunger; in addition, it creates a good feeling between people. Other bomzhi become tolerable, and moreover, once in a while alcohol transforms even potentially threatening outsiders into perfectly enjoyable human beings. The mere fact that a person drinks—regardless of the amount—is an indication of his or her fellow humanness; it signals a sympathetic inability to cope with inhuman conditions and an equally agreeable dependence on company and sociability. Without this, I was frequently told, nobody would be able to cope with the combination of unpredictability, humiliation, and endless boredom that characterizes the reality of homeless survival. People who actively struggled against their alcoholism were usually of the same opinion, which explains their frequent relapses.

Alcohol was also considered a prerequisite for hope. Hope is an amorphous understanding, however, and the Grand Hope of the Soul is not really the same thing as the small, practical anticipation of the outcome of practical achievements, which were, at most, concluded by a tentative: "Well, *sometimes* it works, doesn't it?" I took such comments as cautious acknowledgments of the possibilities inherent in uncertainty as such, for even when the most plausible outcome of most practical endeavors is failure and further humiliation, something good *may* in fact happen. After a few sips of Bomi in good company, by contrast, hope brightened the future—and thus also the present—in a very explicit way, but less realistic: to rob a New Russian and get out of "this life" *no matter how,* the intervention of a truly good fellow human *no matter how,* or for any miracle to happen—*no matter how.* The predilection for miracles is in no way limited to homeless articulations of hope; indeed, it is intrinsic to established Russian notions of soul. As Pesmen explains it, the soul is perceived to be constantly longing elsewhere, to another world of sorts, and hope is a manifestation of this yearning (Pesmen 2000, 60–68). Hence it is the unattainability as such, the inversion of the ordinary here-and-now and a salvation of sorts, that constitutes hope in a true sense. As a vital aspect of soul, hope is in itself humanizing, and then it does not matter much *what* one is actually hoping for. Accordingly, I often found hope directed at itself; people were simply hoping for more hope, although as a momentary euphoric eruption, the Grand Hope would fade as soon as the hangover began. During its short but intensive existence, it still resurrected many a person from deep pits of grief and hopelessness, convincing them—if only for the moment—that they were humans too.

Adaptation is a matter of striking the golden mean, of not going too far in any sense. Many people managed to balance alcohol consumption and sociability evenly, in a way that allowed them to work, keep themselves clean, and avoid having their belongings stolen. Others oscillated between reckless binges and stretches of sensible industriousness, leaving everything to the Fates when they drank and working hard afterwards. Vova was of this kind, at least in the beginning. Later, bingeing took over, and the people he hung out with were increasingly letting themselves go too. He never commented on his own condition, and when I or others confronted him, he simply denied that he was acting any differently. Nonetheless, I think that he intended his sojourn at Botkin Hospital as a detoxification as well as a treatment of a stomach problem; at least this was the case with many other heavy drinkers who understood that their lives occasionally depended on a sudden removal from their everyday contexts.

Vova decided to leave the station and St. Petersburg after I left. A mate of his knew somebody in Vyborg who could put the two of them up for the winter, he said. He made it sound as if he wanted a change of climate in general, but I suspected that he did not want to return to an existence as an "anybody and everybody" at the station after more than ten months as a guide to the Swedish *korrespondent*. The regulars who considered him to be a braggart on the skids would probably forget and forgive very soon, but the police would no longer take me into consideration when they took him to the precinct. I also guessed that he wanted a break from himself. The stay at Botkin Hospital lasted for two weeks only, and he had no realistic prospects of being admitted again in the near future. He was in much better shape when he left the hospital, but with my departure as a pretext, he spent the last weeks of my stay pretty much the same way he had before the hospitalization. I do not think that a transfer to another town was likely to help him: with his exceptional capacity to adjust to different kinds of people, he would probably end up in a drinking gang within ten minutes after leaving the train, regardless of his destination. Vova had a strong predilection for Grand Hopes, however, and always found new people and new pastures promising in some sense or other; Vyborg would, he assured me, be a place for rest, restraint, and restoration of health.

Adaptation was, as should be clear by now, tantamount to death in the opinion of Irina, since it was precisely her incapacity to get used to "this life" that still told her who she was. Nonetheless, she seemed to soften up in the end, but I do not know if this was for good or for bad. I doubt that she was as detached from other homeless people as she claimed to be, but I did not see her hanging out with others until the very end of my fieldwork. Nor did she accept help from others, and well-intentioned advice about where to find clothes, cheap days in the bania, hairdressers who would cut hair for free, and so forth, generally did not penetrate her veneer of disillusion. She did not even like Anna and the handful of others who overtly sympathized with her because they too shared the plight of homeless intellectuals.

To my surprise, she eventually accepted company and support, moreover from a most unlikely person, one who by no definition could be called

"cultured." Nastia was a tall, sturdy, and permanently inebriated former soc-
cer player in her mid-twenties, with cropped hair, a loud bass voice, and
distinctly male clothes. Irina and I met her for the first time in the station
yard as she ran from person to person bellowing: "Help me with a ruble for
a drink, won't you—I *need* it, I *swear* I need it!" Apparently she knew who I
was, because she flung herself at me and embraced me firmly, showering me
with wet kisses until I gave her the ruble and she ran off again. Irina gazed
at Nastia with a blend of horror and fascination, and I asked her jokingly:
"Seems as if she likes me—do you think she's lesbian?" "Lesbian?" said Irina
with feigned surprise. "Do you think she's *female?*"

A week later I came to the station, only to see Nastia cruising the yard
as usual, begging every person present for a drink (which is all I ever heard
her say), but now and then she exchanged some words with Irina. Irina, in a
relatively good mood, told me that Nastia had taken her to her own sleeping
place, an apartment currently under renovation where she had good relations
with the artisans. "But it's a *khata!*" Irina exclaimed with aversion, using the
Russian term meaning "den of thieves" and describing the flow of shady
figures who came and went, exchanging items that quite obviously did not
belong to them. Nevertheless she stayed on. Nastia was, "*in spite of everything*"
—Irina made a face—"a good girl" who helped her out with food and all
sorts of things.

At the time, I was hoping that Irina's final acceptance of another homeless
person would help her, even though Nastia's drinking habits were a sign that
the odd companionship would not last. Irina needed knowledge as well as
material support, and I knew that there were plenty of people with whom
she would get along even better than with Nastia, if only she gave them the
chance. I left for Sweden not long afterwards and met Irina again only in
September 2000, on another visit to St. Petersburg. This was also the last time
I saw her. My hopes were not redeemed. She was skinnier than ever, dressed
in soiled and mismatched clothes, and her fingernails showed no trace of
nail polish. Judging from the nylon scarf wrapped round her head, she had
undergone the humiliating reception procedure at Botkin Hospital a month
or so earlier, and she mentioned a recent hospital stay. I avoided the topic
and asked for Nastia instead. Irina did not answer but proceeded with her
usual litanies about not being able to adapt and having all her things stolen
at night. It was more incoherent now than the year before, and less witty and
sarcastic—Irina had been genuinely funny—but perhaps she was a bit drunk.
Now and then she sipped from a bottle of cheap wine offered by another old
homeless woman. Before, she never drank in the daytime. The whole situation was depressing, and I grew exasperated by her old rhetoric. In practice,

she *did* get used to bomzh life and bomzhi, and as it appeared she did so more than necessary. I guessed that she could not forgive herself for it: by hanging out with Nastia or the woman with the wine, Irina had allowed herself to be immersed in the sameness that she had opposed throughout her life, first as *sovkovost'* (*sovok*-ness) and later as homelessness, and apparently she no longer considered herself worthy of life. Willpower was never Irina's strong point, but now she appeared to have lost her self-respect as well, and the woman I saw had once and for all ceased treading water.

I do not discuss the final demise of people I knew in this chapter (the epilogue reveals the little information I have about their further fates) but death is nonetheless a common theme. My informants frequently drew the parallel themselves, talking about those who had let themselves go as virtually dead, on the way to death, or "creeping up from down there" (with a gesture toward the ground), as some kind of restless corpses banished even from their own graves. Sameness, another recurring theme, in this specific context is akin to death. I have interpreted the efforts of certain women and men to be more than just anonymous anybodies by the way they dress, which I see as resistance to elimination in a social sense. To most other people, however, the "mere" humanness resented by the well-dressed still offered some dignity, because all that it required was the minimum of self-respect and willpower needed to keep oneself reasonably clean. In this sense, this understanding of "perhaps bomzh, but looking like a human being" pushes back at the humiliation and exclusion that the homeless experience every day. Those who settle for this "mere" humanness may appear as optimally undifferentiated, judging from the ways in which they look, behave, and talk, but they resist sameness too. In their case, however, the struggle takes place on the very verge of physical elimination, resisting the total anonymity of death.

I have described "this life" as a merciless force that pulls everybody in the same direction, eliminating individual human traits and replacing them with one and the same face. To end this story with its very beginning, this face was among the first ones I saw. It appeared on the several dozen photos that a pair of civilian policemen brought to Nochlezhka in September 1997, when I was a volunteer there. They wanted to compare the pictures with the ones in the archive. Nochlezhka never cooperates with the police in the search for wanted or suspected people, but this time the identification concerned unknown dead bodies, so they agreed. It took a long time, and I do not remember if they made any matches, or indeed how that would even be possible. The heavily bloated, bruised, and soiled physiognomies differed from each other only by the occasional tuft of beard or wisp of hair, which were also the only traits indicating the sex of the diseased.

This is the face of homelessness to me. I did not confront any more dead bodies during my main fieldwork, notwithstanding Vova's eager attempts to acquaint me with the corpses that appeared at the station. Nevertheless, I met enough men and women who increasingly resembled these photos as they gradually let themselves go, and it was their faces and the faces from the photos that first came into my mind that day when Raia said that all homeless faces in the end turn out the same—the one and single face of the bomzh.

Conclusion

A different title for this study could have been "Makeshift Humans in a Provisional Present," because improvisation and temporariness constituted the essential dilemma of Vova, Irina, and the others, while at the same time this was all they could resort to. For them, being human was being needed by others, but their homeless reality was too permeated with unpredictability and distrust for neededness to appear. Makeshift solutions therefore became the *sine qua non* of physical survival as well as of human dignity, while it simultaneously prevented their attempts to feel human from becoming more than "instead of the real thing," or "for the time being." In a more general sense, "makeshiftness" also deprived them of their homes and their essential humanness in the first place, for the large-scale society that simultaneously expelled them and set the terms for their survival was, in a manner of speaking, provisional as well. Not only was the period of transition or transformation in itself an interim of sorts, but the salient disjunction between the ideology and the actuality of the Soviet system inspired makeshift solutions at the systemic and the individual levels alike, and some of these were vital factors in shaping the conditions for the production of homelessness before as well as after the downfall.

Homelessness is always a waste of sorts, an unintended consequence of social ordering as such. In this sense the Soviet project distinguished itself mainly by its proportions and its exclusively theoretical base—the grandiose dream of a brave new world created straight from a written blueprint. Based on centralized expert design, the new social system was dependent on meticulous organization and, thereby, surveillance in order to adapt an intractable reality to the grand visions. Force and coercion were basic instruments for the regime to impose its will, but as a system of social welfare developed, extralegal violence was replaced with laws, and subjects were increasingly kept in place by soft governance. The propiska was a crucial instrument throughout: it identified the presumably undeserving renegades, who were then deported or contained, at first arbitrarily and later through criminalization, but it also distributed resources to the deserving and legible subjects who had the good sense to stay put.

However, in a number of vital respects, the state did not manage to realize in practice the theoretical objectives that in fact were the prerequisite for its ability to control. Living space—the foundation of surveillance—remained scarce, and as it was transferred from undeserving subjects to more deserving citizens, the renegades were made invisible to the system and, thereby, rendered criminal. The support of the state was absent in practice in many other domains where the needs of the subjects ostensibly should be cared for, which forced people to find their own makeshift solutions to these disjunctions. And the leeway for such improvisations increased as time passed. The peripheries of the country were not, for instance, supplied with the resources needed to prevent the inhabitants from independent attempts to improve their position in territorial stratification, an act of disobedience that, on the other hand, was compensated by the fact that it supplied the cities with an expedient pool of easily dismissed reserve labor.

In the unspoken deal between state and people, resources that the state could not provide were instead secured through informal social networks in which friends and family constituted the core. As a main source of social support, "one's own" were the primary unit of identification and loyalty, that is, home in a transferred sense. To many, they were in addition the only provider of a literal home, insofar as a local propiska only could be acquired through the nuclear family. However, in an immense country with a long history of population movements, large networks of near and dear ones cannot be taken for granted. At times, moreover, the system obstructed the options of close ones to help each other by limiting the composition of households or by depriving young people of relatives altogether by replacing vulnerable parents with orphanages. People without supportive intimate networks faced a multitude of social disadvantages, not least since loneliness and lack of social attachment were in fact criminalized by detour of homelessness, and weak or nonexistent families were thus a common dilemma of those who spent the last decades of the Soviet regime in a neverending circuit between homelessness and the Zone.

Their plight did not end until after the downfall, when many forms of state repression disappeared. Homelessness was no longer criminalized, but the introduction of a market economy and the disintegration of the Soviet Union added new social disjunctions to the old ones. Intimate social networks were reshuffled by new inequalities, and former understandings of neededness were renegotiated as ingrained schemes of "who should help whom in which way and when" no longer applied. While the capacity of grassroots to protect each other diminished, the structures of legal protection eroded, and as lawlessness proliferated, novel routes to attics and basements appeared. Some of them admittedly became less common toward the end of the decade, such as the notorious real estate frauds, but there were no remedies for the escalating poverty, the increasing deterioration of state welfare and protection, and the impoverishment of already disfavored peripheries. In addition to the debilitated capacity of the state to supervise and organize society, old and ingrained deficiencies came to the fore as they eventually could be discussed openly. The decay, disorder, and dirt that most Russians lamented at the time were thus leftovers from the past to the same extent that they were a result of social change: poverty, dirty and neglected public spaces, dilapidated housing, vagrancy, corruption, and the sudden appearance of all sorts of "human waste."

I have used the metaphors of leftovers and dirt somewhat uncritically for two reasons. As emic concepts, they were used consistently to negotiate neededness and social belonging. Waste suggests superfluity and banishment from some sort of totality, and this is without doubt how my informants were largely perceived—by themselves as well as others. Second, allusions to refuse convey important aspects of the actual conditions for homeless survival—living off discarded items and undesired chores; sleeping in places of little interest to most others; being treated "like shit" as the ultimate prey of deception, extortion, and verbal and physical abuse. These qualities notwithstanding, dirt as a metaphor conceals continuity and commonality, dimensions that are equally important for an understanding of how these people actually kept themselves alive. The dichotomy "inclusion/exclusion" is blurred if the social totality to which inclusion pertains is disintegrated, which is precisely what is highlighted by terms such as *razval,* "downfall," or *bardak,* "chaos." If home in a broad sense is continuity, familiarity, and security, the capacity to understand and negotiate the world in which one lives, then most Russians in the 1990s were, in a manner of speaking, homeless. In this sense, my informants were merely victimized twice: deprived of the ultimate anchors of continuity—close ones, a place of one's own, a propiska—in a more common framework of confusion and disorientation.

At the conceptual level, the otherness of bomzhi was not reduced by this similarity in kind. As a category, they were set apart a priori by the Soviet construction of the unattached and itinerant as criminals, but the circumstances depriving them of their homes were not seen as exceptional in the least. Free will, or rather ill will, thus remained as a popular explanation of their fates. At the practical level, however, bardak erased differences by bringing together those excluded from the official social structure and those who merely circumvented it. In spite of discrimination and exploitation, there was no absolute boundary between homeless and non-homeless methods of survival. The odd jobs and the entrepreneurism of station regulars and others were part and parcel of a ubiquitous system of illegal or at least informal practices permeating society, always mediated by "good relations" and various forms of more or less self-invented entrepreneurship, be it at the micro or macro level. In De Certeau's terms, the homeless were merely positioned in the most marginal, dead-end tufts in this tangle of tactics, where the profit was so small that others found it negligible (De Certeau 1984).

Besides the general disrespect of the law, an important precondition for these interactions was an urban environment that did not conscientiously separate social categories from each other. Poverty was too widespread to be treated as an abomination, and spatial divisions were often diffuse. Areas aimed at consumption or residency were not meticulously organized to eliminate other activities, and social interfaces were in effect permeable too. That different people mingled in the same places created possibilities for spontaneous deals and unplanned interactions, a crucial component of this makeshift existence that was additionally encouraged by established cultural conceptualizations of dusha "soul," or what I have called fellow humanness. Since it ignores social distinctions, this "way of feeling about and being in the world," in Pesmen's words, has an undeniable practical efficiency in a makeshift context, as it opens up the scope for spontaneous approaches and unconventional solutions by mere reference to the shared quality of being human (2000, 9). The homeless thus invested considerable effort in summoning the potentially rewarding souls of passersby, more or less temporary employers, janitors and residents, policemen in need of pacification, indifferent bureaucrats, charity workers, remaining relatives or friends, and other homeless people.

In a simplified sense, Vova and the others may be said to have been excluded from the system but not from society, if the latter is seen as the functionally existing socioeconomic relationships of their own habitat. As a comparison, homeless people in more affluent societies are often included in the state system but excluded from society. They are dependent on state welfare or charity (even if it is frequently insufficient) because their unpredictable lives ruin their chances at the ordinary housing and labor markets, while the relative disorder opening up for "makeshift inclusion" is prevented by a punctilious organization of economy and of urban space (and, while we're at it, also of people's minds, for any micro-entrepreneurism presupposes a certain degree of openmindedness and goodwill, even in cultural contexts less dedicated to soul than the Russian one). I refrain from all speculations about which mode of homelessness is worse to endure—the only answer is that hell takes many forms—and I do not wish to trivialize the danger and the exploitation inherent in the risky autonomy of my Russian informants. Nevertheless, the shared social and economic space with non-homeless actors was essential, and not only to their physical survival. It was also crucial to their opportunities to feel—if only for a moment—that they were humans too, a makeshift neededness that I wish befell more of their Western counterparts, as much as I wish that the Russian homeless enjoyed the same civil rights as their "homed" compatriots and at least a rudimentary system of social support. The question is whether it is possible to combine the best aspects of two entirely different worlds: to provide a necessary level of protection and still give leeway for autonomy and individual initiatives.

In the case of the St. Petersburg homeless, I fear that the opposite is taking place. They are expelled both from the system and from society in the aforementioned sense, as the "eurospacing" of their former environments circumscribes their options for independent action without any substantial forms of public support appearing in their stead. I profoundly understand that people do not want to live with Sasha's campfire above their heads, and I assume that the vast majority of the travelers passing through the Moscow Station prefer to be spared Fyodor's drunken temper and Vova's requests for a ruble. Nonetheless I am seriously concerned about all the people who seem to have disappeared entirely. Judging by the present look of former homeless hangouts, it was not only Raia who was aesthetically impossible; her "employers" as well as a fair part of their clientele appear to have become redundant in the process too. Perhaps these sturdy elderly women have new and better jobs, and it is just that I do not recognize the clients now that they are better dressed. And perhaps Raia is making herself needed somewhere else, in a different way. It is for further research to find out what the emerging metropolitan design means to everyday homeless existence, but the tendency as such indicates that future researchers on homelessness in Russia will be able to use the synonym "street people" with more ease than I could.

It is also up to further studies to investigate future causation patterns. Migration remains a crucial factor, insofar as the basic function of the registration system still is to protect the centers from discontented and socially marginalized peripheries. Future investigations should pay particular attention to the increasing number of migrant workers from other CIS countries, a category that is subject to an unstable legal status, extreme labor exploitation, and a proliferating nationalist rhetoric whose hostility makes the disparaging comments about bomzhi sound almost kind-hearted. Another factor that may take on new proportions is the abolishment of state subsidies and the ongoing reforms of the housing system. As mentioned in chapter 1, the bulk of the housing sector is currently being privatized, and the aim of the authorities is now to make housing cooperatives take full charge of the apartment blocs. It remains to be seen how these associations will deal with households unable to pay for common expenses and how the developing system of housing allowances and so-called social apartments will work out in practice—a task that can only be completed by detailed qualitative social research. In general, the question remains if, and how, the present regime will deal with the old paradox of housing as a "civil duty" when it is not a social right, and what kind of disjunctions—and hence provisional solutions—a reform of the present system will imply.

My frequent use of the word "makeshift" does not pertain to processes at the state level so much as to the struggle of individuals to maintain a sense of being human. The St. Petersburg homeless understood this as being recognized as somebody special with something particular to offer in some sort of social whole, most desirably the close unit of people of one's own. Their dilemma was twofold: since they were apparently *not* needed to begin with—or else they would not be homeless—they were cast as suspect, with the result that nobody *wanted* to need them. Even if someone against all odds did so, the chronic contingency of their everyday existence inhibited real neededness, because some minimal measure of continuity is necessary if mutual strangers are to find out how useful they may be to each other. In contrast, homelessness, or "this life," was more or less constituted by disruption: the dangers that homeless people die from, the chances that keep them alive, and the endless flow of replaceable anybodies and everybodies who facilitate survival as well as disappointment or death. All that remained was the project of putting together a humanness of sorts with whatever bits and pieces happened to be available: jobs, tasks, and things undesired by others, places of interest to nobody else, fragile and fading ties to remaining close ones, or other "wasted humans."

The result could never become more than an improvised emergency solution, for every supposedly humanizing move could always backfire into rejection, exploitation, and humiliation. To maintain a sense of self-respect, the homeless therefore modified the conventional criteria for what it is to be human. Everything—assets as well as personal traits or values—that could not be realized in their own everyday lives was disqualified as not applicable, or at least intensely negotiated because of some ambiguity. Among bomzhi, social backgrounds were thus as irrelevant to one's human status as inapplicable skills, good health, or—even—feminine performances, for which the homeless stage did not offer the necessary props.

The homeless hierarchy of relevance certainly rendered a stroke of mercy to a reality that efficiently eliminated most manifestations of respectability or worthiness. At the same time, however, it aggravated the social quagmire in which people tried to stay afloat, for its forgiving stance actually legitimized violations of what most people regarded as common decency. Displacement and external contingencies made it difficult to be accountable in the first place. This incapacity merged with the stigma attached to bomzhi as a category and the latent distrust of strangers in general. Reduced expectations, prejudice, and personal disappointments justified infringements on other people or their possessions, with the logic that "if you cannot act like a human all the same, you need not try to." This led to the predictable vicious circle that undermined relationships between homeless people as well as their contacts with non-homeless actors.

The only humanizing property that remained indisputable was immune to unpredictability and distrust, independent as it was not only of social inclusion but also of continuity as such: the mere capacity to act, to work in the broadest sense. Work proved one's good intentions, as a way to speak back to the popular prejudice that to this day frames homelessness as the result of free choice. Intentionality is admittedly an ambiguous category in such denunciations; *becoming* and *remaining* homeless is framed as an act of will, while bomzhi as *persons* are described as no more than flaccid lumps of conditioned reflexes, and the paradoxical outcome is that it takes a lot of willpower to get rid of it. To the homeless, in contrast, ultimate degradation stemmed not from volition but from the lack of it. Work proved one's entitlement to a place in the "real" world, and the energy to go through with it stemmed from willpower, which, in turn, depended on self-respect, the conviction that one was worthy of a real life. Without this essential spark of humanness, one let oneself go, lost the will to live, which immediately was reflected on the surface of one's own body—the only arena for the manifestation of self-respect that by definition could not be swept away in the general surge of unpredictable events. Process was more emphasized than result, since the actual fruits of "body work" were as perishable as anything else. The credo was thus not "you are what you do" so much as "you are what you *are doing,*" and the most significant parameter for humanness was, in the end, not *being* clean, but *keeping* oneself clean. The issue was thus not "to fake it 'til you make it," because faking it *was* making it.

Nonetheless, such a reduced understanding of what it takes to be a human did not satisfy the essential want of being needed. You can take solace in the assurance that you are at least keeping yourself clean, or you can state it to others and have it accepted. Nevertheless, the mere capacity to act cannot be more than a *measure* of humanness, a proof that you still *deserve* a place in the social world of others. It makes nobody *feel* like a human any more than the principal entitlement to food emits flavors in the mouth or fills an empty stomach. Neededness cannot be severed from humanness without bloodshed and severe pain, and the result is of necessity crippling. Most people I knew, with the exception of a few purportedly self-made men, thus found it deeply tragic, or even perverted, that staying human had to be a solitary project. As a reminder of loneliness, vulnerability, and a hostile external world, the phrase "at least I keep myself clean" mercilessly revealed the magnitude of their loss.

This is why fellow humanness was so crucial. As a social modality, it provides an instant experience of unity and equal worth that is independent of the prerequisites for humanness understood as social agency, of which the homeless were deprived all the same. People who feel soulful are intimate without familiarity and continuity; they pay no regard to willpower but elevate weakness instead, and they can lend themselves to an anti-rationalism that at least lends a touch of humor to the inevitable disorder and unpredictability of the surrounding world. This mode of humanness was, admittedly, makeshift in the sense that it served as a temporary haven from something more enduring and burdensome, but as a set of shared cultural notions it was nonetheless always possible to activate; the only precondition was someone else in equal need of being "fellow."

Fellow humanness was, on the one hand, a prerequisite for social agency, since nobody could endure the unrealistic demands and merciless pressure of materialistic striving without an occasional break. In essence, however, the two modalities are inherently at odds with each other. Souls are conceptualized as being on a perpetual escape from the everyday material concerns of *byt,* and the generosity of fellow humans is always on a collision course with the self-preserving instincts of social agents. The homeless merely take this eternal dilemma to its extreme, for love towards one's neighbor cannot be but an obstacle to one's own resurrection, and the neighbor is, moreover, always a stranger until he or she has been converted into a fellow human, which is most conveniently achieved by a ten-ruble potion available in a nearby kiosk or pharmacy. Soulful sprees, in turn, threaten not only drudgingly collected material resources but the capacity to work in the first place, and too often, the thirst for life in the end quenches its own essential spark—willpower.

From my first visit to Russia in 1989 onward, I have habitually perceived soul or fellow humanness merely as "another way of relating to things." It is not exotic or special in its actual expressions, since these appear in other cultural contexts too. Western strangers drink themselves into friendship, and not only in Russia are various personal problems remedied by alcohol. Intimacy is used to achieve material benefits everywhere, and people of all times and places have taken pride in victimization or turned to other worlds when the existing reality has suffocated them. What initially struck me was rather the intensity and frequency of it all and that one could *do* things with it—that Vova could wring money out of strangers *only* if he told them that he craved for alcohol is only one example. Moreover, the disparate manifestations were neatly wrapped into a coherent but unspoken attitude to life, one that made sense precisely because of its *lack* of conventional logic.

Since then almost two decades have passed, and the people have changed, along with the society in which they live. Although the sense for soul for more than two centuries has constituted a coveted and renowned foundation for perceptions of Russian "culture," the articulations and the practical uses of soulfulness that I have described were in some sense leftovers too. The research on which I have most relied extensively on, by Pesmen and by Ries, pertain to the perestroika era and the early years of transition, a time of fundamental upheaval, when new contrasts were intensely negotiated and tampered with by word and deed, and notions of soul, suffering, and Russianness were useful instruments in the attempts to deal with it all (Ries 1997; Pesmen 2000). Cash had not yet suffocated an economy theretofore largely administered within a conceptual framework of friendly favors and generosity, and people still had some time left to socialize. Already in 1994, however, an informant of Ries complains, somewhat paradoxically: "All that lamenting was a luxury! Now we haven't got the time!" (1997:162). I heard similar exclamations throughout the 1990s. People found it increasingly difficult to find the time to meet and *obshchat'sa,* because they were now materially dependent on other currencies and so had to work all the time. With the exception of my informants, that is, who were as displaced temporally as much as spatially and who still survived from an economy—itself a leftover, one constituted by manifest leftovers—in which one of the most crucial assets was one's capacity to convince others that they were one's fellow humans.

I would appreciate some ethnographic sequel to the aforementioned works (and my own) about the further fates of the Russian soul, to see how it fares among people to whom the notion of "before" relates not to the Soviet period but to the past bardak of transition; who grew up in a social climate of rampant competition instead of stultifying stagnation; who are not ashamed of materialist success and power; and who may not look upon powerlessness and suffering as something entirely inescapable. Nor does this generation necessarily look upon Russia, and thereby its soul, through the ironic prism of the fool Vanya, who defeats Germans and Englishmen not by exploiting his strength or wisdom but by turning common sense topsy-turvy. The economic upswing of the Putin years resulted in an increased national self-confidence, and a rampant nationalist discourse eagerly embraces concepts such as "the Russian soul" or "the Russian idea," but now with overtones of superiority, revenge, and triumph. The pitch of that voice is light years from the self-lacerating snickers of the drinking gangs at the Moscow Station and at the soup kitchens, but possibly there will still be other, less hostile articulations providing some consolation—and perhaps even a ruble or two—to those who are bound to fall through the inevitable cracks of whichever social design the "new" Russia has next in store.

Epilogue

Sadly, I know very little about the subsequent destinies of my band of station regulars and soup kitchen clients. Many, but far from all, nourished a hope of once again becoming needed—tentatively, realistically—but a substantial number of people evaporated into thin air even during my fieldwork in 1999, for good or ill. Nobody knows, for neither the dead nor the formerly homeless return to tell their stories.

I am still in touch with Armen, the Salvation Army regular whom the reader encounters with a Bible on a staircase in chapter 3, while he still survived from selling plastic bags and helping his clients dodge the tax inspection. Apparently he worked up a good reputation, because a year or so later the proprietor of a liquor store offered him a job, and Armen rented a dilapidated room where he has lived ever since. He has neither ID documents nor Russian citizenship, but a lawyer has told him that his problems can easily be solved for a sum of money that Armen would need a few years to save—provided that inflation does not diminish its worth in the meantime. Until then, he is trapped in the liquor store, which he says is less of a problem than the planned renovation of the area where he lives. Few other rooms are cheap enough for his tiny off-the-books salary, so he might have to return to the attics, if there are any left.

Armen says that the old Salvation Army policy of forgiving and tolerance has been replaced with demands on discipline and reform; since he finds this inhuman, he goes there only for Sunday services. A few of our common acquaintances are still around. His former stairway partner Ivan still lacks a propiska but works at a rehabilitation center for alcoholics that the Salvation Army runs in the countryside. Lyosha, seen in chapter 5 battling his recurrent problems over drinking, sleeping places, and domestic girlfriends, was an occasional visitor at the Salvation Army until a couple of years ago, but has disappeared entirely since then, much to my annoyance, as I was very fond of him.

From Armen I also received news about Nadia and Sergei for a few years. I heard nothing of them after a phone call from Nadia in 2004, but three years later she wrote me a long letter, and we are still in touch. Their story roughly continues as follows: they never got their children back, but instead they had another one. The last time I met them, they were living with baby Pasha in a damp basement that came with a *dvornik* job, and they were both in good spirits. Then everything went wrong. They lost the job and had to give Pasha up too, fortunately to the same foster parents who were caring for his older brother. Sergei, whom I knew as a sober alcoholic with very occasional relapses, took up the bottle again and began to beat Nadia, for how long I do not know. Then a miracle intervened—for Nadia, that is. A cousin of hers arrived as a godsend from a distant town, and then Nadia's mother unexpectedly turned up from Ukraine, where she had moved with Nadia's wretched stepfather after deceiving Nadia over her share of their common apartment. Nadia bears her no grudge—evidently the stepfather was not very nice to the mother either—and the three women shared a room for some time, making a living from different cleaning jobs. The series of such unexpected occurrences was completed by the equally sudden appearance of an old male acquaintance of Nadia's, who happened to have a propiska as well as an apartment, and they fell in love and got married. Nadia now has a propiska, lives happily with her husband, and works as a mail carrier. Sergei, she said in a very matter-of-fact manner on the phone in 2004, had drunk himself into the *durdom,* "the loony bin," only to be beaten to death in a stairway not long after he was discharged from the hospital.

I visited the soup kitchen for the last time in 2003. A few old acquaintances were still there. The former doorkeeper Evgenia, who in chapter 4 prefers a stairway to her domestic friend out of shame, eventually received a monthly income when the pension system was made independent from the propiska in 2002. Now she was sharing an shockingly expensive room with another homeless woman. She mentioned that Marina, the well-dressed shelter resident and job-hunter, had had another heart attack and finally obtained a place in Mother Teresa's home for elderly and disabled homeless people. Viktoria was still married, I was told, and Galia still kept the job as a dvornik that she secured in chapter 2, now with the adjoined propiska but also with a tough job and failing health.

Ksenia left the soup kitchen already in 1999, after her argument with the staff about their pilfering. By pure coincidence, I ran into her at a cafe in the autumn of 2000. Her wretched boyfriend threw *her* out, she told me, when he met a woman who in addition to a flat and a propiska also had a car. Ksenia was not bitter about it, because almost immediately she was compensated for a room that she had once lost due to a prison sentence and Article 60. She could not move in since the neighbors in the *kommunalka,* wanting the room for themselves, had filed charges, but Ksenia could still register there, and thanks to the propiska she found a job washing dishes and was thereby able to rent another room to live in. By then, she had a new and sympathetic boyfriend twelve years her junior. "And *his* marriage isn't even happy," she summarized her former boyfriend's fate.

After my last, quite depressing encounter with Irina in October 2000, I went to the Moscow Station. Some faces were still familiar. (A year later, more or less everybody was replaced.) Andrei Half-Finger told me that Zhanna had already disappeared from the station when I left in 1999 and was apparently back in her hometown. Her sister Katia the Colonel had ended up behind bars soon afterward, following a clumsy attempt to steal money from a client. Artistic Anna, who killed lice with hair bleach in chapter 6, was staying with a domestic man somewhere near the station. She told me that the young rascal Zina, who loved to play cat and mouse with the police, swapped the station for Vosstania Square as she substituted heroin for Ldinka, and had since died of an overdose. Only two weeks later her brother passed away from alcohol poisoning. He was always following in her footsteps, Anna said with the laconic fatalism of a true station regular, so it was only logical. A handful of other hard-drinking youngsters were dead too, and so was Dima, who used to live in the ruined bunker with his common-law wife Liuba. She had a new man by now, as young and handsome as her Dima used to be. Olga was purportedly around somewhere, while her ex-boyfriend Kostia was still wiping tables for a kiosk.

Everybody I talked to said that Vova was dead. I said that he planned to leave the city after I left, but the station regulars stubbornly insisted that he was no longer alive although nobody could tell me exactly how or when. But death was, I recalled, the standard explanation for the disappearance of people who were considered too old or too ugly to have married, and Vova certainly belonged in that category. Nor was this the first time he had died. At least three times, he once told me, he had entered the station only to be given notice of his own recent demise. Twice he even attended the funeral feast. I give him the benefit of the doubt, for if you cannot know, you can always hope. And where there is hope, there is—perhaps—life too.

The logic may not be all that convincing, but I find it quite human.

NOTES

Introduction

1. Burawoy and Verdery (1999) recommend "transformation," since the term suggests an open-ended process of change rather than the allegedly predictable transition to a Western society that was forecast by the architects of shock therapy and market capitalism in the early 1990s. I agree with this but sometimes use the term "transition," since it is a more established reference to this particular period of time.

2. The estimation with regard to Russia as a whole was made by Médecins Sans Frontières in the mid-1990s, but I do not know on what basis. The numbers pertaining to St. Petersburg are based on data from hospitals, morgues, and the police collected by Médecins Sans Frontières and the NGO Nochlezhka in 1994. As for the latter, 200,000 is in my opinion more plausible, since a lack of a local propiska (as explained in chapter 1) is more common in large cities than elsewhere. According to the same organizations in 2002, the number of literally roofless people in St. Petersburg was about nine thousand, but I have no idea how this number was estimated.

3. Snow and Anderson suggest that homelessness has a residential dimension as well as a familial-support dimension and a moral-worth dimension (1993, 7–10). This makes sense from the perspective of the homeless, whose everyday reality is determined by the lack of a place to stay of their own, the lack of intimate networks capable of supplying assistance, and experiences of humiliation. Analytically, however, I prefer to see the housing issue as a nodal point since it is always determined by one's position in a social order of some kind.

4. In contrast to political scientists such as Robert D. Putnam, who regard social capital as an asset not of individuals but of a state or a country constituted by a strong civil society and engaged and responsible citizens.

5. In 1999, Nochlezhka's register contained some twenty thousand names, including information about the causes of homelessness, chronic diseases, prison sentences, orphanage backgrounds, and local versus nonlocal origin. Here I use new entries in 1998 and 1999 for statistical purposes rather than the entire archive, since it is impossible to know how many of the registered people are still homeless.

6. Other researchers have been more successful in finding solitude at charities or at a police precinct where homeless people were kept waiting for new ID documents (see the end of chapter 1). In particular, Stephenson (2006) has turned individual narratives into detailed analyses of processes of displacement from the Soviet time onward. I thought of the police department too and also the Sisters of Mother Teresa, who run a home for old or disabled homeless people, but after some consideration, I decided not to include these places in my already large and fragmented field. Access to both of them would have required considerable effort that I could utilize better

elsewhere, and in addition I wanted deeper contacts with the people I already knew, not new contacts.

7. The word *antropolog* in Russian is normally interpreted as "physical anthropologist," so I normally said *sotsiolog* to avoid confusion with a scientist who measures skulls (cf. Markowitz 2000, 24). Since I did not use questionnaires or structured interviews, few informants associated my work with social science anyway. Most of them took me to be a journalist (*korrespondent*).

8. They all knew that I might use the pictures in my book, but I have nonetheless avoided including photographs of people who to my knowledge live different lives now or who may since have developed a different opinion about being portrayed in a book about a social category as stigmatized as bomzhi.

Chapter 1. "Excrement of the State"

1. In 1956, there were restrictions on new inhabitants in forty-eight cities (Buckley 1995). These included all of the republic capitals and most cities with a population of five hundred thousand or more, as well as certain regions of strategic significance (Zaslavsky 1982). Outside these "closed" cities and regions, the propiska functions merely as a device for the administration of social benefits, not as an instrument to prevent people from moving in.

2. Only in 2005 did a new Housing Code make such evictions legally possible, but as I write this in mid-2008, the new law is still being put into systematic practice. In 2006, while living in St. Petersburg for a few months, I heard gossip about a few cases but could find no documentation. The people I talked to assumed that these evictions were carried out as examples, to deter others from rent evasion.

3. Of all the homeless people I met, 42 percent in all (35 percent of the women and 49 percent of the men) had been incarcerated for a period of more than six months before 1995. Of all first-time registrations at Nochlezhka in 1999, 60 percent of the men and 16 percent of the women gave "imprisonment" as the formal reason for lacking a propiska.

4. In St. Petersburg in 1999, the fines equaled the cost of an ice cream cone and served mainly as a pretext for the police to harass people (usually the homeless or persons of Caucasian origin), while even stricter rules were applied in Moscow (Lemon 1998; Pilkington 1998, 41). In 2004, the interim before a temporary registration is compulsory was increased from 10 to 90 days, while the fines for violating the rules were increased by a factor of 25. The authorities may have decided to focus on long-term movements rather than brief journeys since nobody registered them anyway. According to Gromov (2004), the prolonged interim was instead the consequence of a change of the registration rules for foreign guest workers intended to enable Ukrainians working in Russia to vote for the Russian favorite Viktor Yanukovich in the Ukrainian national election of 2004.

5. Statement from the Constitutional Court of the Russian Federation No. 8–11, June 23, 1995, according to printed information to released prisoners distributed by Nochlezhka, St. Petersburg.

6. According to Gutov and Nikiforov (2004), however, these categories were drastically reduced among the homeless in Moscow too in the late 1990s. Statistics from Médecins Sans Frontières in Moscow show that the proportion of "forced

migrants" and "refugees" among the clients diminished from 5 percent to 0.8 percent between 1995 and 2000.

7. Another obstacle was the lack of consensus in different parts of Russia about who should be granted these statuses. In addition, a deregistration stamp, *vypiska,* from the place of departure for many years was required to prove that the applicant had definitely moved, which obviously is a practical problem for people who leave in a hurry or who are persecuted (Pilkington 1998, 212n). According to Nazarova (2000), only 1.3 million of the 5 million people who left the "near abroad" for Russia between 1990 and 1997 are officially registered as "forced migrants" or as "refugees."

8. According to Neidhart, in St. Petersburg in 1997 there were still 200,000 kommunalki housing 1 million people, or 20 percent of the population (2003, 132). For ethnographic accounts of kommunalka life, see Boym (1994), Gerasimova (1999), and Utekhin (2001) as well as the website "Communal Living in Russia: A Virtual Museum of Soviet Everyday Life," created by Ilya Utekhin, Alice Nakhimovsky, Slava Papemo, and Nancy Ries, at http://kommunalka.colgate.edu/.

9. The Housing Code of 2005 finally abolished the subsidies by making municipal tenants as well as owners of privatized apartments pay the full cost of their housing. I do not know how quickly the rents were planned to increase (a system of housing allowances is expected to take care of the needs of the poor), but a stop to free privatization is planned for 2010, and municipal tenants now are more than eager to privatize. In addition, homeowners are encouraged to form housing cooperatives that will take over the full responsibility (and the full cost) of their apartment blocs, since stairways, yards, and so forth have remained municipal property.

10. Legally, the sanitary norm should not determine registrations even in the municipal housing sector. The Constitutional Court has repeatedly affirmed that the limitations set by the norm contradict the constitutionally granted freedom of movement, but administrative offices as well as the lower courts persistently ignore these precedents (*Kommersant,* October 11, 1995; March 12, 1998; February 20, 1999).

11. A suggestion for further research is how this essentially illegal practice has evolved into a full-fledged and publicly flaunted business. In 2007, the center spread of the main newspapers displayed colorful advertisements from respectable solicitor's offices at Nevsky Prospekt, charging US$700 for a permanent registration.

12. Cf. *Trud,* April 28, 2000.

13. Cf. *St. Petersburg Times,* December 1–7, 1997.

14. According to members of the organization *Komitet zashchitii prav potrebitelei na rynke nedvizhimosti* (Committee for the Defense of the Rights of Consumers at the Estate Market), personal conversation, September 2000. Also cf. *Trud,* April 28, 2000; *Izvestiia,* February 28, 2000.

15. Cf. Gilinsky and Sokolov (1993); Sokolov (1994); Yulikova and Skliarov (1994); Beigulenko (1999); Zykov (1999); Zav'ialov and Spiridonova (2000); Gutov and Nikiforov (2004); Osinskii, Khabaeva, and Baldaeva (2004).

16. *O sotsial'noi reabilitatsii lits zanimaiushchikhsia brodiazhnichestvom,* "On the Social Rehabilitation of People Engaged in Vagrancy" (2000), and *O vnesenii izmenenii i dopolnenii v otdel'nye zakonodatel'nye akty Rossiiskoi Federatsii po voprosam sotsial'noi profilaktiki brodiazhnichestva,* "On the Implementation of Change and Effectuation in Special Legal Acts of the Russian Federation on the Question of the Social Prevention of Vagrancy" (2003).

17. *O preduprezhdenii bezdomnosti, brodiazhnichestva, ograchenii brodiazhnichestva, sotsial'noi podderzhke bezdomnykh i lits, zanimaiushchikhcia brodiazhnichestvom,* "On the Prevention of Homelessness, Vagrancy, [on] the Restriction of Vagrancy, [on] Social Support of the Homeless and Persons Engaged in Vagrancy." Available at http://pomogi-bezdomnym.ru, accessed January 16, 2009.

18. *O profilaktike brodiazhnichestva i sotsial'noi reabilitatsii lits bez opredelennogo mesta zhitel'stva, roda zaniatii i sredstv k syshchestvovaniiu,* "On the Prevention of Vagrancy and Social Rehabilitation of Persons Without a Specific Place of Residence, Type of Occupation and Means of Survival." In spite of being based on human and civil rights, the new draft law does not mention the propiska, and it uses the phrases "vagrancy" and "without a specific place of residence," although scrupulously avoiding the acronym bomzh. Its definition of vagrancy is akin to conventional understandings of homelessness, framed as a voluntary or involuntary situation in which one is compelled to live in surroundings not organized for human habitation. The understanding "without a specific place of residence" is somewhat vague and refers to people who have no legal right to a living space or who "cannot realize" their existing rights. However, most probably these definitions will be altered before the draft law is presented to the Duma. It is available at http://pomogi-bezdomnym.ru, accessed January 16, 2009.

19. Such a volunteerist view is reflected also in Russian academic texts that otherwise emphasize the socio-structural roots of homelessness (Beigulenko 1999, 224; Zykov 1999, 157). Stephenson and Karlinsky, even harsher critics of the state, bring up individual intentions as well, but merely to dismiss them as plausible causes (Stephenson 1996, 26; Karlinsky 2004, 30). Whether or not the authors agree, they know that individual volition must be addressed because of the firm entrenchment of the idea.

20. Sometimes "vagrants" were kept at mental hospitals, and Soviet psychiatry also had a term for an incurable lust to wander, *dromomania* (cf. Gilinsky and Sokolov 1993). Medicalizing discursive strands were perhaps nascent, but in my own experience, nobody assumed that bomzhi were mentally ill, nor was the mental health system part of the shared social memory of those who were homeless in the Soviet period.

21. Until 2002, when the propiska ceased to be a precondition for receiving pensions; unregistered pensioners are now supposed to be cared for by the local district where they "occupy themselves" (Karlinsky 2004).

22. From many private conversations with Igor Karlinksi, jurist, and Maxim Egorov, chairman of Nochlezhka, between 2001 and 2005.

23. *Spetspriem raspredelitel'* may be translated as "filtering station," since, in the Soviet era, it dispatched those in custody on to wherever they presumably belonged: Muscovites to Moscow, orphans to orphanages, and so forth (Bodungen 1994). My informants referred to the place only by its Soviet address, Kalaeva 11, stubbornly ignoring the fact that the street had long since been renamed to Zakhar'evskaia ulitsa.

Chapter 2. Refuse Economics

1. I thought that the access to medical care in the case of TB had to do with some sort of communicable disease act, but in 2004 staff at Nochlezhka told me that it was becoming increasingly difficult for people with acute TB to receive hospitalization.

2. Pel'meni are dumplings similar to ravioli, one of the few ready-made foodstuffs in Russia at the time, and a *pel'meni kombinat* is a common kind of factory. The factory could deduct the costs for charity, and I assume that the sum reported to the tax authorities usually exceeded the real one by a considerable amount.

3. The Legal Code on Work, based on the Constitution of 1993, prohibits any limitation of an individual's right to employment that is not tied to purely professional qualifications. Until 2002, a law from the Soviet era simultaneously prohibited employment of people without a propiska and imposed fines on employers who broke the rule (Paragraph 181 of the Code of Administrative Violations). A new law should have precedence over an old one, but rather than enduring endless court cases, employers avoided the problem entirely by keeping to the old system. The old law is abolished now, but employers still need a propiska, since taxes are paid to the local authorities at the place of registration of their staff, and unregistered employees thus imply tax evasion. Furthermore, in order to be hired, an applicant must produce a number of other documents that are provided only at the place of registration, such as insurance certificates or military registration documents (Karlinsky 2004, 34).

4. This is according to Galina Lindquist, who in the 1970s worked at a chemistry institute and, once a month, at the baza together with her colleagues (personal communication).

5. Cf. Bridger, Kay, and Pinnick (1996); Pine (1996); Rotkirch and Haavio-Mannila (1996); Sperling (1999); Ashwin (2000); Silverman and Yanowitch (2000); and Lindquist (2003). It should be added, however, that most researchers on the topic focus on the early 1990s, but the situation with respect to female employment seems to have changed since then. Statistics from Goskomstat since the year 2000 show no significant difference in the unemployment of men and women respectively; more detailed research is needed to understand the reality behind these numbers.

6. A pioneer camp is a summer camp for children. In Soviet times, most children were members of the Pionery, the Pioneer Movement, an organization tied to the Communist Party, and spent part of the summer at the summer camps of the Pioneers. To this day, summer camps for children tend to be referred to as "pioneer camps."

7. In 1999, the price of a local train ticket to the more distant stations was often three times as much (around thirty rubles) as the fixed fine for not paying (eight rubles), so the standard practice everybody did—not only the homeless—was to get on the train and then pay the fines when the controllers appeared, just as if they were tickets.

8. The sex trade was not something that I could just bring up out of context and expect people to talk about. The "mundane muddle" at my field sites generally prevented chats about things of such intimacy, and I readily agree that in cases like this, my choice of method was not to my advantage. Indiscreet questions are easier to make in a one-time interview, in part because the unlikelihood of the parties ever meeting again can encourage a frankness that is less common between long-term acquaintances.

9. Homosexual prostitution seems common among adult homeless men in the United States, but I never heard of it among my own male informants (Bahr 1973; Snow and Anderson 1993; Dordick 1997). To my knowledge, in Russia younger categories of men—homeless or not—are more likely to engage in prostitution than the

mainly middle-aged cohort with which I worked. This observation is confirmed by Maya Rusakova, criminologist at Institute of Sociology, RAN, St. Petersburg, private conversation, April 2002.

Chapter 3. Perilous Places

1. Wright (1997) juxtaposes refuse space with leisure space, spaces for consumption and relaxation, and functional space used for some sort of transport. I see no analytical point in the distinction since from the vantage point of the homeless, the two kinds of space do not differ. Snow and Anderson (1993) contrast prime space with marginal space, but I find Wright's term refuse space more suitable since it does not imply geographical marginality—on the contrary, refuse space is situated in the heart of the city, usually inside residential houses.

2. I think of place as concrete site units such as "the stairway to the ticket hall at the station" or "the attic where Sasha lived," while space is more abstract: attics in general, or a particular type of place (for instance refuse space). I am not entirely consistent, since the writers from whom I borrow the concepts refuse space and prime space use "space" in both senses.

3. Ruble mentions that due to the socialist economy, the number of entryways along Nevsky Prospekt declined by two-thirds between 1914 and the 1980s (1995, 23). Subsequently, the new profusion of doors—larger doors, replaced doors, new doors—and larger shop windows are, after the ubiquitous advertisements, the most conspicuous sign of the post-Soviet market economy.

4. "The crosses," from the shape of the two major buildings of this notorious prison.

5. I am not sure about the degree of coercion in this case. Papik was also ordered to help to move the corpse, but he bluntly refused and apparently suffered no ill consequences. Vova, on the other hand, did not mind, since he wanted to have a closer look at the body to see if he knew the person and to establish the cause of death.

6. Judging from the breath of many of them, Vova was not entirely lying. Drinking at work was common among station employees, but more than these guards—who never spoke or moved in a drunken fashion—the cleaners and the porters seemed constantly tipsy. Station regulars frequently accused the police of drinking at work, but I never observed this myself.

7. I heard too many accounts about these deportations in too many different contexts to doubt their existence.

8. Judging from most non-homeless Russians I know, none of the forms of abuse mentioned here are restricted to the homeless. Their situation is merely a heightened form of the conditions that everybody share. In defense of the police one may mention low wages and, as a result, a serious turnover problem, insufficient recruitment standards and education, and in addition massive workloads and poor working conditions with regard to material and technology (see Human Rights Watch 1999).

9. I heard no other pacification stories touching on sexual desire, but in Vova's conceptual universe (and probably the police officer's too), sex between males is what it is in the Zone: a way for the strong to humiliate the weak. Rape emasculates the penetrated party and dispatches him to the bottom ranks of the Zone hierarchy,

helplessly and infinitely, while the rapist's masculine prestige remains untouched. The code is so rigid that camp authorities sometimes stage rapes in order to get rid of powerful and potentially troublesome prisoners (Abramkin 2001).

10. As three hundred rubles at the time was the minimum monthly rent for a room, the more affluent inhabitants found such accommodation, whereas the others took to the stairways in the vicinity of the station. The new chairs had, moreover, rigid armrests to prevent people from lying down to sleep, although I noticed with a certain satisfaction a year or two later that many of them had been sawn off. This hall is probably still an occasional refuge for many homeless people, but hardly as a permanent sleeping place.

Chapter 4. No Close Ones

1. In Dement'eva's Moscow study, only 4 to 5 percent of all detdomovtsy are "orphans in full" (1992, 67ff.). The rest either remember their parents well or keep in continuous contact with them, and 51 percent of the total number of children in her study returned to their parents after leaving school. Since her study concerns the late Soviet period, it elucidates the background of my adult informants more than the situation of contemporary orphans. For more information about the formal procedures with regard to public care of children, see Harwin (1996).

2. After being notified by schools, relatives, or neighbors, a supervision committee may declare a parent unfit for parenthood and deprive the parent of his or her right to be a custodian of the child, after which the child goes to live with relatives or to an orphanage.

3. I never met Oksana. She was interviewed by others in connection with the "Tell Us Your Life" contest (*Na Dne* 1999). Proceeding on the premise that written narratives are comparable with spoken ones, a few students of sociology were recruited to approach homeless people and conduct interviews (I do not know their names, but I am grateful for the work they did). In the end these were not included, but the material fell into my hands. I have *Na Dne*'s permission to use interviews where the interviewees give their consent to publishing, as Oksana did. I know her family well since they still were living in Nochlezhka's shelter when I began my fieldwork.

4. The question is whether *motherhood* is conceived of as eternal, while *fatherhood* can expire, or if it is simply that children in need consider parenthood to be eternal while poor parents—fathers as well as mothers—think of it as liable to termination.

5. Already in the 1980s, Shlapentokh argued that the role of grandmothers is decreasing, and I often hear that today's babushki want to live their own lives, instead of slaving in the service of their children, backing up his argument with statistics showing that "only" 41 percent of the respondents consider the babushka to be a resource of significance (1984, 193–95). To me, 41 percent is, on the contrary, quite enough to establish that grandmothers are still a force to be counted on, which tends to be the conclusion of most Westerners observing Russian family life at close distance (Caldwell 2004, 66–67).

6. Formally, unregistered children have no right to education. The details of how this works out in practice are a little unclear. Viktoria blamed the school problem on their constant moves, not on their status, but I was told by another mother

that her sons (who lacked a propiska but not a home) were admitted to one school only. She knew, she said indignantly, that this school was selected because it already had a bad reputation due to the children from a nearby orphanage.

Chapter 5. Friend or Foe?

1. The adult male Zone is not in the least equal, but many ex-cons like to remember it as such. The prisoners organize themselves into three hierarchical layers (*masti,* playing card suits), with the leaders (*avtoritety*) at the top, a majority of ordinary men (*muzhchiny*) in the middle, and the outcasts (*opushchennye*) at the very bottom (Abramkin 2001; Samoilov 1993). The plight of the latter is bleak, to say the least, but ex-cons who had been spared this fate tend to repress the existence of outcasts in favor of the equality and internal cohesion of "the men" in their own *mast'* (Essig 1999, 8–13; Abramkin 2001, 53–54). Reportedly, youth prisons and female prisons and camps are not unaffected by bullying, but their social organization is less rigid and more varied than in the case of their adult male counterparts (Polivanova 2000, 29; Abramkin 2001, 36).

2. At that time, 225 rubles a month, equivalent to about eight U.S. dollars, one hundred packs of cheap cigarettes, or fifty loaves of bread.

Chapter 6. Dirt, Degradation, and Death

1. Grammatically, the form "opushchennyi" indicates the agency of a different party: "that which has been lowered" (by something else). "Opustivshii" implies that the subject is the cause of its own fate, "that which has lowered itself." Opustivshii should apply in the homeless context, but both words were used, perhaps because the ubiquitous Zone experience colored the language.

2. Distinct divisions into hetero and homo are not as self-evident in Russia as in the West, nor is the attached Western vocabulary (Essig 1999). The loan word *lesbianka* is used by representatives of a social class that Raia probably confronted only in the courtroom, and neither she nor other women with same-sex desires ever used it.

3. "Class" is still a somewhat unwieldy term in the post-Soviet Russian context. Blue-collar workers prefer to talk about themselves as "workers" only. The term "middle class" is increasingly used, but it refers to wealth rather than to white-collar employment or attainment of culture, and the social strata implied are by Russian standards quite wealthy.

4. Needless to say, there is no dental care for the homeless. They sometimes talked about having aching teeth pulled out, but I never found out where this might be done. However, dental care is a problem for non-homeless Russians too. The general practitioners are fundamentally distrusted, notorious as they are for painful and unprofessional treatments (anyone who has seen a set of Soviet steel teeth is likely to agree) and what remains is private—and expensive—clinics. Private dentists distance themselves from the public, or "Soviet," dental tradition by calling themselves *stomatologi,* a more high-tech designation than the old *zubnoi vrach,* literally "tooth doctor."

5. The most notorious part of the Zone is Mordovia, not Siberia as Westerners tend to believe. The concentration of camps is extreme, and many of them have special security of different types. The name always makes me think of Mordor, Sauron's abode in J. R. R. Tolkien's *The Lord of the Rings,* and judging from the stories, Mordovia is not far off.

BIBLIOGRAPHY

Abramkin, Valery, and Iu. V. Chizhov. 1992. *Kak vyzhit'v sovietskoi tiurme v pomoshch' yzniku.* Krasnoiarsk, Russia: Vostok.

Abu-Lughod, Lila. 1990. "The Romance of Resistance: Tracing Transformations of Power through Bedouin Women." *American Ethnologist* 17: 41–55.

Agamben, Giorgio. 1998. *Homo Sacer: Sovereign Power and Bare Life.* Stanford, CA: Stanford University Press.

Alpern, Liudmila. 2000. *Zhenshchiny v rossiiskoi tiur'me.* Moscow: Obshchestvennyi tsentr sodeistviia reform ugolovnogo pravosudiia.

Ambrose, Peter, Berth Danemark, and Boris Grinchel. 1998. *A Comparative Study of Housing Privatisation in Russia, Sweden, and the U.K.* Örebro, Sweden: University Centre for Housing and Urban Research.

Amster, Randall. 2003. "Patterns of Exclusion: Sanitizing Space, Criminalizing Homelessness." *Social Justice* 30(1): 195.

Ashwin, Sarah. 2000. "Introduction: Gender, State, and Society in Soviet and Post-Soviet Russia." In *Gender, State, and Society in Soviet and Post-Soviet Russia,* edited by Sarah Ashwin. London: Routledge.

Attwood, Lynne. 1990. *The New Soviet Man and Woman: Sex-Role Socialization in the USSR.* Basingstoke, U.K.: Macmillan/Centre for Russian and East European Studies, University of Birmingham.

———. 1997. "'She Was Asking for It': Rape and Domestic Violence against Women." In *Post-Soviet Women: From the Baltic to Central Asia,* edited by Mary Buckley. Cambridge, U.K.: Cambridge University Press.

Axenov, Konstantin. 2002. "Spatial Saturation as Adaptation of a Post-Socialist City to Market Relation in Retail Trade and Services: The Case of St. Petersburg." In *Die Städte Russlands im Wandel: Raumstrukturelle Veränderungen am Ende des 20. Jahrhunderts,* edited by I. Brade. Leipzig: Institut für Länderkunde.

Azhgikhina, Nadezhda, and Helena Goscilo. 1996. "Getting Under Their Skin." In *Russia, Women, Culture,* edited by Helena Goscilo and Beth Holmgren. Bloomington: Indiana University Press.

Bahr, Howard M. 1973. *Skid Row: An Introduction to Disaffiliation.* New York: Oxford University Press.

Ball, Alan M. 1994. *And Now My Soul Is Hardened: Abandoned Children in Soviet Russia, 1918–1930.* Berkeley: University of California Press.

Bauman, Zygmunt. 2004. *Wasted Lives: Modernity and Its Outcasts.* Cambridge, U.K.: Polity Press.

Beigulenko, Yana. 1999. "Homelessness in Russia: The Scope of The Problem and the Remedies in Place." In *Homelessness: Exploring the New Terrain,* edited by Patricia Kennet and Alex Marsh. Bristol, U.K.: Policy Press.

Birdsall, Karen. 1999. "'Everyday Crime' at the Workplace: Covert Earning Schemes in Russia's New Commercial Sector." In *Economic Crime in Russia,* edited by Alena Ledeneva and Marina Kurkchiyan. The Hague: Kluwer Law International.

Bodungen, Alexei. 1994. *Homelessness in Russia: A Report.* New York: Charities Aid Foundation.

Borneman, John. 1991. *After the Wall: East Meets West in the New Berlin.* New York: Basic Books.

Bourdieu, Pierre. 1984. *Distinction: A Social Critique of the Judgement of Taste.* London: Routledge and Kegan Paul.

———. 1986. "The Forms of Capital." In *Handbook of Theory and Research for the Sociology of Education,* edited by John G. Richardson. New York: Greenwood Press.

———. 1990. *The Logic of Practice.* Stanford, CA: Stanford University Press.

Boym, Svetlana. 1994. *Common Places: Mythologies of Everyday Life in Russia.* Cambridge, MA: Harvard University Press.

———. 1995. "From the Russian Soul to Post-Communist Nostalgia." In "Identifying Histories: Eastern Europe before and after 1989." Special issue, *Representations* 49: 133–66.

Bridger, Susan, Rebecca Kay, and Kathryn Pinnick. 1996. *No More Heroines? Russia, Women, and the Market.* London: Routledge.

Bruno, Marta. 1998. "Playing the Co-operation Game: Strategies around International Aid in Post-Socialist Russia." In *Surviving Post-Socialism: Local Strategies and Regional Responses in Eastern Europe and the Former Soviet Union,* edited by Sue Bridger and Frances Pine. London: Routledge.

Buckley, Cynthia. 1995. "The Myth of Managed Migration: Migration Control and Market in the Soviet Period." *Slavic Review* 54(4): 896–916.

Burawoy, Michael, and Katherine Verdery. 1999. "Introduction." In *Uncertain Transition: Ethnographies of Change in the Postsocialist World,* edited by Michael Burawoy and Katherine Verdery. Lanham, MD: Rowman and Littlefield.

Caldwell, Melissa. 2004. *Not By Bread Alone: Social Support in the New Russia.* Berkeley: University of California Press.

Chalidze, Valery. 1977. *Criminal Russia: Essays on Crime in the Soviet Union.* New York: Random House.

Collier, Stephen J. 2001. "Post-Socialist City: The Government of Society in Neo-Liberal Times." Ph.D. dissertation, University of California, Berkeley.

Condee, Nancy. 1999. "Body Graphics: Tattooing the Fall of Communism." In *Consuming Russia: Popular Culture, Sex, and Society since Gorbachev,* edited by Adele Marie Barker. Durham: Duke University Press.

Connell, Robert W. 1995. *Masculinities.* Berkeley: University of California Press.

Creutziger, Clementine G. K. 1996. *Childhood in Russia: Representations and Reality.* Lanham, MD: University Press of America.

Davidova, Nadia. 2004. "Poverty in Russia." In *Poverty and Social Exclusion in the New Russia,* edited by Nick Manning and Nataliya Tikhonova. Burlington, VT: Ashgate.

Davis, Mike. 1990. *City of Quartz: Excavating the Future in Los Angeles.* Reprint, London: Pimlico, 1998.

De Certeau, Michel. 1984. *The Practice of Everyday Life.* Berkeley: University of California Press.

Dement'eva, I. F. 1992. "Sotsial'naia adaptatsia detei-sirot: problemy i perspektivy v usloviiakh rynka." *Sotsiologicheskie Issledovaniia* 10: 62–70.

De Soto, Hermine, and Nora Dudwick. 2002. "Eating from One Pot: Survival Strategies in Moldova's Collapsing Rural Economy." In *When Things Fall Apart: Qualitative Studies of Poverty in the Former Soviet Union,* edited by Nora Dudwick, Elizabeth Gomart, and Alexandre Marc. Washington, D.C.: World Bank.

Dibel', V. 2003. "Pasportnaia sistema Rossii." Obozrevatel' 5(160). Available at www.nasledie.ru/oboz/05_03/5_15.htm, accessed September 20, 2008.

Dordick, Gwendolyn A. 1997. *Something Left to Lose: Personal Relations and Survival among New York's Homeless.* Philadelphia: Temple University Press.

Douglas, Mary. 1966. *Purity and Danger: An Analysis of the Concepts of Pollution and Taboo.* London: ARK Paperbacks.

Dudwick, Nora. 2002a. "No Guests at Our Table: Social Fragmentation in Georgia." In *When Things Fall Apart: Qualitative Studies of Poverty in the Former Soviet Union,* edited by Nora Dudwick, Elizabeth Gomart, and Alexandre Marc. Washington, D.C.: World Bank.

———. 2002b. "When the Lights Went Out: Poverty in Armenia." In *When Things Fall Apart: Qualitative Studies of Poverty in the Former Soviet Union,* edited by Nora Dudwick, Elizabeth Gomart, and Alexandre Marc. Washington, D.C.: World Bank.

Erofeev, Venedikt. 1991. *Moskva—Petushki.* St. Petersburg: Izdatelstvo "Soiuz," Soiuz Internatsionalistov.

Essig, Laurie. 1999. *Queer in Russia: A Story of Sex, Self, and the Other.* Durham: Duke University Press.

Fitzpatrick, Sheila. 1994. *Stalin's Peasants: Resistance and Survival in the Russian Village after Collectivization.* Oxford: Oxford University Press.

Foucault, Michel. 1977. *Discipline and Punish: The Birth of the Prison.* London: Allen Lane.

———. 1990. *The History of Sexuality. Vol. 1, The Will to Knowledge.* Harmondsworth: Penguin.

———. 1991. "Governmentality." In *The Foucault Effect: Studies in Governmentality,* edited by Graham Burchell, Colin Gordon, and Peter Miller. Chicago: University of Chicago Press.

———. 1997. "The Birth of Biopolitics." In *Essential Works of Foucault, 1954–1984. Vol. 1, Ethics: Subjectivity and Truth,* edited by Paul Rabinow. New York: New Press.

Fujimura, Clementine. 2002. "Adult Stigmatization and the Hidden Power of Homeless Children in Russia." *Demokratizatsiia* 10(1): 37–47.

Garcelon, Mark. 2001. "Colonizing the Subject: The Genealogy and Legacy of the Soviet Internal Passport." In *Documenting Individual Identity: The Development of State Practices in the Modern World,* edited by John Torpey and Jane Caplan. Princeton: Princeton University Press.

Gdaniec, Cordula. 2001. "Ostozhenka—A Moscow District in Transition: Reflections of Post-Soviet Restructuring Processes." *Ethnologia Europaea* 31(2): 41–58.

George, Vic. 1980. *Socialism, Social Welfare, and the Soviet Union.* London: Routledge and Kegan Paul.

Gerasimova, Katerina. 1999. "The Soviet Communal Apartment." In *Beyond the Limits: The Concept of Space in Russian History and Culture,* edited by Jeremy Smith. Helsinki: SHS.

Gerasimova, Tatiana. 1998. Opinion poll included in grant application from *Na Dne* street newspaper to Know-How Foundation. In cooperation with the Faculty of Sociology, State University of St. Petersburg. Unpublished.

Gilinskii, Yakov I., and Valery Sokolov. 1993. "Bezdomnost' v Rossii: vchera, segodnia, zavtra." *Peterburgskie Chtenia.* St. Petersburg: Peterburgskii institut pechtati.

Goffman, Erving. 1968. *Asylums: Essays on the Social Situation of Mental Patients and Other Inmates.* Harmondsworth: Penguin.

———. 1993. *Stigma: Notes on the Management of Spoiled Identity.* New York: Simon and Schuster.

Gounis, Kostas. 1992. "Temporality and the Domestication of Homelessness." In *The Politics of Time,* edited by Henry J. Rutz. Washington, D.C.: American Anthropological Association.

Gromov, Andrei. 2004. "Ne igrai v moi igrushki i ne pisai v moi gorshok: Nashe po-raszjenie na Ukraine mozhet obernut'sa pobedoi." Available at www.globalrus.ru/comments/139342, accessed September 20, 2008.

Gutov, R. N., and A. N. Nikiforov. 2004. "Homelessness and Trends in its Development." *Sociological Research* 43(3): 67–74.

Handelman, Stephen. 1997. *Comrade Criminal: Russia's New Mafiya.* New Haven: Yale University Press.

Harris, Grace. 1989. "Concepts of Individual, Self, and Person in Description and Analysis." *American Anthropologist* 91: 599–611.

Harwin, Judith. 1996. *Children of the Russian State: 1917–1995.* Aldershot, U.K.: Avebury.

Heleniak, Timothy. 1997. "Internal Migration in Russia During the Economic Transition." *Post-Soviet Geography and Economics* 38(2): 81–104.

Höjdestrand, Tova. 2004. "The Soviet-Russian Production of Homelessness: *Propiska,* Housing, Privatisation." Available at www.anthrobase.com/Txt/H/Hoej destrand_T_01.htm, accessed September 20, 2008.

———. 2005. "Needed by Nobody: Homelessness, Humiliation, and Humanness in Post-Socialist Russia." Ph.D. dissertation, University of Stockholm.

Human Rights Watch. 1999. *Crisis in the Criminal Justice System.* Available at www.hrw.org/reports/1999/russia/Russ99o-10.htm, accessed September 20, 2008.

Humphrey, Caroline. 2000a. "An Anthropological View of Barter in Russia." In *The Vanishing Rouble: Barter Networks and Non-Monetary Transactions in Post-Soviet Societies,* edited by Paul Seabright. Cambridge, U.K.: Cambridge University Press.

———. 2000b. "How is Barter Done? The Social Relations of Barter in Provincial Russia." In *The Vanishing Rouble: Barter Networks and Non-Monetary Transactions in Post-Soviet Societies,* edited by Paul Seabright. Cambridge, U.K.: Cambridge University Press.

———. 2001. "Inequality and Exclusion: A Russian Case Study of Emotion in Politics." *Anthropological Theory* 1(3): 331–53.

———. 2002a. "Does the Category 'Postsocialist' Still Make Sense?" In *Postsocialism: Ideals, Ideologies, and Practices in Eurasia,* edited by Chris M. Hann. London: Routledge.

——. 2002b. *The Unmaking of Soviet Life: Everyday Economies after Socialism.* Ithaca: Cornell University Press.

Humphreys, Robert. 1999. *No Fixed Abode: A History of Responses to the Roofless and the Rootless in Britain.* Basingstoke, U.K.: Macmillan.

Hunt, Kathleen. 1998. *Abandoned to the State: Cruelty and Neglect in Russian Orphanages.* New York: Human Rights Watch.

Isupova, O. G. 2004. "The Relinquishment of Newborns and Women's Reproductive Rights." *Russian Social Science Review* 45(3): 40–57.

Ivleva, Irina, and Oleg Pachenkov. 2003. "Street Traders in St. Petersburg." In *Everyday Economy in Russia, Poland, and Latvia,* edited by Karl-Olov Arnstberg and Thomas Borén. Södertörn Academic Studies. Stockholm: Almqvist and Wiksell International.

Järvinen, Margaretha. 1993. *De nye hjemlose, kvinder, fattigdom, vold.* Holte, Sweden: Soc-Pol.

Johnson, Janet. 2001. "Privatizing Pain: The Problem of Woman Battery in Russia." *NWSA Journal* 13(3): 153–68.

Karlinsky, Igor. 2004. *An Analysis of the Social and Legal Situation of the Homeless in Contemporary Russia.* St. Petersburg: Delta.

Kay, Rebecca. 1997. "Images of an Ideal Woman: Perceptions of Russian Womanhood through the Media, Education, and Women's Own Eyes." In *Post-Soviet Women: from the Baltic to Central Asia,* edited by Mary Buckley. Cambridge, U.K.: Cambridge University Press.

Kennet, Patricia. 1999. "Homelessness, Citizenship, and Social Exclusion." In *Homelessness: Exploring the New Terrain,* edited by Patricia Kennet and Alex Marsh. Bristol, U.K.: Policy Press.

Kiblitskaya, Marina. 2000. "'Once We Were Kings': Male Experiences of Loss of Status at Work in Post-Communist Russia." In *Gender, State, and Society in Soviet and Post-Soviet Russia,* edited by Sarah Ashwin. London: Routledge.

Klimova, S. G. 2002. "Kriterii opredeleniia grupp 'my' i 'oni.'" *Sotsiologicheskie issledovaniia* 6: 83–95.

Koegel, Paul. 1992. "Through a Different Lens: An Anthropological Perspective on the Homeless Mentally Ill." *Culture, Medicine, and Psychiatry* 16: 1–22.

Konstantinov, Andrei, and Malkolm Dikselius. 1997. *Banditskaia Rossiia.* St. Petersburg: Bibliopolis.

Kotkin, Stephen. 1995. *Magnetic Mountain: Stalinism as a Civilization.* Berkeley: University of California Press.

Kukhterin, Sergei. 2000. "Fathers and Patriarchs in Communist and Post-Communist Russia." In *Gender, State, and Society in Soviet and Post-Soviet Russia,* edited by Sarah Ashwin. London: Routledge.

Ledeneva, Alena V. 1998. *Russia's Economy of Favours: Blat, Networking, and Informal Exchange.* Cambridge, U.K.: Cambridge University Press.

Ledeneva, Alena V., and Marina Kurkchiyan, eds. 2000. *Economic Crime in Russia.* The Hague: Kluwer Law International.

Lemon, Alaina. 1998. "'Your Eyes Are Green like Dollars': Counterfeit Cash, National Substance, and Currency Apartheid in 1990s Russia." *Cultural Anthropology* 13(1): 22–55.

Likhodei, O. A. 2003. "Sub'ektivnye faktory marginalizatsii." Paper given at the conference *Tsennosti sovetskoi kul'tury v kontekste global'nykh tendentsii XXI veka*. Institute for International Business and Communications, St. Petersburg, June 6, 2003. Available at www.ibci.ru/konferencia/page/statya_k22.htm, accessed September 20, 2008.

Lindquist, Galina. 1994. "Feminism as a Threatening Message: The Story of a Russian Urban Intellectual Woman." *Ethnos* 51(1–2): 7–35.

———. 2003. "Selling and Buying Power: The Economy of a Magic Centre in Moscow." In *Everyday Economy in Russia, Poland, and Latvia*, edited by Karl-Olov Arnstberg and Thomas Borén. Södertörn Academic Studies. Stockholm: Almqvist and Wiksell International.

———. 2005. *Conjuring Hope: Healing and Magic in Contemporary Russia*. New York: Berghan Books.

Lovell, Anne M. 1992. "Seizing the Moment: Power, Contingency, and Temporality in Street Life." In *The Politics of Time*, edited by Henry J. Rutz. Washington, D.C.: American Anthropological Association.

Lyon, David. 2006. *Theorizing Surveillance: The Panopticon and Beyond*. Cullompton, U.K.: Willan.

Madison, Bernice Q. 1968. *Social Welfare in the Soviet Union*. Stanford, CA: Stanford University Press.

Malkki, Liisa. 1992. "National Geographic: The Rooting of Peoples and the Territorialization of National Identity among Scholars and Refugees." *Cultural Anthropology* 7(1): 24–44.

———. 1997. "News and Culture: Transitory Phenomena and the Fieldwork Tradition." In *Anthropological Locations: Boundaries and Grounds of a Field Science*, edited by Akhil Gupta and James Ferguson. Berkeley: University of California Press.

Manning, Nick, and Nataliya Tikhonova. 2004. "Russia in Context." In *Poverty and Social Exclusion in the New Russia*, edited by Nick Manning and Nataliya Tikhonova. Burlington, VT: Ashgate.

Markowitz, Fran. 1991. "Russkaia Druzhba: Russian Friendship in American and Israeli Contexts." *Slavic Review* 50(3): 637–45.

———. 2000. *Coming of Age in Post-Soviet Russia*. Urbana: University of Illinois Press.

Mathieu, Arline. 1993. "The Medicalization of Homelessness and the Theater of Repression." *Medical Anthropology Quarterly* 7(2): 170–84.

Matthews, Mervyn. 1989. *Patterns of Deprivation in the Soviet Union under Brezhnev and Gorbachev*. Stanford, CA: Hoover Institution Press.

———. 1993. *The Passport Society: Controlling Movement in Russia and the USSR*. Boulder, CO: Westview Press.

Medvedev, Sergei. 1999. "A General Theory of Russian Space: A Gay Science and a Rigorous Science." In *Beyond the Limits: The Concept of Space in Russian History and Culture*, edited by Jeremy Smith. Helsinki: SHS.

Mil'ianenkov, Lev. 1992. *Po tu storonu zakona: entsiklopediya prestupnogo mira*. St. Petersburg: Redaktsia zhurnala "Damy i gospoda."

Na Dne. 1999. *Tell Us Your Life / Rasskazhi svoiu istoriu*. St. Petersburg: Isdatelskii dom Na Dne.

Nazarova, E. A. 2000. "Osobennosti sovremennych protsessov migratsii." *Sotsiologicheskie Issledovaniia* 7: 106–11.

Nazpary, Joma. 2002. *Post-Soviet Chaos:Violence and Dispossession in Kazakhstan.* London: Pluto Press.

Neidhart, Christoph. 2003. *Russia's Carnival: The Smells, Sights, and Sounds of Transition.* Lanham, MD: Rowman and Littlefield.

Novikova, Irina. 2000. "Soviet and Post-Soviet Masculinities: After Men's Wars in Women's Memories." In *Male Roles, Masculinities and Violence,* edited by Ingeborg Breines, Robert Connell, and Ingrid Eide. Paris: UNESCO Publishing.

Ortner, Sherry B. 1995. "Resistance and the Problem of Ethnographic Refusal." *Comparative Studies in Society and History* 37(1): 173–93.

Osborn, Robert J. 1970. *Soviet Social Policies: Welfare, Equality, and Community.* Homewood, IL: Dorsey Series in Political Science.

Osinskii, Ivan I., Indra M. Khabaeva, and Irina B. Baldaeva. 2004. "The Homeless." *Sociological Research* 43(3): 54–66.

Passaro, Joanne. 1996. *The Unequal Homeless: Men on the Streets, Women in their Place.* New York: Routledge.

Pesmen, Dale. 2000. *Russia and Soul: An Exploration.* Ithaca: Cornell University Press.

Peterson, Nadya L. 1996. "Dirty Women." In *Russia, Women, Culture,* edited by Helena Goscilo and Beth Holmgren. Bloomington: Indiana University Press.

Pilkington, Hilary. 1994. *Russia's Youth and its Culture: A Nation's Constructors and Constructed.* London: Routledge.

———. 1998. *Migration, Displacement, and Identity in Post-Soviet Russia.* London: Routledge.

Pine, Frances. 1996. "Redefining Women's Work in Rural Poland." In *After Socialism: Land Reform and Social Change in Eastern Europe,* edited by Ray Abrahams. Oxford: Berghahn.

Polivanova, M. M. 2000. "Vliianie prebyvaniia v zakliuchenii na lichnost' zhenshchiny." In *Tiur'ma—ne zhenskoe delo,* edited by Ludmila Alpern. Moscow: Obshchestvennyi tsentr sodeistviia reform ugolovnogo pravosudiia.

Popov, V. P. 1995a. "Pasportnaia sistema v SSSR (1932–1976)." *Sotsiologicheskie Issledovaniia* 8: 3–14.

———. 1995b. "Pasportnaia sistema v SSSR (1932–1976)." *Sotsiologicheskie Issledovaniia* 9: 3–13.

Prokof'eva, L. M., and M. F. Valetas. 2002. "Otsy i ikh deti posle razvoda." *Sotsiologicheskie Issledovaniia* 28(6): 111–15.

Redmond, Gerry, and Sandra Hutton. 2000. "Poverty in Transition Economies: An Introduction to the Issues." In *Poverty in Transition Economies,* edited by Sandra Hutton and Gerry Redmond. London: Routledge Studies of Societies in Transition.

Ries, Nancy. 1994. "The Burden of Mythic Identity: Russian Women at Odds with Themselves." In *Feminist Nightmares: Women at Odds—An Anthology of Essays on the Problematics of Sisterhood,* edited by Susan Ostrov Weisser and Jennifer Fleischner. New York: New York University Press.

———. 1997. *Russian Talk: Culture and Conversation during Perestroika.* Ithaca: Cornell University Press.

Rivkin-Fish, Michele. 2005. *Women's Health in Post-Soviet Russia: The Politics of Intervention.* Bloomington: Indiana University Press.

Robben, Antonius C. G. M. 1995. "Seduction and Persuasion: The Politics of Truth and Emotion among Victims and Perpetrators of Violence." In *Fieldwork Under Fire: Contemporary Studies of Violence and Survival*, edited by Carolyn Nordstrom and Antonius Robben. Berkeley: University of California Press.

Rosengren, Anette. 2003. *Mellan ilska och hopp: om hemlöshet, droger och kvinnor.* Stockholm: Carlsson.

Rotkirch, Anna, and Elina Haavio-Mannila, eds. 1996. *Women's Voices in Russia Today.* Aldershot, U.K.: Dartmouth.

Roudakova, Natalia, and Deborah S. Ballard-Reisch. 1999. "Femininity and the Double Burden: Dialogues on the Socializing of Russian Daughters into Womanhood." *Anthropology of East Europe Review* 17(1).

Ruble, Blair A. 1995. *Money Sings: The Changing Politics of Urban Space in Post-Soviet Yaroslavl.* Cambridge, U.K.: Cambridge University Press.

Sahlins, Marshall. 1984 [1974]. *Stone Age Economics.* London: Tavistock.

Samoilov, Lev. 1993. "Ethnography of the Camp." *Anthropology and Archeology of Eurasia* 32(3): 32–58.

Scott, James C. 1985. *Weapons of the Weak: Everyday Forms of Peasant Resistance.* New Haven: Yale University Press.

———. 1998. *Seeing Like a State: How Certain Schemes to Improve the Human Condition Have Failed.* New Haven: Yale University Press.

Sedlenieks, Klavs. 2003. "Cash in an Envelope: Corruption and Tax Avoidance as an Economic Strategy in Contemporary Riga." In *Everyday Economy in Russia, Poland, and Latvia*, edited by Karl-Olov Arnstberg and Thomas Borén. Södertörn Academic Studies. Stockholm: Almqvist and Wiksell International.

Shilling, Chris. 1993. *The Body and Social Theory.* London: Sage.

Shlapentokh, Vladimir. 1984. *Love, Marriage, and Friendship in the Soviet Union: Ideals and Practices.* New York: Praeger.

———. 1989. *Public and Private Life of the Soviet People: Changing Values in Post-Stalin Russia.* New York: Oxford University Press.

Silverman, Bertram, and Murray Yanowitch. 2000. *New Rich, New Poor, New Russia: Winners and Losers on the Russian Road to Capitalism.* Armonk, NY: M. E. Sharpe.

Simis, Konstantin. 1982. *USSR: Secrets of a Corrupt Society.* London: Dent.

Sinelnikov, Andrei. 2000. "Masculinity á la Russe: Gender Issues in the Russian Federation Today." In *Male Roles, Masculinities, and Violence*, edited by Ingeborg Breines, Robert Connell, and Ingrid Eide. Paris: UNESCO Publishing.

Skeggs, Beverly. 1997. *Formations of Class and Gender: Becoming Respectable.* London: Sage.

Smith, Hedrick. 1976. *The Russians.* London: Sphere Books.

Snow, David A., and Leon Anderson. 1993. *Down on their Luck: A Study of Homeless Street People.* Berkeley: University of California Press.

Snow, David A., and Michael Mulcahy. 2001. "Space, Politics, and the Survival Strategies of the Homeless." *American Behavioural Scientist* 45(1): 149–72.

Sokolov, Valery. 1994. "Homelessness in St. Petersburg." *Petersburg in the Early 90's: Crazy, Cold, Cruel.* St. Petersburg: Blagotvoritelnyi Fond Nochlezhka.

Solovieva, Zoja R. 2001. "Reabilitatsia bezdomnykh: issledovanie 'nochlezhki.'" *Zhurnal sotsiologii i sotsialnoy antropologii* 4(3): 92–108.

Sperling, Valerie. 1999. *Organizing Women in Contemporary Russia: Engendering Transition*. Cambridge, U.K.: Cambridge University Press.

Starikov, Evgenii. 1989. "Marginaly, ili razmyshleniia na staruiu temu: 'Chto s nami proiskhodit?'" *Znamia* 10: 133–62.

Steinwedel, Charles. 2001. "Making Social Groups, One Person at a Time: The Identification of Individuals by Estate, Religious Confession, and Ethnicity in Late Imperial Russia." In *Documenting Individual Identity: The Development of State Practices in the Modern World*, edited by John Torpey and Jane Caplan. Princeton: Princeton University Press.

Stephenson, Svetlana. 1996. "O fenomene bezdomnisti." *Sotsiologicheskie Issledovainia* 8: 26–33.

———. 1997. *Bezdomnye v sotsial'noi strukture bol'shogo goroda*. Moscow: INION RAN.

———. 2000a. "The Russian Homeless." In *Poverty in Transition Economies*, edited by Sandra Hutton and Gerry Redmond. London: Routledge Studies of Societies in Transition.

———. 2000b. "Ulichnye deti i tenevye gorodskie soobshchestva." *Sotsiologicheskii zhurnal* 3–4: 87–97.

———. 2006. *Crossing the Line: Vagrancy, Homelessness, and Social Displacement in Russia*. Basingstoke, U.K.: Ashgate.

Stryker, Rachel. 2000. "Ethnographic Solutions to the Problems of Russian Adoptees." *Anthropology of East Europe Review* 18(2): 79–84.

Taussig, Michael. 1992. *The Nervous System*. New York: Routledge.

Tikhonova, Nataliya. 2004. "Social Exclusion in Russia." In *Poverty and Social Exclusion in the New Russia*, edited by Nick Manning and Nataliya Tikhonova. Burlington, VT: Ashgate.

Torpey, John C. 2000. *The Invention of the Passport: Surveillance, Citizenship, and the State*. Cambridge, U.K.: Cambridge University Press.

Toth, Jennifer. 1993. *The Mole People: Life in the Tunnels beneath New York City*. Chicago: Chicago Review Press.

Turner, Victor. 1974. *Dramas, Fields, and Metaphors: Symbolic Action in Human Society*. Ithaca: Cornell University Press.

Utekhin, Ilia. 2001. *Ocherki kommunalnogo byta*. Moscow: O.G.I.

Vainshtein, Olga. 1996. "Female Fashion, Soviet Style." In *Russia, Women, Culture*, edited by Helena Goscilo and Beth Holmgren. Bloomington: Indiana University Press.

Verdery, Katherine. 1996. *What Was Socialism, and What Comes Next?* Princeton: Princeton University Press.

Wagner, David. 1993. *Checkerboard Square: Culture and Resistance in a Homeless Community*. Boulder, CO: Westview Press.

Wardhaugh, Julia. 2000. *Sub City: Young People, Homelessness, and Crime*. Aldershot, U.K.: Ashgate.

Wedel, Janine. 1986. *The Private Poland*. New York: Facts on File.

White, Stephen. 1996. *Russia Goes Dry: Alcohol, State, and Society*. Cambridge, U.K.: Cambridge University Press.

Wierzbicka, Anna. 1992. *Semantics, Culture, and Cognition: Universal Human Concepts in Culture-Specific Configurations*. New York: Oxford University Press.

Wright, Talmadge. 1997. *Out of Place: Homeless Mobilizations, Subcities, and Contested Landscapes.* Albany: State University of New York Press.

Yakubovich, V., and I. Kozina. 2000. "The Changing Significance of Ties: An Exploration of the Hiring Channels in the Russian Transitional Labor Market." *International Sociology* 15(3): 479–500.

Yulikova, E. P., M. A. Novikova, and A. L. Marshak. 1997. *Problemy lits opredelennogo mesta zhitel'stvo (bomzh) i puti ikh resheniia.* Moscow: Ministerstvo tryda i sotsialnogo razvitija Rossijskoj Federatsii: Tsentralnoe otraselevoe biuro Naytjno-Technitjeskoj informatsii i propagandy.

Yulikova, E. P., and V. F. Skliarov. 1994. "Sotsial'naia zashchita bomzhi." *Sotsiologicheskye Issledovanya* 10: 137–39.

Yurchak, Alexei. 2006. *Everything Was Forever, Until It Was No More: The Last Soviet Generation.* Princeton: Princeton University Press.

Zabelina, Tatiana. 1996. "Sexual Violence towards Women." In *Gender, Generation, and Identity in Contemporary Russia,* edited by Hilary Pilkington. London: Routledge.

Zaionchkovskaia, Zh. 1998. "Vynuzhdennye migranty iz stran SNG i Baltii." *Sotsiologicheskie Issledovaniia* 6: 55–59.

Zaslavsky, Victor. 1982. *The Neo-Stalinist State: Class, Ethnicity, and Consensus in Soviet Society.* New York: M. E. Sharpe.

Zav'ialov, F. N., and E. M. Spiridonova. 2000. "Uroven i obraz zhizni bomzhei." *Sotsiologitjeskie Issledovaniia,* no. 2.

Zdravomyslova, Elena, and Elena Chikadze. 2000. "Scripts of Men's Heavy Drinking." *Idatutkimus* 2: 35–52. Available at www.indepsocres.spb.ru/zdrav1.htm, accessed September 20, 2008.

Zykov, Oleg. 1999. "Russia." In *Homelessness in the United States, Europe, and Russia,* edited by Carl. O. Helive and Wilfred Konstmann. London: Bergin and Garvey.

INDEX

Page numbers in *italics* indicate photographs.